PRENTICE HALL
WRITING AND
GRAMMAR

Extra Grammar
and Writing Exercises

Grade Seven

PEARSON

Prentice
Hall

Boston, Massachusetts,
Upper Saddle River, New Jersey

ISBN 0-13-361626-6

1 2 3 4 5 6 7 8 9 10   10 09 08 07

Contents

Introduction

Extra Grammar and Writing Exercises provides your students with ample practice in a broad range of topics. To engage students of different ability levels, each worksheet covers a topic by providing two or three exercise banks, arranged in order of difficulty. This arrangement allows you to select exercises appropriate to your studentsí needs.

Here is a summary of the contents of each section:

- **The Elements of Writing** provides extra practice in paragraph development and sentence structure; unity, coherence, and transitions in writing; sentence problems, such as fragments and run-on sentences; recognition of various parts of a sentence; word choice; tone and mood; voice; and figurative language.

- **Problem Solver** focuses on the errors that students most commonly make: run-on sentences, sentence fragments, subject-verb agreement, verb forms, pronoun problems, problems with modifiers, and missing commas.

- **Grammar, Usage, and Mechanics** provides extensive practice in all major grammar, usage, and mechanics topics, arranged in alphabetical order from Abbreviations to Voice.

- **Vocabulary for Standardized Tests** helps students build vocabulary while giving them practice in a variety of test formats.

The Elements of Writing

Paragraph Structure

Parts of a Paragraph: Topic Sentences

EXERCISE A: For the paragraph below, choose the better of the two topic sentences. Write the letter of the answer.

> **Example:** A popular nutritionist visits schools to talk about calcium. Last year this nutritionist volunteered at a soup kitchen.
>
> a. One of my best friends is studying to be a nutritionist.
>
> b. Many nutritionists take their civic duties seriously.
>
> **Answer:** b

First dig a hole six inches deep. Place the bulb with its root facing down. Cover the bulb and water it generously.

a. Tulips and hyacinths grow from bulbs.
b. Planting bulbs is quite simple.

EXERCISE B: For each paragraph, write a topic sentence that ties the details together.

> **Example:** I return books to the shelves, and I record information on the computer. Soon I hope to be allowed to read during story hour.
>
> **Answer:** I have a job at our local library.

1. Many people bring their boats to sail or fish on Lake Pierre. Vacation homes line the shores of the lake. Tourists visit the many shops and restaurants along the shore road.
2. A riding mower allows you to sit down and mow. Many people like the ease of a self-propelled mower. Of course, the best exercise and the least pollution comes with an old-fashioned push mower.

EXERCISE C: For each topic, create a topic sentence. Then use it as the basis of a short paragraph of your own. Underline your topic sentence.

1. A generous deed
2. My practice schedule
3. Building nests
4. One hateful chore
5. The worst show on TV

Parts of a Paragraph: Supporting Sentences

EXERCISE A: Write whether each sentence *supports* or *does not support* this topic sentence: The Chao Phraya is Thailand's most vital river.

> **Example:** The rainy season in Thailand lasts from June until October.
> **Answer:**   does not support

1. The Chao Phraya runs from northern Thailand to the Gulf of Thailand.
2. Thailand is about the size of the state of Texas.
3. Many people have built their homes along the banks of the river.
4. Many Thai homes have wood walls and tin roofs.

EXERCISE B: Read each topic sentence in the left-hand column. Write the letter of a sentence in the right-hand column that supports the topic sentence.

> **Example:** 1. Our book group has been meeting every month for a year.
>
>   a. We meet during lunch period in the cafeteria.
>
> **Answer:** a.

___ 1. Everyone in our group has different reading preferences.

___ 2. The group has helped me extend my reading habits.

___ 3. There are many ways to begin each discussion.

___ 4. It isn't difficult to start a book group.

a. Sometimes I like to read my favorite passage out loud for the group.

b. All you need to do is gather a few people and agree on a reading list.

c. I have read and evaluated twelve fascinating books this year.

d. I like to read mysteries, but Avi always picks fantasy novels.

EXERCISE C: Each of the following paragraphs has a topic statement and one supporting statement. Write one more supporting statement for each paragraph.

> **Example:** There are many unusual pets in the store at the mall. They have cages or tanks for ferrets, tarantulas, and boa constrictors.
> **Answer:** Aquariums contain sponges, sea horses, and angelfish.

1. People should think carefully before selecting a pet. They should consider how much time they have to take care of the pet.
2. Keeping fish can be very simple or very complicated. A goldfish can be happy in a medium-sized bowl.
3. I think it is true that pets sometimes resemble their owners. I know a man who looks exactly like his bulldog.
4. Our catalog offers the finest in animal accessories. You can purchase the very best food, toys, and grooming aids.

Parts of a Paragraph: Concluding Sentences

EXERCISE A: For the paragraph below, choose the better of the two concluding sentences. Write the letter of your answer.

Example: Few people would paint their houses the way the Dobbs family did. They used an aqua base. Then they painted the trim dark red.

    a. The door was left navy blue.

    b. The total effect causes passers-by to gawk.

Answer: b

Vacuuming the car is easy. Pull out the floor mats and vacuum underneath. Then vacuum each mat. Make sure to reach beneath and between the seats.

a. Vacuuming once or twice a month will keep things tidy.
b. You should wash your car to remove salt and dirt.

EXERCISE B: For each paragraph, write a concluding sentence that sums up the details.

Example: It is impossible to keep a beach house clean. Sand gets into all the cracks. Dogs and children carry in grasses and other debris.

Answer: It may be best just to forget about cleaning up.

1. Carl's campaign for school president is going well. He has posters everywhere. His campaign speech was enjoyed by all. Many students are working toward his election.
2. Dog-training school was a good investment. My puppy learned to sit, stay, and lie down. He no longer chews the furniture or begs for food.

EXERCISE C: Write a paragraph for each topic sentence below. Conclude the paragraph with a strong concluding sentence. Underline your concluding sentence.

1. Ballet should be considered a sport.
2. I learned to cook from a teacher who couldn't.
3. If you take vitamins, do you need to eat vegetables?
4. Build a lemonade stand for fun and profit.
5. There really are only three kinds of pets.

Recognizing Effective Paragraphs

EXERCISE A: Choose the more effective paragraph for the topic below. Write the letter of the paragraph and explain what makes it more effective.

Example: Learning to ride a bike

a. It takes some skill to learn to ride a bike. You need good balance, and you need a certain fearlessness. Once it all clicks, however, riding becomes second nature.

b. Bike riding can be learned in a day. Just have someone hold the bike. Push off, and go! Training wheels are useless. It's like skating.

Answer: a; it is more coherent.

Answering the phone politely

a. My brother is always answering my phone. He doesn't care what he says. Also, it's important to be polite, which he doesn't understand.

b. Answering the phone is an exercise in manners. Speak clearly and precisely. Use polite language, and take messages when asked to do so.

EXERCISE B: Rewrite the paragraph to improve its unity, coherence, and transitional expressions.

Mowing the lawn is a terrible chore. Why don't we get sheep instead? I would rather play ball. The grass just grows back, anyway. I don't like weeding, either.

EXERCISE C: Select five topics from the ones below. For each topic write a paragraph that demonstrates unity, coherence, and the use of good transitional expressions.

1. Dental health
2. My school-related nightmare
3. My favorite subject
4. A day I'll never forget
5. The meaning of courage
6. My scariest moment
7. How to make a _____
8. Why voting is important
9. The most beautiful sight
10. How I am like and unlike my best friend

Unity, Coherence, Transitions

Unity

EXERCISE A: Write whether each sentence supports topic sentence *A* or topic sentence *B*. If a sentence supports neither topic, write *N*.

A. We use the Arabic numbering system.
B. Zero is an important numeral.

Example: It is a decimal system based on the number 10.
Answer: A

1. During the 700's, the Arabs conquered parts of India and learned the system there.
2. Not a part of the Arabic numeral system at first, zero appeared in the late 800's.
3. Brahmi has special symbols for numbers from 10 to 100 that are multiples of ten.
4. Zero was necessary as a placeholder in columns where there was no amount.
5. During the next 300 years, the Arabs spread the system throughout their empire.

EXERCISE B: Revise the following paragraph by deleting five details (entire sentences or parts of sentences) that do not support the topic.

Do you know how commonplace, yet unique, paper is? Just think! Early paper, made from rags, was not easily manufactured. We use it to write on, wrap gifts, dry our hands, eat off it, drink out of it, wrap garbage in it, and fill boxes we're mailing, although lots of people really waste it. In the 1960's, for a short while, paper even showed up as clothing! The Chinese made paper from bamboo and mulberry stalks. Today's paper is inexpensive and plentiful—not like early paper, which had to be pounded together—but its properties are so special that there's really no good substitute for it. Today's paper is a mat of millions of tiny pressed fibers.

EXERCISE C: Revise the paragraph. Delete any nonsupportive details, and add two supporting sentences of your own.

One wonder that Columbus took back to Europe was a natural substance that West Indian natives used to make waterproof shoes. These were the earliest "sneakers." European inventors first used it to rub out pencil marks, giving the substance the name by which we know it— rubber. For more than 200 years, inventors tried to find other uses for rubber. Many inventors went broke. However, it became soft and sticky when hot, brittle and stiff when cold. In 1839, quite by accident, American inventer Charles Goodyear, who went to prison because of his debts, added sulfur to natural rubber, making it usable for thousands of products—more than fifty thousand, in fact. Today, _____.

Coherence Through Time Order

EXERCISE A: In these sentences, Alice tells how her adventures in Wonderland began. Write the sentences in correct time order.

1. The rest, as they say, is history.
2. No sooner had I crawled through the hole than down I fell—down, down, down.
3. One lovely afternoon my sister was reading history to me in the meadow.
4. Never having seen a rabbit with a watch, I immediately followed him.
5. Suddenly, a white rabbit came running by, looking at his watch.

EXERCISE B: Write the sentences in correct time order.

1. The earliest peoples probably communicated with sounds and gestures.
2. Invention of languages was the first great breakthrough in spoken communication.
3. During the 1800's, the telegraph, the telephone and the typewriter further advanced written communication.
4. Then came alphabets, whose symbols stood for sounds.
5. Gradually, picture-writing systems developed to symbolize things and ideas.
6. Radio and TV in the first half of the 1900's speeded up spoken communication.
7. The next true breakthrough in written communication was the printing press.
8. Written communication followed the invention of spoken languages.
9. Drawings and paintings to tell stories were the first steps toward written language.
10. Computers and satellites in the latter half of the 1900's again improved the speed of communication.

EXERCISE C: Revise this anecdote so that it is in correct time order. Write it correctly.

(1) When we left in the morning, the sun was shining. (2) Snow began to fall, gently at first and then more heavily. (3) As the day wore on, however, and we came nearer Colorado, clouds, heavy with snow, covered the sun. (4) The highway was hidden under snow, and we inched along at less than one mile per hour for about half an hour! (5) One Thanksgiving, we were returning to our home in New Mexico from my grandmother's in Kansas. (6) Finally, ahead of us and to the right, we saw a very faint light. (7) Less than an hour after the first snowflake appeared, we couldn't see five feet ahead of us. (8) Carefully, we pulled off the road, braking to a stop—nearly through the window of a little roadside cafe! (9) As we caught our breath, we watched, astonished, as six other cars followed us. (10) We hadn't seen them behind us through the heavy snow.

Coherence Through Space Order

EXERCISE A: Rewrite each phrase, adding a word that expresses a logical spatial relationship between objects.

    Example: books _____ the shelf
    Answer: books <u>on</u> the shelf

1. feet _____ shoes
2. branches _____ the trunk
3. fence _____ the yard
4. lid _____ pan
5. the stop sign _____
6. napkin _____ the fork
7. catcher _____ home plate
8. bicycle lane _____ traffic
9. the airplane _____
10. picture _____ the wall

EXERCISE B: Read each sentence; then write a second sentence that expresses the spatial relationship asked for in the parentheses.

    Example: I lay looking up at the spreading branches of the tree. (under)
    Answer: Under me, the ground felt firm and springy.

1. Camilla sat in the airport terminal, fascinated by the activity around her. (left)
2. The United States fills the middle of the North American continent. (up)
3. Wrapped in the hot night air, Kareem waited for the fireworks to start. (above)
4. The climber reached the top of the mountain. (under)
5. In Disney World at last, Danny breathed deeply with eagerness. (in front of)
6. The Ferris wheel ground to a halt. (at the top)
7. Sitting on the side of the boat, Sarah tightened her oxygen tank. (below)
8. At the head of the table, the prince's mouth began to water. (in front of)
9. The old wizard shook his head, not believing what he saw. (far away)
10. As the thunder boomed, Valerie jumped. (nearby)

EXERCISE C: Rewrite the paragraph, using space order to make it coherent. Add sentences where indicated by the suggestions in parentheses.

    At the state park, Vanessa and Vicky bounded from the car. Looking around, they took stock of the activities that beckoned. Precisely in the middle, of course, sparkled Horseshoe Lake. (to the immediate left) Farther down, tennis and volleyball courts lay waiting for players. (lake's far end) To the right, a concrete pathway separated the restaurant from the picnic area with its tables and barbecue pits. (along the lake's right edge) Below, was the bathhouse. (behind the bathhouse) (beside the bathhouse)

Coherence Through Other Kinds of Order

EXERCISE A: Write whether each sentence is an example of *cause-effect order, comparison-contrast order, particular-to-general order,* or *general-to-particular order.* Also write any transitional words that signal a relationship.

> **Example:** Jeremy refused to eat his asparagus; consequently, he had no dessert.
> **Answer:** cause-effect   consequently

1. Identical twins look exactly alike; on the other hand, fraternal twins often don't.
2. Green vegetables are nutritious; broccoli, in particular, is stuffed with vitamins and minerals.
3. Jody liked physical exercise; thus, she joined a health club.
4. Spinning winds are part of many kinds of storms, such as tornadoes.
5. Snow White, Cinderella, and Sleeping Beauty are good examples of the helpless heroine waiting to be rescued.
6. Our old house had a huge front window; in contrast, our new home has many small, single windows.
7. Matt was a good planner; therefore, the committee put him in charge.
8. I go for bright colors; for example, I'll buy almost anything that's orange.
9. Mount Rushmore is a unique monument; there's no other like it in the world.
10. Because Fred was a poor cook, he helped the cleanup committee.

EXERCISE B: For sentences 1-2, write whether each is a *cause* or an *effect.* Revise the sentences by adding the missing part. Revise sentence 3 so that it shows a contrast. For sentence 4, write whether it is a *particular* or *general* statement. Revise the sentences by adding the other part.

1. Don fell asleep during history class.
2. Piles of paper and books sat in every room.
3. The fastest way to travel is by air.
4. T-shirts, hats, mugs, and bumper stickers all can be printed with ad slogans.

EXERCISE C: Write a paragraph about any one of the following topics. Make sure that your paragraph follows a logical order.

1. Similarities between bees and wasps
2. The results of not paying attention
3. The differences between your two sets of grandparents
4. Why "absence makes the heart grow fonder"

Coherence Through Transitional Expressions

EXERCISE A: Rewrite each pair of sentences as a single sentence. Include the transitional word in parentheses and add the necessary punctuation.

> **Example:** I am afraid of heights. I get dizzy just sitting on a horse. (for instance)
> **Answer:** I am afraid of heights; <u>for instance</u>, I get dizzy just sitting on a horse.

1. Paper is common, cheap, and good at its many jobs. It has no substitute. (for these reasons)
2. Kentucky's Mammoth Caves are protected by the federal government. They are protected by the United Nations. (moreover)
3. No law states that only Presidents can appear on our money. Most U.S. coins have had Presidents' portraits on them. (nevertheless)
4. The late 1950's and early 1960's produced some "wild and crazy" dances. Teens danced to the Twist, the Pony, the Swim, and the Chicken. (for example)

EXERCISE B: Rewrite each sentence, supplying the transitional expression that best links the two clauses.

on the other hand   in particular   however   in fact   after all

> **Example:** We'll leave the baby with Bob; _____, he's not going to the fair.
> **Answer:** We'll leave the baby with Bob; <u>after all</u>, he's not going to the fair.

1. Broccoli is a poor source of calcium; _____, it's an excellent source of vitamins C and A.
2. In 1772, a Baltimore, Maryland, storekeeper caused a sensation when he came out carrying the first umbrella in America; _____, the police had to be called!
3. Most of my family suffers from hay fever in the spring; I, _____, seem to be immune.
4. I don't understand why you're so mad about tearing that shirt; _____, you never liked it anyway.

EXERCISE C: Rewrite the paragraph, adding appropriate transitional expressions.

French toast is a favorite breakfast dish in the United States; _____, it's a favorite dish in many countries. It goes by various names. In England, _____, where it originated, it's known as "Poor Knights." Penniless, aging English knights of the 1300's became quite clever at "stretching" food—_____, stale, leftover bread. The knights soaked the stale bread in a mixture of milk, eggs, sugar, and sherry, fried it, and then served it with melted butter. The origin of the name "Poor Knights" is easy to understand; _____, poor knights invented the dish. _____, no one can explain why Americans call it "French toast."

Sentences

Recognizing Subjects and Predicates

EXERCISE A: Rewrite each sentence. Draw a line between the subject and the predicate.

> **Example:** Everyone in my family enjoys going to the zoo.
> **Answer:** Everyone in my family | enjoys going to the zoo.

1. The zoo is open seven days a week.
2. My brother likes the monkeys best.
3. The big Siberian tiger is my favorite.
4. Many of the animals go outside in warm weather.
5. The zookeepers feed the animals and clean the cages.
6. My friends and I enjoy visiting the farm inside the zoo.
7. People were feeding special food to the goats.
8. My father bought a yellow balloon for my sister Lisa.
9. Lisa released the balloon into the air.
10. We will go to the zoo again next weekend.

EXERCISE B: Determine whether each group of words is a sentence. If the words form a sentence, write the predicate. If they do not, write *not a sentence*.

> **Example:** The boys swam in the lake.
> **Answer:** swam in the lake

1. The children frolicked merrily on the banks of the stream.
2. The older children, playing word games and talking quietly among themselves.
3. Filled to the brim with good things to eat.
4. The smell of burnt marshmallows perfumed the air.
5. Barbecued chicken, sizzling hot dogs, and thick, juicy hamburgers.

EXERCISE C: Write a sentence that uses each phrase as its subject.

> **Example:** A glass of lemonade
> **Answer:** <u>A glass of lemonade</u> can be very refreshing on a warm summer's day.

1. the magician
2. my best friend
3. that little cat
4. Marla's teacher
5. green vegetables
6. some boys
7. seventh-graders
8. my favorite memories
9. three sailboats
10. the elephants

Name _____ Class _____ Date _____

Recognizing Effective Sentences

EXERCISE A: Each sentence below is ineffective. Write the main problem with each one—that *it is not clear and concise*, that *it does not contain a complete thought*, or that *it does not emphasize the main idea*.

> **Example:** People who collect fossils, of whom you may know some, need to have patience (and a great deal of it) in order to find the fossils that they seek in pursuing their fossil-collecting hobby.
> **Answer:** It is not clear and concise.

1. The speaker, whose name is not important here, seemed to drone on and on and on, and—as sometimes happens in such situations—the boy's attention began to wander and drift.
2. My brother disagreeing and we arguing anyway.
3. Everyone got up to leave, and the lecture was over at last.
4. Being able to hold an audience's attention is one of the most important.

EXERCISE B: Rewrite each sentence so that it is clear and concise, conveys a complete thought, and emphasizes the main idea properly.

> **Example:** Like a jackhammer, his heart began to pound, and, in the pit of his stomach, he felt a knot tightening.
> **Answer:** His heart began to pound like a jackhammer, and he felt a knot tightening in the pit of his stomach.

1. Teddy heard the opening notes, and, as it was his favorite song, he clapped as the band began to play them.
2. Freedom of speech and freedom of religion are two important ones.
3. Because of the blizzard, which some people say was the worst in that part of the country in twenty years, our flight was delayed.
4. Today, a team of dedicated, hard-working archaeologists is working hard to restore the Great Sphinx, which, needless to say, they are very concerned about, to its original condition, making it the way it used to be.

EXERCISE C: Write a paragraph about one of the topics below. Make sure that each sentence in the paragraph is clear and concise, that it conveys a complete thought, and that it emphasizes the main idea properly.

1. An event in your community
2. A person you admire
3. A peaceful scene
4. An issue that you care about

Sentence Problems

Sentence Fragments

EXERCISE A: Label each item as *sentence* or *fragment*.

> **Example:** They discovered gold in the old creek bed. Working all day.
> **Answer:** fragment

1. The miners had sifted pans of silt all day.
2. Jasper stood up and stretched.
3. From the bottom of the creek.
4. Something flashed in the sun.
5. Sparkling at him through two feet of water.
6. To catch his breath or move.
7. He slowly lowered the pan into the creek above the glint.
8. With a gentle, circular motion, he swished the pan.
9. A nugget of gold nestled in the bottom.
10. Fingers trembling with excitement.

EXERCISE B: Write whether each fragment needs a *subject*, a *verb*, or a *main clause* to become a sentence.

> **Example:** Carried it all the way home.
> **Answer:** subject

1. If you want to learn to play canasta.
2. It difficult to play.
3. Learned to play with a friend of mine.
4. Who became my second shadow.
5. Also taught me to ski.
6. She the better skier.
7. Rides a bike better, too.
8. However, I the better skater.
9. If you have a good friend.
10. Are lucky.

EXERCISE C: If an item contains only sentences, write *Correct*. If it contains fragments, rewrite the item to correct the fragments.

> **Example:** The word *comet* comes from a Greek word. Meaning "long-haired."
> **Answer:** The word *comet* comes from a Greek word meaning "long-haired."

1. Every seventy-six years, Halley's Comet is visible. To us here on Earth.
2. It was seen in 1910, when Earth actually passed. Through part of its tail.
3. Fearing poisonous gases, many people became hysterical.
4. Some even bought "comet pills." To protect themselves.
5. Of course. Halley's Comet is a harmless mass. Of ice, gas, and dust.

Run-on Sentences

EXERCISE A: Label each item as *sentence* or *run-on*.

> **Example:** Do you know about Harriet Tubman she was once a slave.
> **Answer:** run-on

1. She escaped in 1849 she risked her life to save other slaves.
2. Tubman would lead slaves north using the "Underground Railroad."
3. The Underground Railroad was a system of helping slaves to escape, it existed 1830–1860.
4. During the Civil War, she served the Union as a nurse and a scout.
5. She was a brave woman, she was also a big help to the army.

EXERCISE B: Correct the run-on sentences. For the first two sentences, use an end mark and a capital. For the third sentence, use a comma and a conjunction. For the last sentence, use a semicolon to correct the run-on.

> **Example:**   George Washington was elected President on April 20, 1789, thirty-five years of public service already lay behind him.
> **Possible Answers:** George Washington was elected President on April 20, 1789. Thirty-five years of public service already lay behind him.
> George Washington was elected President on April 20, 1789, and thirty-five years of service already lay behind him.
> George Washington was elected President on April 20, 1789; thirty-five years of service lay behind him.

1. He served two terms as President, he inspired confidence.
2. John Adams had also served his country well before he became the second President of the United States he took office in 1796.
3. Thomas Jefferson served as President from 1801 to 1809 he may be best known as the author of the Declaration of Independence.
4. Jefferson was interested in science and geography he arranged an expedition to have the Louisiana Purchase explored.

EXERCISE C: Rewrite each run-on. Use an end mark and a capital letter, a comma and a coordinating conjunction, or a semicolon to correct the error.

1. Have you ever read *A Wind In the Door*, it's a great science-fiction story about a little boy named Charles Wallace and his sister Meg.
2. Charles Wallace is having trouble in school, he's also seriously ill and getting sicker every day.
3. Determined to help her brother, Meg asks for help from the school principal, she learns that an alien has taken over his mind!
4. Meg gets help from her friend Calvin and a dragon-like creature from another planet, meeting the alien is Meg's first step to saving her brother.

Stringy Sentences

EXERCISE A: Rewrite each item as two complete, separate sentences.

Example: My brother Rudy went to the dentist and Rudy asked the dentist questions about braces and Rudy wanted to know how long he might be wearing them.
Answer: My brother Rudy went to the dentist and asked him questions about braces. Rudy wanted to know how long he might be wearing them.

1. The dentist showed Rudy X-ray pictures of his teeth and the dentist gave him a booklet to read and at that point the dentist showed Rudy pictures of some of his former patients.
2. The dentist explained that there were some things that Rudy could do to shorten the time he would need braces and that included brushing his teeth regularly and not to mention eating the right snacks.

EXERCISE B: Rewrite each item to correct stringy sentences.

Example: Our neighbors just got a new dog and it's mostly white with a few black marks and it's got a long, furry tail.
Answer: Our neighbors just got a new dog. It's mostly white with a few black marks and a long, furry tail.

1. When they brought the dog home it barked all night and nobody on our block could sleep and the dog wouldn't stop barking.
2. And then after a while the dog calmed down and then he wasn't so bad to have next door and then we even became friends.
3. I asked my neighbors if it were okay to give the dog some treats and they said I could and they showed me which kind to get.
4. I taught that dog a lot of tricks, like he can sit up, and beg, and I also taught him to jump through a hoop.
5. Eventually, the dog even became friendly with our cat, the two animals would eat together, and they would play together, and sometimes even sleep side-by-side on the bed.

EXERCISE C: List five things you would like to do after school. Write a paragraph using the items on your list. As you edit, correct stringy sentences.

Choppy Sentences

EXERCISE A: Combine two or more choppy ideas by using one or more conjunctions.

> **Example:** Sammy likes to play baseball. He practices every day. Sammy hopes to make it to the professional leagues.
>
> **Answer:** Sammy likes to play baseball. He practices every day <u>because</u> he hopes to make it to the professional leagues.

1. Sammy has played in Little League. He has played short stop. He has played second base.
2. Sammy has won several awards. He has won a trophy for batting. He has received a trophy for his defense. Sammy was named Most Improved Player this year.
3. Sammy likes to listen to baseball games on the radio. He watches games on television. Going to the stadium is Sammy's favorite way to watch the team.
4. Sammy wants to know about his favorite players. He reads the newspaper. Sammy reads magazines about sports.
5. Sammy has recently received an encyclopedia about baseball. He reads a few entries in it every day. Sammy wants to be a sports announcer or a sports journalist someday.

EXERCISE B: Rewrite the paragraph, correcting choppy sentences. Your finished paragraph should contain five sentences.

> **Example:** The workers are repairing a bridge in our neighborhood. The bridge is at the end of the street. It will take four months to repair. The workers have built a toolshed on our street.
>
> **Answer:** The workers are repairing a bridge at the end of the street. Because it will take four months to repair, the workers have built a toolshed on our street.

The trucks arrived today. The bulldozers. They brought graders. The foreman arrived. The supervisor arrived. The whole crew was there by eight o'clock. They broke up the concrete. They hauled away stones. They cleared the site. They put up fences. They posted warnings. They closed the road as they worked.

EXERCISE C: Think of a job that might require a variety of tools. List four tools you might need to complete this job; then write a paragraph explaining how you would use these tools. Edit your writing to correct choppy sentences.

Wordy Sentences

EXERCISE A: Write the letter of the less wordy sentence in each pair.

   Example: a. Gus is a student who deserves to be class president.

   b. Gus deserves to be class president.

   Answer: b

1. a.   Gus participates in sports in spite of the fact that these activities require plenty of time.
   b.   Gus participates in sports although these activities require plenty of time.
2. a.   You can trust Gus to do the right thing.
   b.   What I want to say is that Gus is a person whom you can trust to do the right thing.
3. a.   Gus is well liked on account of the fact that he is thoughtful not only to his teammates but also to his classmates.
   b.   Gus is well liked because he is thoughtful to his teammates and his classmates.
4. a.   The reason why my parents compare me with Gus is because we were born on the same day.
   b.   The reason that my parents compare me with Gus is because we were born on the same day.

EXERCISE B: Rewrite the sentences, eliminating wordiness.

   Example: The wolverine is one of the most ferocious hunters in the places that are woods in spite of the fact that it is smaller than most of the prey that it hunts.
   Answer: The wolverine is one of the most ferocious hunters in the woods although it is smaller than most of its prey.

1. The reason why a wolverine is fierce is because its jaws and teeth are very strong.
2. Wolverines are feared on account of the fact that they have strong, sharp claws.
3. A wolverine is an animal that is very seldom found in a starving condition.
4. What I mean is they are clever hunters and in fact are fearless.

EXERCISE C: Rewrite the paragraph, deleting words that do not add meaning.

   Lasers are becoming more common in spite of the fact that many people view them with a kind of suspicion. The reason why lasers are used in surveying is that they can be focused accurately. Because of the fact that lasers have proven useful in space, people now find jobs for lasers here on earth. What I want to say is that you will see lasers at work in grocery stores, in museums, and in hospitals. So it's like they are not so special or unique anymore.

Empty Sentences

EXERCISE A: If an item contains ideas that are repeated, write *repetition*. If an item needs supporting details, write *details*.

> **Example:** The discovery of gold in California brought people to search for gold. News of gold caused many miners to come to California.
> **Answer:** repetition

1. People came from all over to search for gold. Some people traveled a long way to search for gold.
2. The long journey to the gold fields was really something.
3. Miners paid a high price for expensive food and shelter.
4. Most of the prospectors came away luckless. They never found any gold.
5. The California gold rush began in 1848 or 1849. It occurred in the mid-nineteenth century.

EXERCISE B: Revise each item. Delete empty sentences that repeat ideas stated elsewhere. Add supporting details to sentences that make unsupported statements of fact.

> **Example:** Most moths survive because of their hearing. Moths have sharp ears.
> **Answer:** Most moths survive because of their hearing.

1. Moths have different enemies.
2. If a moth is detected by a bat, it will turn its wings so that the edges are pointed toward the bat. It faces its edges toward the bat.
3. The wings of a moth are thin. They have a fine edge, which makes them difficult to see.
4. Moths are good escape artists because moths are good at getting out of danger.
5. Moths can flee quickly. They can fly away before you know it.

EXERCISE C: Choose an animal and list four ways in which that animal defends itself. Then write a paragraph explaining how the animal protects itself from its predators. Make sure that your paragraph contains no empty sentences.

Lack of Parallel Structure

EXERCISE A: Write whether each sentence is *parallel* or *not parallel*. If it is not parallel, write the word or phrase that needs rephrasing.

> **Example:** I saw a movie that was interesting, exciting, and a real thrill to watch.
> **Answer:** not parallel   a real thrill to watch

1. It began with a fight among creatures from Jupiter, Venus, and Martians.
2. The Martians were intelligent, kind, and with a lot of courage.
3. The creatures from Jupiter wanted resources, to expand their territory, and, finally, to conquer the universe.
4. Choosing sides, helping their allies, and deciding the final outcome was up to the Venusians.

EXERCISE B: Rewrite each sentence that is not parallel in structure. If a sentence is parallel, write *Correct*.

> **Example:** Gwendolyn Brooks, who is a poet and she writes novels, is a great writer!
> **Answer:**   Gwendolyn Brooks, who is a poet and novelist, is a great writer!

1. Brooks has been named "Woman of the Year" and winning the Pulitzer Prize.
2. She has written fifteen books of poetry and one novel.
3. Her writing is moving, interesting, and it makes you think.
4. Brooks also sponsors a contest that offers prizes to ten high-school poets and ten poets who are in grade school.

EXERCISE C: Combine the following pairs or groups of sentences. Make sure that each new sentence is parallel in structure.

> **Example:** Some volcanoes are caused by gases breaking through an opening in the earth's crust. Lava and pieces of rock can break through it, too.
> **Answer:**   Some volcanoes are caused by gases, lava, and pieces of rock breaking through the earth's crust.

1. Lava can take the form of hot, melted rock. Lava can also take the form of hard, cooled rock.
2. A volcano might be active. It might also be dormant. It might also be extinct.
3. There are eight active volcanoes on Jupiter. Many volcanoes are active on Mars, too.
4. The study of volcanoes is fascinating. It's important to study volcanoes.

Confusing Shifts of Verb Tenses and Pronouns in Sentences

EXERCISE A: Choose the word that correctly completes each sentence.

> **Example:** Maples are my favorite trees. They provide much shade. (Its, Their) leaves turn
> colors in autumn.
> **Answer:** Their

1. Walnuts are important trees, too. They produce sweet-tasting nuts. They (will grow, grow) rapidly.
2. Willows are often found near water. (It is, They are) usually seen by the edge of a pond or lake.
3. Birches have paper-like bark. They (grow, have grown) in groups of three. They are easy to identify.
4. Cedars are a variety of evergreen trees. (It, They) have needles even through cold winters. The wood (has, will have) a distinctive fragrance.
5. Cedar chests are wonderful pieces of furniture. (It, They) often hold the memories of a lifetime.

EXERCISE B: Rewrite the items, correcting unnecessary changes in verb tenses and personal pronouns.

> **Example:** Botanists study plants in different ways. He will be in a laboratory. He may study
> plants in the field.
> **Answer:** Botanists study plants in different ways: in a laboratory or in the field.

1. Plant pathologists specialize in diseases that are harmful to plants. Your work helps farmers raise successful crops.
2. Some plant pathologists study viruses. They can live on lettuce, causing disease. It has killed the lettuce.

EXERCISE C: Rewrite the paragraph, completing it with appropriate verbs and pronouns.

> **Example:** Dora _____ comic books. _____ trades comic books at conventions.
> **Answer:** Dora <u>collects</u> comic books. <u>She</u> trades comic books at conventions.

Dora _____ a copy of a 1967 comic and traded one of her favorite comic books for it. Dora keeps her special comic books wrapped in plastic. She files _____ in alphabetical order so she can find them easily. Dora draws comics, too, and _____ hopes to become an illustrator. Dora always _____ watercolors in her illustrations.

Sentence Combining

Sentence Combining with Coordinating Conjunctions

EXERCISE A: Write the coordinating conjunction that connects each pair of main clauses. (Do not write conjunctions that serve other purposes.)

> **Example:** Baseball was invented almost two hundred years ago, and people have been playing it ever since.
> **Answer:** and

1. The National League was organized in 1876, and the American League was organized in 1900.
2. Baseball fans might have just one favorite team, or they might have a favorite in each league.
3. Some fans want to prove their devotion, so they memorize a team's statistics.
4. Other fans don't care about statistics, nor do they know much about their team's players.
5. Fans may follow the game in different ways, yet almost everybody cares about the World Series.

EXERCISE B: Combine each pair of simple sentences with one of these coordinating conjunctions: *and, but, or, nor, for, so,* or *yet.*

> **Example:** I don't know much about robots. I'd like to learn.
> **Answer:** I don't know much about robots, but I'd like to learn.

1. Robots are used for different purposes. They come in different shapes and sizes.
2. A robot might do a factory job. It might play the piano in a pizza parlor.
3. A robot might appear in a science-fiction novel. It might be seen in a movie.
4. Some people are scared of robots. There's no need.
5. Robots can do many wonderful things. They'll never replace people!

EXERCISE C: Combine four pairs of simple sentences in the paragraph, using coordinating conjunctions.

> **Example:** Tokyo is the capital of Japan. It's also the world's second largest city.
> **Answer:** Tokyo is the capital of Japan, and it's also the world's second largest city.

Japan consists of four main islands. It also includes many smaller islands. Heavy rains fall frequently in Japan. Typhoons are also common. According to legend, Japan was founded in 660 B.C.; however, records go back only to A.D. 400. Japan is now a major industrial power. The Japanese have kept many of their traditions. They have a democratic form of government. The emperor is still considered the head of state.

Sentence Combining with Subordinating Conjunctions

EXERCISE A: Use the words in parentheses to connect the two sentences. Make sure to use commas where needed.

>   **Example:** I get to Los Angeles. I'll give you a call. (when)
>   **Answer:** <u>When</u> I get to Los Angeles, I'll give you a call.

1. I see Uncle Albert. I'll give him your present. (as soon as)
2. I do anything else. I'm going to have one of Aunt Lily's special sandwiches. (before)
3. She always makes me one. I visit. (whenever)
4. I eat. She tells me all the news. (while)
5. I won't rest. We're all caught up! (until)

EXERCISE B: Use an appropriate subordinating conjunction to combine each pair of sentences. Be sure to use commas correctly.

>   **Example:** Most mammals live on land. Some live in the sea.
>   **Answer:** <u>Although</u> most mammals live on land, some live in the sea.

1. The weather gets colder. Whales migrate to warmer waters.
2. The spring comes. They swim north again.
3. They are always seeking places. They can get food.
4. The dolphin is much smaller than the whale. They are close relations.
5. We should try to protect sea mammals. We can.

EXERCISE C: Write a complex sentence to answer each question. In each sentence, underline the subordinating conjunction that connects ideas.

>   **Example:** When will you study for the test?
>   **Answer:** I'll study for the test <u>as soon as</u> I've finished dinner.

1. Why do you have all those books?
2. How long will you study?
3. What would happen if you didn't study?
4. What will happen if you do study?
5. Where will you study?

Sentence Combining with Compound Subjects and Predicates

EXERCISE A: Write whether each sentence contains a *compound subject* or a *compound predicate*.

Example: Our stories and poems were published in a class magazine.
Answer: compound subject

1. The scientists discovered and perfected a powerful new serum.
2. Either Mom or Dad will chaperone the dance next Friday.
3. Are North, South, East, and West the points of the compass?
4. Ross welcomed me and showed me around but failed to introduce his friends.
5. Your essays and your exercises will be collected and graded.

EXERCISE B: Add each idea in parentheses to the sentence that comes before it. Write the new sentence and label it as having a *compound subject* or a *compound predicate*.

Example: Smoke from the grill drifted through the window. (filled the room)
Answer: Smoke from the grill drifted through the window and filled the room.
(compound predicate)

1. Cars thronged the parking lot. (buses)
2. The rescue ship sped to the scene. (began to search for survivors)
3. On the front lawn, a maple tree provided shade. (a willow)
4. You may wait for us at the library. (go by yourself to the mall)
5. I tasted the asparagus. (chewed, swallowed it quickly)

EXERCISE C: Combine each set of sentences, using a compound subject or a compound predicate. Label the compound element in each sentence.

Example: Sonnets are one form of lyric poetry. Elegies are another.
Answer: Sonnets and elegies are forms of lyric poetry. (compound subject)

1. The glasses did not get clean. The silverware did not get clean either.
2. Spanish explorers conquered the Aztecs. Then they subjugated the people.
3. Rosa may call. Rafael may call you. Richie may call.
4. Amber arrived at the party on time. She didn't stay long.
5. Will you study during this free period? Will you work quietly with your partner? Will you read?

Name _____ Class _____ Date _____

Sentence Variety

Types of Sentence Structure

EXERCISE A: Identify the structure of each sentence as *simple, compound, complex,* or *compound-complex.*

> **Example:** How I enjoy an afternoon of skiing!
> **Answer:** simple

1. Do you glide on cross-country skis, or do you prefer downhill skiing?
2. Skis probably were invented by people who lived in Europe about five thousand years ago.
3. For a long time, skiing was primarily a European activity.
4. After ski lifts were developed in the 1930's, skiing became popular in the United States; it remains so today.

EXERCISE B: Combine each set of simple sentences to make the kind of sentence indicated in parentheses.

> **Example:** I studied a book about sea creatures. I chose the manta ray as the subject for my report. (complex)
> **Answer:** After I studied a book about sea creatures, I chose the manta ray as the subject for my report.

1. The enormous manta ray looks dangerous. It actually is harmless. It feeds on nothing larger than shrimp. (compound-complex)
2. It does not carry poison in its tapered tail. A manta ray still is a very powerful animal. (compound)
3. Mantas often weigh 1.5 tons. They have been measured at as much as 23 feet across. (compound)
4. You may see a manta ray. You go swimming off the coast of Florida. (complex)

EXERCISE C: Combine each set of simple sentences to make a compound, complex, or compound-complex sentence. Label your answer.

> **Example:** Ice skates and roller skates have been around for many years. Skateboards and roller blades are relatively new.
> **Answer:** Although ice skates and roller skates have been around for many years, skateboards and roller blades are relatively new. (complex)

1. The first ice skates were a form of transportation. They probably were made from animal bones tied to the feet with thongs.
2. Skates with wooden blades were used during the Middle Ages. Steel blades were not introduced until the nineteenth century.
3. Roller skates also were introduced in the 1800's. The earliest models used wood instead of steel for wheels.
4. Crude skateboards appeared in the 1960's. In-line skates are the newest skating sensation. They are called roller blades.

Varying Sentence Structure

EXERCISE A: Add a main clause or a subordinate clause to each simple sentence, as directed in parentheses. Identify each new sentence as *compound*, *complex*, or *compound-complex*.

> **Example:** Do you fear dangerous land animals? (main clause)
> **Answer:** Do you fear dangerous land animals, <u>or do some fish scare you</u>? (compound)

1. Sharks are perhaps the most feared fish in the world. (main clause)
2. A shark can attack silently and suddenly. (subordinate clause)
3. Some people actually like to fish for them! (main clause)
4. Most people fear the poison of a rattlesnake's bite. (main clause, subordinate clause)
5. Would you run? (subordinate clause)

EXERCISE B: Add to each simple sentence or combine each set of simple sentences to make the kind of sentence indicated in parentheses.

> **Example:** C.S. Lewis wrote a wonderful series of children's books. (compound)
> **Answer:** <u>C.S. Lewis is best remembered for his religious books, but he also</u> wrote a wonderful series of children's books.

1. Lewis wrote literary essays, autobiographical works, science fiction, and children's books. (compound)
2. *The Chronicles of Narnia* is a modern classic. It is a collection of his seven children's novels. (complex)
3. You read the first novel, *The Lion, the Witch, and the Wardrobe*. You become part of the magical land of Narnia. (complex)
4. Talking animals live in Narnia's deep woods. (compound)
5. Four children enter Narnia. They meet Aslan, the great lion. Together they free Narnia from the White Witch's eternal winter. (compound-complex)

EXERCISE C: Write an anecodote about something you did as a child—something that makes you laugh when you think about it now. Include at least one example of each of the four kinds of sentences—simple, compound, complex, and compound-complex—in your anecdote.

Varying Sentence Length

EXERCISE A: Combine each pair of short sentences into one sentence, using any method you wish. Use commas where needed.

> **Example:** One of the loveliest palaces in Europe is the Alhambra. The Alhambra is located in southern Spain.
> **Answer:** One of the loveliest palaces in Europe is the Alhambra, <u>located in southern Spain</u>.

1. The name *Alhambra* is Arabic. It means "crimson castle."
2. Muhammed Al-Ahmar began building the palace. He probably began around A.D. 1238.
3. Many rooms overlook courtyards. The courtyards usually have fountains and sculptures.
4. An American author wrote a book about the Alhambra. The author was Washington Irving.

EXERCISE B: Rewrite the paragraph, combining some of the short sentences. Change some of the information into appositives, phrases, or dependent clauses. The finished paragraph should have ten sentences.

> **Example:** I finally finished my science project. It is due tomorrow.
> **Answer:** I finally finished my science project, <u>which is due tomorrow</u>.

My project involved making dyes. I used onion skins, banana peels, and blackberries. First I boiled the plant parts. The plant parts made a "dye bath." I added chemicals. The chemicals strengthened the color. Copper sulphate brightened the dye. The copper sulphate was a blue powder. Tin dulled the dye. The tin was a yellow powder. I added vinegar and soda. The dye bubbled. Textiles were placed in the dye. They soaked for an hour. The onion skins made the deepest color. The color was a rich gold. The banana peels were a slick brown heap. They were disgusting. The dyes simmered on the stove. They really made a mess of our kitchen!

EXERCISE C: Rewrite each sentence as directed in parentheses.

> **Example:** My best friend _____ recently saved my life. (Add an appositive.)
> **Answer:** My best friend, <u>Royce Glazer</u>, recently saved my life.

1. My best friend has _____ _____ _____ hair. (Add three adjectives.)
2. Once _____ _____ I had a close call. (Add two prepositional phrases.)
3. A car _____ nearly hit me. (Add a participial phrase.)
4. _____ Royce yelled, just in time. (Add a quotation.)

Varying Sentence Beginnings

EXERCISE A: Rewrite each sentence, moving the underlined word or words to a different position in the sentence. Add commas where needed.

> **Example:** *Alice in Wonderland*, <u>written by a Lewis Carroll</u>, is an amusing book.
> **Answer:** <u>Written by Lewis Carroll</u>, *Alice in Wonderland* is an amusing book.

1. Carroll, <u>a shy math teacher</u>, wrote the book to entertain children.
2. Alice is reading in the garden <u>at the beginning of the story</u>.
3. A white rabbit dashes across the lawn, <u>muttering to himself</u>.
4. He disappears down a hole when <u>Alice follows him</u>.
5. "Where did he go?" <u>Alice wonders</u>.
6. Alice, <u>unafraid and curious</u>, tumbles in after him.
7. Alice finds a tiny bottle <u>at the bottom of the hole</u>.
8. The words on the bottle read, "<u>Drink me</u>."
9. Alice, <u>upon swallowing the liquid</u>, grows very small.
10. <u>Meanwhile</u>, the rabbit had disappeared again.

EXERCISE B: Use each item to write a sentence about your favorite book or movie. Then rewrite the sentence, moving the item to a different location.

> **Example:** my favorite movie
> **Answers:** <u>My favorite movie</u>, *Home Alone*, was a big box-office hit.
>
> *Home Alone*, <u>my favorite movie</u>, was a big box-office hit.

1. at the beginning of the movie
2. as the story unfolds
3. adding excitement to the plot
4. by the way
5. when the movie ends

EXERCISE C: Complete each sentence with a word or words that answer the question in parentheses. Then rewrite the sentences, repositioning the word or words that you added.

> **Example:** We stopped at the card shop. (When did you stop?)
> **Answers:** We stopped at the card shop <u>on our way home</u>.
>
> <u>On our way home</u>, we stopped at the card shop.

1. Hillary was looking for a Mother's Day card. (Who is Hillary?)
2. She complained. (What did she say?)
3. Hillary and I examined several cards. (How did you examine them?)
4. She paid for the card at the counter. (What did she do before paying?)

Word Choice

Using Connotation and Denotation

EXERCISE A: Choose the word in parentheses that gives each sentence a more positive connotation.

>   **Example:** Mr. Tyrone's work has always been (adequate/satisfactory).
>   **Answer:**   satisfactory

1. Throughout the interview, Mr. Tyrone felt (sedate/relaxed).
2. He (believed/suspected) that he had interviewed well.
3. Finally, the interviewer (took/chose) Mr. Tyrone for the job.
4. Mr. Tyrone was (delighted/happy) to accept.
5. His new boss predicted a (good/prosperous) future for Mr. Tyrone.

EXERCISE B: Change one or more words in each sentence to create the impression indicated.

>   **Example:** Create a more mysterious impression: The old brick building sat in the
>   overgrown lot.
>   **Answer:**   The ancient brick building hid in the weedy lot.

1. Create a more positive impression: You could tell that the comedy was a success because the audience looked happy.
2. Create a more negative impression: The movie was bad because the ending was so likely.
3. Create a milder impression: I thought the film was loathsome because it was extraordinarily tedious.
4. Create a more humorous impression: My favorite movie has a cast of silly characters.
5. Create a more somber impression: The movie shows a vivid picture about the unpleasantness of war.

EXERCISE C: Change the impression of the paragraph by replacing ten words. Choose your own impression, or select one of the following: positive, negative, mysterious, or humorous.

>   **Example:** The magician's tricks were very amusing.
>   **Answer:**   more positive: The magician's tricks were completely astonishing.

When I look out my window, I see a field of white snow covering the farm. It is not yet morning, and no one else is awake. One dog runs across the snow, looking for scraps. A sound of wind rushes through the air.

Choosing Specific, Concrete Words

EXERCISE A: Replace each underlined word with a more specific or concrete term.

> **Example:** The garden <u>house</u> is a <u>nice</u> place to have a <u>meal</u>.
> **Answer:** The gazebo is a delightful place to have a picnic.

1. Alana brought a large wicker hamper <u>filled</u> with <u>good</u> food.
2. Mr. Márquez <u>got</u> into the water.
3. His swimming strokes were <u>good</u> and <u>easy</u>.
4. Then the ants <u>showed up</u> and <u>covered</u> the food.
5. The picnickers <u>put</u> their food into a <u>boat</u> and <u>went</u> to a raft in the middle of the lake.

EXERCISE B: Rewrite each sentence. Replace vague or abstract terms with specific, concrete words.

> **Example:** Leroy made a stack out of blocks.
> **Answer:** Leroy <u>constructed</u> a <u>tower</u> out of blocks.

1. Pamela works at a good child-care center found right in town.
2. Her job gives her happiness.
3. The children at the center are a bunch of different ages.
4. Pamela is a good worker because she is good with children.
5. A child-care center should always serve good food for snacks and meals.
6. Abigail, has a cold, so she is not at the center today.
7. The people who are responsible for the children try to make sure that the children do not come into contact with many illnesses.
8. It takes a lot of clever thinking to get a two-year-old's attention.
9. The wall of blocks fell down when the children came up to it.
10. The children laughed because the wet puppet looked funny.

EXERCISE C: Rewrite the paragraph, replacing vague or abstract terms with specific, concrete words.

> **Example:** The artist's work was meant to be read to people.
> **Answer:** The <u>writer's poetry</u> was meant to be read <u>aloud</u>.

The Harlem Renaissance of the 1920's was a time of big literary interest. The period got its name from the African-American region of New York called Harlem. Many bright people were part of this movement, such as Claude McKay, Countee Cullen, and Langston Hughes. The period included people who produced art, people who wrote novels, and people who wrote poems.

Varieties of English

Formal and Informal English

EXERCISE A: Write whether each sentence uses *formal* or *informal* English. If it uses informal English, identify the colloquialism used.

> **Example:** Don't tinker with the controls, please.
> **Answer:** informal   tinker

1. The control panel is delicate.
2. We will scoot out of here in five minutes.
3. The astronauts are ready to roll.
4. They have been preparing for months.
5. Several of them have the jitters.

EXERCISE B: Write the more formal word or phrase from the choice in parentheses.

> **Example:** The law was (declared, called) unconstitutional.
> **Answer:** declared

1. Many (kids, students) are reading below average.
2. (You, One) may not use school buildings after hours.
3. I felt (up, happy) about my test results.
4. My homework assigment (gave me chills, unnerved me).
5. (Lots of, Many) students complained to the teacher.
6. Perhaps (we'll, we shall) protest formally.
7. (Who's going to, Who will) help me draft a letter?
8. I (do not care, couldn't care less) if he fails me.
9. (Flunking out, Failing) seems unlikely, however.
10. I must (stand up for, defend) what is right.

EXERCISE C: Rewrite each sentence in informal English.

> **Example:** They are involved in many athletic endeavors.
> **Answer:** They play a lot of sports.

1. We spent a memorable evening at the theater.
2. Artists must register to participate.
3. Did the attorneys negotiate a settlement?
4. Audience participation was encouraged.

Slang and Clichés

EXERCISE A: Match each slang or clichéd expression with its more formal meaning.

Example: 1. far out   a. splendid
Answer: a.

___ 1. blast
___ 2. like a drowned rat
___ 3. ditsy
___ 4. mess up
___ 5. chill out

a. relax
b. senseless
c. err
d. good time
e. soaked

EXERCISE B: Rewrite each sentence, replacing slang and clichés with more formal language.

Example: The three friends chattered like monkeys.
Answer: The three friends chattered <u>aimlessly</u>.

1. Pay attention! You seem bummed out today.
2. Wasn't his description of the snakes gross?
3. The overloaded rowboat sank pronto.
4. Mom freaked when she saw my report card!

EXERCISE C: Rewrite this part of a letter, replacing the underlined slang with more formal language and the underlined clichés with fresher and more colorful figures of speech.

Example: I love them <u>to the max</u>.
Answer: I love them very much.

Dear Aunt Courtney,

    My friends and I <u>flipped</u> over the <u>cool</u> in-line skates you sent. They were <u>dynamite</u>! I fly <u>like the wind</u> when I wear them.

    The other day, I was <u>partying</u> with some <u>kids</u> from the <u>'hood</u>, and we decided to see a movie. Yolanda wanted to see the one about the giant sea slugs, but I wanted to see something a little <u>more tame</u>. We ended up at a <u>hot new</u> movie, where we all had a <u>blast</u>.

Your niece,

Ruby

Dialect and Jargon

EXERCISE A: Identify each underlined expression as *dialect* or *jargon*.

> **Example:** Why don't you just <u>set a spell?</u>
> **Answer:** dialect

1. We stayed at a <u>B & B</u> in North Carolina.
2. The <u>menfolks</u> went for a walk in the hills.
3. I sat and <u>jawed</u> <u>for a spell</u> with the owner.
4. She told me where I might go <u>antiquing.</u>
5. It was <u>a ways</u> from here.

EXERCISE B: Match each example of dialect or jargon with its more formal and familiar meaning.

> **Example:** 1. I been   a. I have been   b. I am
> **Answer:** <u>a</u>

___ 1. a far piece   a. care
___ 2. 20-20   b. perfect vision
___ 3. boot up   c. ammunition
___ 4. give a hoot   d. a long way
___ 5. ammo   e. start

EXERCISE C: Rewrite each sentence, replacing dialect and jargon with more formal or less technical language. Use a dictionary if needed.

> **Example:** We's expectin' some bad weather.
> **Answer:** We <u>are expecting</u> some bad weather.

1. He been working there for many years.
2. Send me some E-mail when you know the answer.
3. The soldier who vanished was declared AWOL.
4. Did the ref force him to leave the game?
5. I visited friends in the barrio.

Figurative Language

Simile and Metaphor

EXERCISE A: Write whether each sentence contains a *simile* or a *metaphor*. Then write what each figure of speech compares.

> **Example:** Across the sky swept the clouds, herds of woolly sheep.
> **Answer:** metaphor   clouds—herds of woolly sheep

1. The jewels at the queen's throat flashed like blue fire.
2. On that most perfect of summer evenings, the moon was a sugar cookie in the sky.
3. Good grief, Mom! That joke is as stale as week-old bread!
4. When my sister Tiffany dances, she is cat-like in her gracefulness.
5. As I walked past the construction site, jackhammer drumbeats set my pace.

EXERCISE B: Complete each sentence with a simile or metaphor of your own. Label the figure of speech in each sentence.

> **Example:** We set off along the trail, chattering _____.
> **Answer:** We set off along the trail, chattering like squirrels. (simile)

1. Before long, however, my feet began stinging _____.
2. Reid, _____, continued to lead us forward, ignoring my pleas for a few minutes of rest.
3. After a two-hour hike in the sun, a drink of water was _____.
4. It was _____ to my parched throat.
5. With a sigh of gratitude, I eased out of my backpack, _____.

EXERCISE C: Use a simile or metaphor to write a sentence comparing each pair of items. Label the figure of speech in each sentence.

> **Example:** Ms. Johnson's voice/a knife
> **Answer:** Ms. Johnson's voice is as sharp as a knife. (simile)

1. her comments about my report/spicy mustard
2. a tangled web/contradictions in my writing
3. whispering voice/my conscience
4. the way I had written the report/a runaway subway train
5. my computer's beeping/a red flag

Personification and Symbol

EXERCISE A: Write whether each phrase contains an example of *personification* or *symbol*. (At least two phrases contain both.)

> **Example:** the crown of the ancient Egyptian pharaoh
> **Answer:** symbol

1. the royal chariots, rumbling their warning to rebels
2. a circle, sign of perfection
3. a jackal, messenger of death
4. wisdom, speaking to the king through the voice of his young daughter
5. the sun, source of all light and giver of all hope

EXERCISE B: For each item write a phrase or sentence that includes an example of personification. Then use a word or phrase to identify what the item symbolizes to you.

> **Example:** flags
> **Answer:** The flags in the wind opened welcoming arms to the marchers.
>   patriotism;   Mother Country

1. a red rose
2. the sun
3. bass drums
4. the earth

EXERCISE C: Using each item as a springboard, write a sentence with personification. Then write at least two possible symbolic meanings for each item.

> **Example:** an armchair
> **Answer:** The armchair beckoned me invitingly. (personification)
>   comfort, hospitality   (symbolic meanings)

1. the moon
2. a clock
3. a storm
4. a lamp

Answer Key

The Elements of Writing

Paragraph Structure

Parts of a Paragraph: Topic Sentences, EXERCISE A
b

Parts of a Paragraph: Topic Sentences, EXERCISE B
Answers will vary; possible answers are given.
1. Lake Pierre is a great summer attraction.
2. You have many choices when it comes to buying a lawnmower.

Parts of a Paragraph: Topic Sentences, EXERCISE C
Answers will vary; possible topic sentences are given.
1. My brother was rewarded for a generous deed he did.
2. My practice schedule before a recital is grueling.
3. Starlings are building nests in our garage.
4. Washing dishes is one hateful chore that I'd like to see eliminated.
5. I quizzed several students on their choice for the worst show on TV.

Parts of a Paragraph: Supporting Sentences, EXERCISE A
1. supports
2. does not support
3. supports
4. does not support

Parts of a Paragraph: Supporting Sentences, EXERCISE B
1. d
2. c
3. a
4. b

Parts of a Paragraph: Supporting Sentences, EXERCISE C
Answers will vary; possible answers are given.
1. They also should think about how much it will cost to feed the pet.
2. Many other kinds of fish require much larger homes.
3. They are both short, solid, and feisty.
4. You also will find a complete selection of leashes and clothing.

Parts of a Paragraph: Concluding Sentences, EXERCISE A
a

Parts of a Paragraph: Concluding Sentences, EXERCISE B
Answers will vary; possible answers are given.
1. At this rate, his election seems assured.
2. The forty dollars I spent on training was money well spent.

Parts of a Paragraph: Concluding Sentences, EXERCISE C
Answers will vary; possible concluding sentences are given.
1. <u>If a sport requires physical stamina, training, and agility, then ballet should be considered a sport.</u>
2. <u>My cooking teacher was inept, but I did learn some valuable lessons—a few were even about cooking!</u>
3. <u>You may think you don't need to eat vegetables if you take vitamins, but you should still include them in your diet.</u>
4. <u>Building the stand is fun; and once it is constructed, the money will come *pouring* in.</u>
5. <u>Pets that shed, pets that make noise, and pets that do nothing at all—those are the only kinds of pets that exist.</u>

Recognizing Effective Paragraphs, EXERCISE A
b;   It is coherent and unified.

Recognizing Effective Paragraphs, EXERCISE B
Answers may vary; a possible answer is given.

   Mowing the lawn is a terrible chore. I would rather do almost anything else. Why don't we get sheep instead of having me mow? After all, the grass just grows back, anyway.

Recognizing Effective Paragraphs, EXERCISE C
Answers will vary; suggested answers are given for the first two topics.
1. For good dental health, my dentist suggests three things. First, brush two or three times a day. Second, floss. Third, get regular checkups. Following these steps may save your teeth.
2. My worst school-related nightmare begins with me walking into the hallway. I'm on my way to math class for the biggest test of the year. Suddenly, however, I can't remember the room number. Even worse, the hall branches in four directions—all of them exactly alike! As the final bell rings, I wake up in a cold sweat.

Unity, Coherence, Transitions

Unity, EXERCISE A
1. A
2. B
3. N
4. B
5. A

Unity, EXERCISE B
Sentences to be deleted are underlined.

   Do you know how commonplace, yet unique, paper is? Just think! <u>Early paper, made from rags, was not easily manufactured</u>. We use it to write on, wrap gifts, dry our hands, eat off it, drink out of it, wrap garbage in it, and fill boxes we're mailing, <u>although lots of people really waste it</u>. In the 1960's, for a short while, paper even showed up as clothing! <u>The Chinese made paper from bamboo and mulberry stalks</u>. Today's paper is inexpensive and plentiful—<u>not like early paper, which had to be pounded together</u>—but its properties are so special that there's really no good substitute for it. <u>Today's paper is a mat of millions of tiny pressed fibers.</u>

Unity, EXERCISE C

Sentences and/or details to be deleted are underlined. Additional sentences will vary; possible additions are given in parentheses.

One wonder that Columbus took back to Europe was a natural substance that West Indian natives used to make waterproof shoes. <u>These were the earliest "sneakers."</u> European inventors first used it to rub out pencil marks, giving the substance the name by which we know it—rubber. For more than two hundred years, inventors tried to find other uses for rubber. <u>Many inventors went broke.</u> However, it became soft and sticky when hot, brittle and stiff when cold. In 1839, quite by accident, American inventer Charles Goodyear, <u>who went to prison because of his debts,</u> added sulfur to natural rubber, making it usable for thousands of products—more than fifty thousand, in fact. Today, (like the West Indian natives, we also use rubber to waterproof shoes.) (We also use it in new ways—for tires, glue, tubing, and rubber bands.)

Coherence Through Time Order, EXERCISE A

The correct order is 3, 5, 4, 2, 1.

Coherence Through Time Order, EXERCISE B

The correct order is 1, 2, 8, 9, 5, 4, 7, 3, 6, 10.

Coherence Through Time Order, EXERCISE C

Previous positions are shown in parentheses.

(5) One Thanksgiving, we were returning to our home in New Mexico from my grandmother's in Kansas. (1) When we left in the morning, the sun was shining. (3) As the day wore on, however, and we came nearer Colorado, clouds, heavy with snow, covered the sun. (2) Snow began to fall, gently at first and then more heavily. (7) Less than an hour after the first snowflake appeared, we couldn't see five feet ahead of us. (4) The highway was hidden under snow, and we inched along at less than one mile per hour for about half an hour! (6) Finally, ahead of us and to the right, we saw a very faint light. (8) Carefully, we pulled off the road, braking to a stop—nearly through the window of a little roadside cafe! (9) As we caught our breath, we watched, astonished, as six other cars followed us. (10) We hadn't seen them behind us through the heavy snow.

Coherence Through Space Order, EXERCISE A

Answers will vary; possible answers are given.
1. feet <u>squeezed into</u> shoes
2. branches <u>above</u> the trunk
3. fence <u>around</u> the yard
4. lid <u>on</u> pan
5. the stop sign <u>to the right</u>
6. napkin <u>under</u> the fork
7. catcher <u>behind</u> home plate
8. bicycle lane <u>across from</u> traffic
9. the airplane <u>overhead</u>
10. picture <u>hanging on</u> the wall

Coherence Through Space Order, EXERCISE B

Answers will vary; possible answers are given.

1. To her left was the ticket agent's counter.
2. To the north, Canada stretches all the way to the "top" of the world.
3. Above him, the full moon watched over the celebration below.
4. The valley with its little stream lay far below him.
5. In front of him stretched Main Street, lined with shops on either side.
6. Stuck at the top, his seat swinging slightly, George gulped and refused to look down.
7. Below her, the clear turquoise water rippled with brightly colored fish.
8. In front of him lay a huge platter of steaming roasted meat.
9. In the distance, a huge swirl of orange and purple clouds was forming.
10. Suddenly, a lightning bolt struck the tree stump just two feet away.

Coherence Through Space Order, EXERCISE C

Answers will vary; possible answers are given. Additions are underlined.

At the state park, Vanessa and Vicky bounded from the car. Looking around, they took stock of the activities that beckoned. Precisely in the middle, of course, sparkled Horseshoe Lake. To the immediate left was the popular little pancake restaurant. Farther down, tennis and volleyball courts lay waiting for players. At the far end of the lake, half a dozen boats crowded around a small dock. To the right, a concrete pathway separated the restaurant from the picnic area, with its tables and barbecue pits. The pathway continued along the right side of the lake. Below, was the bath house. Behind it, a wooded area with a trail beckoned casual hikers. Beside it, a winding bicycle path began.

Coherence Through Other Kinds of Order, EXERCISE A

1. comparison-contrast; on the other hand
2. general to particular; in particular
3. cause-effect; thus
4. general to particular; such as
5. particular to general
6. comparison-contrast; in contrast
7. cause-effect; therefore
8. general to particular; for example
9. comparison-contrast; no other
10. cause-effect; because

Coherence Through Other Kinds of Order, EXERCISE B

Answers will vary; possible answers are given.

1. cause; Because he had stayed up late, Don fell asleep during history class, so he missed the homework assignment. (*Effect* is a possible answer.)
2. effect; Piles of paper and books sat in every room since no one had had time to pick them up. (*Cause* is a possible answer.)
3. The fastest way to travel is by air; it is much faster than a car or even a fast train.
4. particular to general; T-shirts, mugs, and bumper stickers all can be printed with ad slogans; almost any surface can carry advertising.

Coherence Through Other Kinds of Order, EXERCISE C

Paragraphs will vary; a possible paragraph, on the third topic, is given.

Though they're both related to me, my two sets of grandparents are very different from each other. Grandma and Grandpa Reed live in a big house in a farming community in Kansas; Grandma and Grandpa Gould own a condo in West Palm Beach, Florida. They're both retired, but the Reed farm is quite active. Though all my grandparents love music, the Reeds' tastes run to country music, while the Goulds prefer classical music. It will be fun to see what other differences arise when we all get together next July!

Coherence Through Transitional Expressions, EXERCISE A

1. Paper is common, cheap, and good at its many jobs; <u>for these reasons,</u> it has no substitute.
2. Kentucky's Mammoth Caves are protected by the federal government; <u>moreover,</u> they are protected by the United Nations.
3. No law states that only Presidents can appear on our money; <u>nevertheless,</u> most U.S. coins have had Presidents' portraits on them.
4. The late 1950's and early 1960's produced some "wild and crazy" dances; <u>for example,</u> teens danced to the Twist, the Pony, the Swim, and the Chicken.

Coherence Through Transitional Expressions, EXERCISE B

Some answers may vary.

1. Broccoli is a poor source of calcium; <u>on the other hand,</u> it's an excellent source of vitamins C and A.
2. In 1772, a Baltimore, Maryland, storekeeper caused a sensation when he came out carrying the first umbrella in America; <u>in fact,</u> the police had to be called!
3. Most of my family suffers from hay fever in the spring; I <u>however,</u> seem to be immune.
4. I don't understand why you're so mad about tearing that shirt; <u>after all,</u> you never liked it anyway.

Coherence Through Transitional Expressions, EXERCISE C

Answers will vary; possible answers are given.

French toast is a favorite breakfast dish in the United States; <u>in fact,</u> it's a favorite dish in many countries. It goes by various names. In England, <u>for example,</u> where it originated, it's known as "Poor Knights." Penniless, aging English knights of the 1300's became quite clever at "stretching" food—<u>in particular,</u> stale, leftover bread. The knights soaked the stale bread in a mixture of milk, eggs, sugar, and sherry, fried it, and then served it with melted butter. The origin of the name "Poor Knights" is easy to understand; <u>after all,</u> poor knights invented the dish. <u>On the other hand</u>, no one can explain why Americans call it "French toast."

Sentences

Recognizing Subjects and Predicates, EXERCISE A

1. The zoo | is open seven days a week.
2. My brother | likes the monkeys best.
3. The big Siberian tiger | is my favorite.
4. Many of the animals | go outside in warm weather.
5. The zookeepers | feed the animals and clean the cages.
6. My friends and I | enjoy visiting the farm inside the zoo.
7. People | were feeding special food to the goats.
8. My father | bought a yellow balloon for my sister Lisa.
9. Lisa | released the balloon into the air.
10. We | will go to the zoo again next weekend.

Recognizing Subjects and Predicates, EXERCISE B

1. frolicked merrily on the banks of the stream
2. not a sentence
3. not a sentence
4. perfumed the air
5. not a sentence

Recognizing Subjects and Predicates, EXERCISE C

Answers will vary; possible answers are given.
1. <u>The magician</u> performed her act.
2. <u>My best friend</u> lives next door.
3. <u>That little cat</u> is very friendly.
4. <u>Marla's teacher</u> gives a lot of homework.
5. <u>Green vegetables</u> are delicious.
6. <u>Some boys</u> become lifelong friends.
7. <u>Seventh-graders</u> work hard.
8. <u>My favorite memories</u> are of our camping trip.
9. <u>Three sailboats</u> drifted lazily down the river.
10. <u>The elephants</u> had huge tusks.

Recognizing Effective Sentences, EXERCISE A

Answers will vary; possible answers are given.
1. It is not clear and concise.
2. It does not contain a complete thought.
3. It does not emphasize the main idea.
4. It does not contain a complete thought.

Recognizing Effective Sentences, EXERCISE B

Answers will vary; possible answers are given.
1. Teddy clapped as he heard the band play the opening notes of his favorite song.
2. Freedom of speech and freedom of religion are two of the most important guarantees of the Bill of Rights.
3. Our flight was delayed by the blizzard, which some people say was the worst in that part of the country in twenty years.
4. Today, a team of dedicated, hard-working archaeologists is restoring the Great Sphinx to its original condition.

Recognizing Effective Sentences, EXERCISE C

Paragraphs will vary; a possible paragraph for the second topic is given.

I feel very fortunate to know my great-grandmother, Mary Harris. She was born on the first day of the twentieth century—January 1, 1901—and every conversation with her is a living history lesson. More important, she has always displayed characteristics that I want for myself. She showed strength in managing a Texas ranch with her late husband. She showed faith in going on after losing three of her five children in a fire. She showed love in raising a neighbor child who was orphaned in the same fire. The lessons of her life, then and now, teach my heart as well as my mind.

Sentence Problems

Sentence Fragments, EXERCISE A
1. sentence
2. sentence
3. fragment
4. sentence
5. fragment
6. fragment
7. sentence
8. sentence
9. sentence
10. fragment

Sentence Fragments, EXERCISE B

1. main clause
2. verb
3. subject
4. main clause
5. subject
6. verb
7. subject
8. verb
9. main clause
10. subject

Sentence Fragments, EXERCISE C

Answers may vary slightly; possible answers are given.

1. Every seventy-six years, Halley's comet is visible to us here on Earth.
2. It was seen in 1910, when Earth actually passed through part of its tail.
3. Correct
4. Some even bought "comet pills" to protect themselves.
5. Of course, Halley's Comet is a harmless mass of ice, gas, and dust.

Run-on Sentences, EXERCISE A

1. run-on
2. sentence
3. run-on
4. sentence
5. run-on

Run-on Sentences, EXERCISE B

1. He served two terms as President. He inspired confidence.
2. John Adams had also served his country well before he became the second President of the United States. He took office in 1796.
3. Thomas Jefferson served as President from 1801 to 1809, but he may be best known as the author of the Declaration of Independence.
4. Jefferson was interested in science and geography; he arranged to have the Louisiana Purchase explored.

Run-on Sentences, EXERCISE C

1. Have you ever read A Wind In the Door? It's a great science-fiction story about a little boy named Charles Wallace and his sister Meg.
2. Charles Wallace is having trouble in school; he's also seriously ill and getting sicker every day.
3. Determined to help her brother, Meg asks for help from the school principal, but she learns that an alien has taken over his mind!
4. Meg gets help from her friend Calvin and a dragon-like creature from another planet. Meeting the alien is Meg's first step to saving her brother.

Stringy Sentences, EXERCISE A

Answers may vary slightly; possible answers are given.

1. The dentist showed Rudy X-ray pictures of his teeth and gave him a booklet to read. Then the dentist showed Rudy pictures of some of his former patients.
2. The dentist explained there were some things that Rudy could do to shorten the time he would need braces. That included regular brushing and eating the right snacks.

Stringy Sentences, EXERCISE B
Answers may vary slightly; possible answers are given.
  1. When they brought the dog home, it barked all night. Nobody on our block could sleep because the dog wouldn't stop barking.
  2. After a while, the dog calmed down, and then he wasn't so bad to have next door. We even became friends.
  3. I asked my neighbors if it were okay to give the dog some treats. They said I could, and they showed me which kind to get.
  4. I taught that dog a lot of tricks. He can sit up, beg, and jump through a hoop.
  5. Eventually, the dog even became friendly with our cat. The two animals would eat and play together. Sometimes they would even sleep side-by-side on the bed.

Stringy Sentences, EXERCISE C
Answers will vary slightly; possible answers are given.
  1. watch television
  2. read a book
  3. call a friend
  4. play a game
  5. make something
    After school I have a lot of choices of things to do. On Tuesdays and Thursdays I often watch television. If there's nothing good on television, then I might read a book or call a friend. I like to play video games at home, too. Sometimes I make things with the scrap wood that we have in our basement.

Choppy Sentences, EXERCISE A
Answers may vary slightly; possible answers are given.
  1. Sammy has played short stop <u>and</u> second base in Little League.
  2. Sammy has won awards for batting <u>and</u> defense. He was named Most Improved Player this year.
  3. Sammy likes to listen to baseball games on the radio <u>and</u> watch games on television, <u>but</u> going to the stadium is Sammy's favorite way to watch the team.
  4. Sammy reads the newspapers <u>and</u> magazines <u>because</u> he wants to know about his favorite players.
  5. Sammy has recently received an encyclopedia about baseball. He reads a few entries in it every day <u>because</u> he wants to be a sports announcer or a sport journalist someday.

Choppy Sentences, EXERCISE B
Answers may vary; possible answers are given.
    The trucks arrived today, bringing bulldozers and graders. The foreman and then the supervisor arrived. By eight o'clock, the whole crew was there. They broke up the concrete, hauled away stones, and cleared the site. They put up fences, posted warnings, and closed the road as they worked.

Choppy Sentences, EXERCISE C
Answers will vary; possible answers are given.
    Cooking: (a) pots, (b) bowls, (c) spoons, (d) knives
    When I am cooking, I rely on having good tools. The first thing I look for is a sharp knife for chopping and slicing. Then I usually have mixing bowls of different sizes. A set of copper pots can be handy, as is a long-handled spoon.

Wordy Sentences, EXERCISE A
Answers will vary; possible answers are given.
  1. b   2. a   3. b   4. b

Wordy Sentences, EXERCISE B
1. A wolverine is fierce because its jaws and teeth are very strong.
2. Wolverines are feared because they have strong, sharp claws.
3. A wolverine rarely starves.
4. They are clever, fearless hunters.

Wordy Sentences, EXERCISE C
Lasers are becoming more common although many people view them with suspicion. Lasers are used in surveying because they can be focused accurately. Because lasers have proven useful in space, people now find jobs for lasers here on earth. You will see lasers at work in grocery stores, in museums, and in hospitals. They are not so special anymore.

Empty Sentences, EXERCISE A
1. repetition
2. details
3. details
4. repetition
5. repetition

Empty Sentences, EXERCISE B
Answers will vary; possible answers are given.
1. Moths have different enemies. They are the favorite foods of birds and bats. Some frogs eat moths, too.
2. If a moth is detected by a bat, it will turn its wings so that the edges are pointed toward the bat.
3. The fine edge of the moths' wings makes them difficult to see.
4. Moths are good escape artists.
5. Moths can flee quickly.

Empty Sentences, EXERCISE C
Answers will vary; possible answers are given.
Falcons
1. talons
2. beak
3. flight
4. vision

A falcon is known as a predator, but it has several important weapons of defense, too. It uses its powerful, hooked beak to peck and bite. Its sharp talons will scratch an enemy. The falcon also uses its ability to fly to escape danger in a hurry. The falcon's keen eyesight helps it spot distant trouble.

Lack of Parallel Structure, EXERCISE A
Answers may vary slightly; possible answers are given.
1. not parallel, Martians
2. not parallel, with a lot of courage
3. not parallel, resources
4. parallel

Lack of Parallel Structure, EXERCISE B
1. Brooks has been named "Woman of the Year" and has won the Pulitzer Prize.
2. Correct
3. Her writing is moving, interesting, and thought-provoking.
4. Brooks also sponsors a contest that offers prizes to ten high-school poets and ten grade-school poets.

Lack of Parallel Structure, EXERCISE C
Answers may vary; possible answers are given.
1. Lava can take the form of hot, melted rock or hard, cooled rock.
2. A volcano might be active, dormant, or extinct.
3. There are eight active volcanoes on Jupiter and many active volcanoes on Mars.
4. The study of volcanoes is fascinating and important.

Confusing Shifts of Verb Tenses and Pronouns in Sentences, EXERCISE A
1. grow
2. They are
3. grow
4. They, has
5. They

Confusing Shifts in Verb Tenses and Pronouns in Sentences, EXERCISE B
Answers may vary slightly; possible answers are given.
1. Plant pathologists specialize in diseases that are harmful to plants. Their work helps farmers raise successful crops.
2. Some plant pathologists study viruses. The viruses can live on lettuce, causing disease and often killing it.

Confusing Shifts in Verb Tenses and Pronouns in Sentences, EXERCISE C
Answers will vary; possible answers are given. Additions are underlined.

Dora <u>found</u> a copy of a 1967 comic and traded one of her favorite comic books for it. Dora keeps her special comic books wrapped in plastic. She files <u>them</u> in alphabetical order so she can find them easily. Dora draws comics, too, and <u>she</u> hopes to become an illustrator. Dora always <u>uses</u> watercolors in her illustrations.

Sentence Combining

Sentence Combining with Coordinating Conjunctions, EXERCISE A
1. and
2. or
3. so
4. nor
5. yet

Sentence Combining with Coordinating Conjunctions, EXERCISE B
1. Robots are used for different purposes<u>, so</u> they come in different shapes and sizes.
2. A robot might do a factory job, <u>or</u> it might play the piano in a pizza parlor.
3. A robot might appear in a science-fiction novel, <u>or</u> it might be seen in a movie.
4. Some people are scared of robots, <u>but</u> there's no need.
5. Robots can do many wonderful things, <u>yet</u> they'll never replace people!

Sentence Combining with Coordinating Conjunctions, EXERCISE C
Some answers may vary slightly, possible answers are given.

Japan consists of four main islands, <u>but</u> it also includes many smaller islands. Heavy rains fall frequently in Japan, <u>and</u> typhoons are also common. According to legend, Japan was founded in 660 B.C.; however, records go back only to A.D. 400. Japan is now a major industrial power, <u>yet</u> the Japanese have kept many of their traditions. They have a democratic form of government, <u>but</u> the emperor is still considered the head of state.

Sentence Combining with Subordinating Conjunctions, EXERCISE A
Some answers may vary slightly; possible answers are given.
1. <u>As soon as</u> I see Uncle Albert, I'll give him your present.
2. <u>Before</u> I do anything else, I'm going to have one of Aunt Lily's special sandwiches.
3. She always makes me one <u>whenever</u> I visit.
4. <u>While</u> I eat, she tells me all the news.
5. I won't rest <u>until</u> we're all caught up!

Sentence Combining with Subordinating Conjunctions, EXERCISE B
Some answers may vary slightly; possible answers are given.
1. <u>When</u> the weather gets colder, whales migrate to warmer waters.
2. <u>As soon as</u> the spring comes, they swim north again.
3. They are always seeking places <u>where</u> they can get food.
4. <u>Although</u> the dolphin is much smaller than the whale, they are close relations.
5. We should try to protect sea mammals <u>whenever</u> we can.

Sentence Combining with Subordinating Conjunctions, EXERCISE C
Answers will vary; possible answers are given.
1. I have all these books <u>because</u> I'm studying for a test.
2. I'll study <u>until</u> I know all the answers.
3. <u>If</u> I didn't study, I might not do well.
4. <u>Since</u> I'm studying hard, I expect to do well.
5. I'll study <u>wherever</u> I can find a place to concentrate.

Sentence Combining with Compound Subjects and Predicates, EXERCISE A
1. compound predicate
2. compound subject
3. compound subject
4. compound predicate
5. compound subject, compound predicate

Sentence Combining with Compound Subjects and Predicates, EXERCISE B
Answers may vary slightly; possible answers are given.
1. Cars and buses thronged the parking lot. (compound subject)
2. The rescue ship sped to the scene and began to search for survivors. (compound predicate)
3. On the front lawn, a maple tree and a willow provided shade. (compound subject)
4. You may wait for us at the library or go by yourself to the mall. (compound predicate)
5. I tasted the asparagus but chewed and swallowed it quickly. (compound predicate)

Sentence Combining with Compound Subjects and Predicates, EXERCISE C
Answers may vary; possible answers are given.
1. Neither the glasses nor the silverware got clean. (compound subject)
2. Spanish explorers conquered the Aztecs and then subjugated the people. (compound predicate)
3. Rosa, Rafael, or Richie may call. (compound subject)
4. Amber arrived at the party on time but didn't stay long. (compound predicate)
5. Will you study, work quietly with your partner, or read during this free period? (compound predicate)

Sentence Variety

Types of Sentence Structure, EXERCISE A
1. compound
2. complex
3. simple
4. compound-complex

Types of Sentence Structure, EXERCISE B
1. <u>Although</u> the enormous manta ray looks dangerous, it actually is harmless, and it feeds on nothing larger than shrimp.
2. It does not carry poison in its tapered tail, <u>but</u> a manta ray still is a very powerful animal.
3. Mantas often weigh 1.5 tons, <u>and</u> they have been measured at as much as 23 feet across.
4. You may see a manta ray <u>if</u> you go swimming off the coast of Florida.

Types of Sentence Structure, EXERCISE C
1. The first ice skates, <u>which probably were made from animal bones tied to the feet with thongs</u>, were a form of transportation. (complex)
2. Skates with wooden blades were used during the Middle Ages<u>, but</u> steel blades were not introduced until the nineteenth century. (compound)
3. <u>Although</u> roller skates also were introduced in the 1800's, the earliest models used wood instead of steel for wheels. (complex)
4. Crude skateboards appeared in the 1960's<u>, but</u> in-line skates, <u>which are called roller blades,</u> are the newest skating sensation. (compound-complex)

Varying Sentence Structure, EXERCISE A
Answers will vary; possible answers are given.
1. Sharks are perhaps the most feared fish in the world, <u>and they certainly have my respect</u>. (compound)
2. <u>Because it is a skilled hunter</u>, a shark can attack silently and suddenly. (complex)
3. <u>Sharks can be deadly</u>, yet some people actually like to fish for them! (compound)
4. Most people <u>who know about snakes</u> fear the poison of a rattlesnake's bite; <u>they walk cautiously in rattlesnake habitats</u>. (compound-complex)
5. <u>If you saw a rattlesnake on top of your sleeping bag</u>, would you run? (complex)

Varying Sentence Structure, EXERCISE B
Answers will vary; possible answers are given.
1. Lewis wrote literary essays, autobiographical works, science fiction, and children's books, <u>but I like his children's books best</u>.
2. The *Chronicles of Narnia*<u>, which</u> is a collection of his seven children's novels, is a modern classic.
3. <u>When</u> you read the first novel, *The Lion, the Witch, and the Wardrobe*, you become part of the magical land of Narnia.
4. Talking animals live in Narnia's deep woods<u>, and mythical creatures are a normal part of the population</u>.
5. <u>After</u> four children enter Narnia, they meet Aslan, the great lion; <u>and</u> together they free Narnia from the White Witch's eternal winter.

Varying Sentence Structure, EXERCISE C

Anecdotes will vary; a possible anecdote is given. Sentence structures appear in parentheses.

When I was eight years old, I sang in a children's choir. (complex) How I loved to sing—and especially at Christmas! (simple) That Christmas Eve, we sang several carols, and then we concluded with "Silent Night." (compound) As we came to the last verse, the choir started to file out of the church, but I was so wrapped up in the song that I didn't notice. (compound-complex) Soon I was singing all by myself! (simple) The singer who came to get me couldn't help giggling. (complex) How embarrassed I was! (simple)

Varying Sentence Length, EXERCISE A

Answers will vary; possible answers are given.
1. The name *Alhambra,* meaning "crimson castle," is Arabic.
2. Muhammed Al-Ahmar began building the palace, probably around A.D. 1238.
3. Many rooms overlook courtyards, which usually have fountains and sculptures.
4. Washington Irving, an American author, wrote a book about the Alhambra.

Varying Sentence Length, EXERCISE B

Answers will vary; possible answers are given.

My project involved making dyes from onion skins, banana peels, and blackberries. First I boiled the plant parts, making a "dye bath." I added chemicals, which strengthened the color. Copper sulphate, a blue powder, brightened the dye. Tin, a yellow powder, dulled the dye. When I added vinegar and soda, the dye bubbled. Textiles were placed in the dye and soaked for an hour. The onion skins made the deepest color, a rich gold. The banana peels were a slick, brown, disgusting heap. The dyes simmered on the stove, really making a mess of our kitchen!

Varying Sentence Length, EXERCISE C

Answers will vary; possible answers are given.
1. My best friend has thick, red, curly hair.
2. Once on the way to school, I had a close call.
3. A car coming around the curve nearly hit me.
4. "Look out!" Royce yelled, just in time.

Varying Sentence Beginnings, EXERCISE A

Some answers may vary slightly; possible answers are given.
1. A shy math teacher, Carroll wrote the book to entertain children.
2. At the beginning of the story, Alice is reading in the garden.
3. A white rabbit, muttering to himself, dashes across the lawn.
4. When Alice follows him, he disappears down a hole.
5. Alice wonders, "Where did he go?"
6. Unafraid and curious, Alice tumbles in after him.
7. At the bottom of the hole, Alice finds a tiny bottle.
8. "Drink me," the words on the bottle read.
9. Upon swallowing the liquid, Alice grows very small.
10. The rabbit, meanwhile, had disappeared again.

Varying Sentence Beginnings, EXERCISE B

Answers will vary; possible answers are given.
1. At the beginning of the movie, the boy's family is about to leave for Europe./The boy's family is about to leave for Europe at the beginning of the movie.
2. As the story unfolds, his parents accidentally leave him behind./His parents accidentally leave him behind as the story unfolds.
3. Thieves break into his house, adding excitement to the plot./Adding excitement to the plot, thieves break into his house.
4. By the way, his parents miss him./His parents, by the way, miss him.
5. When the movie ends, the family is reunited./The family is reunited when the movie ends.

Varying Sentence Beginnings, EXERCISE C
Answers will vary; possible answers are given.
  1. Hillary, <u>my best friend</u>, was looking for a Mother's Day card./<u>My best friend</u> Hillary was looking for a Mother's Day card.
  2. "<u>I don't see what I want</u>, "she complained./She complained, "<u>I don't see what I want</u>."
  3. Hillary and I <u>quickly but carefully</u> examined several cards./<u>Quickly but carefully</u>, Hillary and I examined several cards.
  4. <u>After making her choice</u>, she paid for the card at the counter./She paid for the card at the counter <u>after making her choice</u>.

Word Choice

Using Connotation and Denotation, EXERCISE A
  1. relaxed   4. delighted
  2. believed   5. prosperous
  3. chose

Using Connotation and Denotation, EXERCISE B
Answers will vary; possible answers are given.
  1. You could tell that the comedy was a hit because the audience sparkled with delight.
  2. The movie was rotten because the ending was utterly predictable.
  3. I thought the film was poor because it was quite dull.
  4. My number-one movie has a cast of lunatic characters.
  5. The movie portrayed an unforgettable picture of the grim reality of war.

Using Connotation and Denotation, EXERCISE C
Answers will vary; a possible answer, for a more mysterious impression, is given.
   When I <u>gaze</u> out my window, I see a <u>quilt</u> of white snow <u>blanketing</u> the farm. It is not yet <u>dawn</u>, and no one else <u>stirs</u>. A <u>lone</u> dog <u>scampers</u> across the snow, <u>searching</u> for scraps. A <u>sigh</u> of wind <u>hangs</u> in the air.

Choosing Specific, Concrete Words, EXERCISE A
Answers will vary; possible answers are given.
  1. Alana brought a large wicker hamper <u>packed</u> with <u>delicious</u> food.
  2. Mr. Márquez <u>plunged</u> into the water.
  3. His swimming strokes were <u>strong</u> and <u>graceful</u>.
  4. Then the ants <u>arrived</u> and <u>attacked</u> the food.
  5. The picnickers <u>dropped</u> their food into a <u>canoe</u> and <u>rowed</u> to a raft in the middle of the lake.

Choosing Specific, Concrete Words, EXERCISE B
Answers will vary; possible answers are given.
  1. Pamela works at a <u>reliable</u> child-care center <u>located conveniently</u> in town.
  2. Her job <u>provides</u> her <u>with a source of satisfaction</u>.
  3. The children at the center are a <u>variety</u> of different ages.
  4. Pamela is a <u>valued employee</u> because she <u>works so well</u> with children.
  5. A child-care center should always serve <u>nutritious</u> food for snacks and meals.
  6. Abigail, has a cold, so she is <u>absent</u> today.
  7. The <u>caretakers</u> try to <u>prevent</u> children <u>from being exposed to</u> many illnesses.
  8. <u>A creative imagination is necessary</u> to <u>capture</u> a two-year-old's attention.
  9. The wall of blocks <u>collapsed</u> when the children <u>attacked</u> it.
  10. The children <u>giggled</u> because the <u>drenched</u> puppet looked <u>ridiculous</u>.

Choosing Specific, Concrete Words, EXERCISE C

Answers will vary; possible answers are given.

    The Harlem Renaissance of the 1920's was a <u>movement</u> of <u>enormous</u> literary <u>activity</u>. The <u>movement took the name of Harlem after the well-known African-American region of New York City</u>. Many <u>creative minds participated in</u> this movement, including Claude McKay, Countee Cullen, and Langston Hughes. The <u>Harlem Renaissance</u> included <u>artists, novelists, and poets.</u>

Varieties of English

Formal and Informal English, EXERCISE A

1. formal
2. informal, scoot out of here
3. informal, ready to roll
4. formal
5. informal, have the jitters

Formal and Informal English, EXERCISE B

1. students
2. One
3. happy
4. unnerved me
5. Many
6. we shall
7. Who will
8. do not care
9. Failing
10. defend

Formal and Informal English, EXERCISE C

Answers may vary; possible answers are given.

1. We saw a great play.
2. Artists who want to join can sign up.
3. Did the lawyers work out a deal?
4. We want you guys to participate.

Slang and Clichés, EXERCISE A

1. d
2. e
3. b
4. c
5. a

Slang and Clichés, EXERCISE B

Answers will vary; possible answers are given.

1. Pay attention! You seem <u>inattentive</u> today.
2. Wasn't his description of the snakes <u>revolting</u>?
3. The overloaded rowboat sank <u>quickly</u>.
4. Mom <u>was very disturbed</u> when she saw my report card.

Slang and Clichés, EXERCISE C

Answers will vary; possible answers are given.

My friends and I <u>loved</u> the <u>wonderful</u> in-line skates you sent. They were <u>magnificent!</u> I fly <u>like a turbojet</u> when I wear them.

The other day, I was <u>having a good time</u> with some <u>neighborhood friends,</u> and we decided to see a movie. Yolanda wanted to see the one about the giant sea slugs, but I wanted to see something a little less <u>revolting</u>. We ended up at <u>a very popular new movie,</u> where we all had a good <u>time</u>.

Dialect and Jargon, EXERCISE A

1. jargon
2. dialect
3. dialect
4. jargon
5. dialect

Dialect and Jargon, EXERCISE B

1. d
2. b
3. e
4. a
5. c

Dialect and Jargon, EXERCISE C

Answers may vary; suggested answers are given.

1. He <u>has been</u> working there for many years.
2. Send me some <u>electronic mail</u> when you know the answer.
3. The soldier who vanished was declared <u>absent without leave</u>.
4. Did the <u>referee</u> force him to leave the game?
5. I visited friends in the <u>Spanish-speaking district</u>.

Figurative Language

Simile and Metaphor, EXERCISE A

1. simile; jewels (flashing of the jewels)—blue fire
2. metaphor; moon—sugar cookie (in the sky)
3. simile; joke (staleness of the joke)—week-old bread
4. simile; Tiffany (Tiffany's gracefulness)—cat (a cat's gracefulness)
5. metaphor; jackhammer (sound of a jackhammer)—drum (beating of a drum)

Simile and Metaphor, EXERCISE B

Answers will vary; possible answers are given.

1. Before long, however, my feet began stinging <u>as if they had been attacked by bees.</u> (simile)
2. Reid, <u>a 15-year-old drill sergeant</u>, continued to lead us forward, ignoring my pleas for a few minutes of rest. (metaphor)
3. After a two-hour hike in the sun, a drink of water was <u>like a dip in a sparkling pool.</u> (simile)
4. It was <u>as sweet as nectar</u> to my parched throat. (simile)
5. With a sigh of gratitude, I eased out of my backpack, <u>a sack of lead hanging from my aching shoulders.</u> (metaphor)

Simile and Metaphor, EXERCISE C

Answers will vary; possible answers are given.

1. Her comments about my report were <u>as tart as spicy mustard</u>. (simile)
2. She pointed out a <u>tangled web of contradictions</u> in my writing. (metaphor)
3. As she spoke, I could hear <u>the whispering voice of my own conscience</u>. (metaphor)
4. When I had written that report, I had been hurrying <u>like a runaway subway train</u>. (simile)
5. The beeping of my computer had been <u>like a red flag</u>, urging me to slow down. (simile)

Personification and Symbol, EXERCISE A

1. personification
2. symbol
3. symbol and personification
4. symbol and personification
5. symbol and personification

Personification and Symbol, EXERCISE B

Answers will vary; possible answers are given.

1. A red rose kissed the dew. morning; love in bloom (symbolic meanings)
2. Bass drums gave the beat to the marchers. warfare (symbolic meaning)
3. The fierce sun proudly shone. fierceness; pride; boldness; glory (symbolic meanings)
4. The earth embraced the seeds. love; generation; Mother Earth; fertility (symbolic meanings)

Personification and Symbol, EXERCISE C

Answers will vary; possible answers are given.

1. The moon smiled at us as it reached its full height.
   happiness; strength (symbolic meanings)
2. The steady movement of the hands of the clock told the time.
   time marching on; unyielding nature of time (symbolic meanings)
3. A raging storm, venting anger and destruction, sped toward the village.
   anger; building rage; swift destruction (symbolic meanings)
4. A lighted lamp in the window spoke of hope and comfort.
   hope; comfort; aid (symbolic meanings)

Problem Solver

Run-on Sentences

Run-on Sentences

EXERCISE A: Revise the sentences, correcting the run-ons.

Example:	This summer our family is going to the beach we like to go there on vacation.
Possible Answers:	This summer our family is going to the beach. We like to go there on vacation.
	This summer our family is going to the beach, for we like to go there on vacation.
	This summer our family is going to the beach; we like to go there on vacation.

1. I like to swim in the ocean, the waves are awesome.
2. My dad collects shells on the beach last year he found a conch.
3. My brother likes to build castles in the sand and so he made one with towers on the wall.
4. My mom always brings a book and she sits under a big umbrella and she reads all day.
5. Lacy loves to surf she can stay in the water for hours.

EXERCISE B: Rewrite the run-on sentences correctly. If a sentence needs no change, write *Correct*.

Example:	Yvonne practices karate after school and Ruben takes piano lessons I usually look after my younger sister.
Possible Answer:	Yvonne practices karate after school. Ruben takes piano lessons. I usually look after my younger sister.

1. Jarrett likes to play soccer and coach the younger players.
2. Adrienne sings in the school chorus, she hopes to have a career as a performer.
3. Judith runs at least a mile every day she is one of the fastest runners on the cross-country team.
4. Aaron delivers newspapers Edward skates and Nora paints.
5. Ashley takes violin lessons Forrest practices soccer.

EXERCISE C: Rewrite the paragraph, revising any run-on sentences.

California condors are vultures and they have huge wings and so they can soar over long distances in search of food. Condors are a threatened species and they may become extinct and so people have captured them and they want to try breeding them and so later they will be able to return the birds to their natural habitat.

Sentence Fragments

Sentence Fragments

EXERCISE A: Rewrite each fragment to make a complete sentence. Be sure to use punctuation correctly.

> **Example:** A new movie about dinosaurs.
> **Answer:** A new movie about dinosaurs <u>opens on Friday</u>.

1. Promising thrills and excitement.
2. Danger and suspense minute after minute.
3. Frightening monsters beyond your imagination.
4. The brave research scientist, working against all odds.
5. With a surprise ending, too!

EXERCISE B: Add words to each fragment to make a complete sentence. If the words make a complete sentence already, write *Correct*.

> **Example:** Tired, hungry, and lost in the wilderness.
> **Answer:** <u>The travelers were</u> tired, hungry, and lost in the wilderness.

1. Pioneer women and their families.
2. Following the trail for hundreds of miles.
3. Made a temporary camp above the banks of the Yellowstone.
4. A friendly clan of Cheyenne.
5. Their leader, a thoughtful but careful man.
6. As if they had been rescued from disaster.
7. Hunting and trapping wild animals.
8. They shared food.
9. The return of good weather.
10. Until they were able to be on their way again.

EXERCISE C: Rewrite the paragraph, revising any sentence fragments.

    Mount Rushmore, an unusual national monument to some famous Americans. Located in the Black Hills of South Dakota. Carved in the side of a mountain. The faces of George Washington, Thomas Jefferson, Theodore Roosevelt, and Abraham Lincoln. Took more than fifteen years to complete.

Subject-Verb Agreement

Subject-Verb Agreement: Compound Subjects

EXERCISE A: Write the verb in parentheses that correctly completes each sentence.

> **Example:** Salt and pepper (is, are) added to many dishes.
> **Answer:** is

1. Either a pen or a pencil (is, are) fine for this quiz.
2. Many a coach and player (has, have) wanted to visit the Hall of Fame.
3. (Is, Are) Louisa May Alcott or Laura Ingalls Wilder the author?
4. The planet's atmosphere and temperature (prevents, prevent) growth.
5. The clarinet or the flutes (is, are) out of tune.

EXERCISE B: Rewrite the sentences, correcting any errors in agreement. If a sentence needs no changes, write *Correct*.

> **Example:** Aline or Joanne serve customers at the snack bar.
> **Answer:** Aline or Joanne <u>serves</u> customers at the snack bar.

1. Dogwood trees and jonquils were blooming everywhere that spring.
2. Some grapes or an orange are waiting to be eaten for a snack.
3. Macaroni and cheese make a good meal on a cold day.
4. Each postcard and photograph remind me of my summer vacation.
5. Many a painter and poet were inspired by love.

EXERCISE C: Combine each pair of sentences. Make sure that the verb in the new sentence agrees with its subject.

> **Example:** The seventh grade holds elections each fall.
>
> The eighth grade holds elections each fall.
> **Answer:** The seventh and eighth grades hold elections each fall.

1. The principal runs the nomination assembly.
   The council president runs the nomination assembly.
2. Many a hand is raised to nominate a candidate.
   Many a voice is raised to nominate a candidate.
3. Pamela writes four names for each office.
   Jamal writes four names for each office.
4. The candidates do not talk together very much.
   Their campaign managers do not talk together very much, either.

Subject-Verb Agreement: Other Agreement Problems

EXERCISE A: In each sentence, the subject is underlined. Write the verb in parentheses that agrees with it.

    Example: Here (is, are) <u>the stickers and stationery you ordered</u>.
    Answer: are

    1. On the envelope (is, are) <u>your name and address</u>.
    2. There (is, are) also special <u>stickers</u> with your picture.
    3. <u>Color</u>, as well as design, (create, creates) a personal effect.
    4. <u>Some</u> of the styles (appear, appears) formal.
    5. Many <u>examples</u> of each style (is, are) available.

EXERCISE B: Write the subject and correct verb of each sentence.

    Example: Some of my favorite songs (is, are) "golden oldies."
    Answer: Some are

    1. From the fifties and sixties (come, comes) many great songs.
    2. There (is, are) some important reasons why I like these songs.
    3. A good beat, as well as clever lyrics, (mean, means) something to me.
    4. My collection of records (features, feature) some of the best bands ever to record.
    5. A strong singer, together with a fresh lead guitarist, (make, makes) the difference between a good band and a great one.

EXERCISE C: Rewrite the sentences, correcting errors in agreement. If a sentence needs no changes, write *Correct*.

    Example: There is some good reasons for preparing a report on a computer.
    Answer: <u>There are</u> some good reasons for preparing a report on a computer.

    1. With a computer comes many advantages.
    2. Often, many drafts of a paper is necessary.
    3. Ease of revision, as well as speed, have long been a key to successful software.
    4. There is some helpful books about word processing.
    5. Any of the aides in the media center have enough computer experience to help you.

Verb Forms

Verbs: Irregular Forms

EXERCISE A: Choose the verb in parentheses that correctly completes each sentence.

> **Example:** Juanita (brang, brought) her photo album to school.
> **Answer:** brought

1. She has some of the best pictures I've ever (seen, saw).
2. She (telled, told) us a little story about each picture.
3. One picture was (taken, took) from an airplane.
4. Juanita and her family (flied, flew) to Chicago for vacation.
5. Even her grandmother had (went, gone).
6. I never (knowed, knew) that Chicago had so many skyscrapers!
7. Juanita and her family had (ridden, rode) the elevated train.
8. It looked as though she (done, did) everything in Chicago!
9. Juanita said that she (buy, bought) souvenirs, too.
10. After lunch, we (heard, heared) about her other travels.

EXERCISE B: Write the correct form of the verb in each sentence.

> **Example:** The sun (rise) at six o'clock that morning.
> **Answer:** rose

1. Two unknown riders (come) along the trail.
2. Not a word was (speak) between them.
3. Had these wranglers (break) the law?
4. The sheriff and his posse (catch) up with them at High Pass.
5. The strangers (begin) to tell their story.

EXERCISE C: Rewrite the paragraph, using the correct form of the underlined verbs.

> **Example:** Last summer, we <u>gone</u> to my cousin's farm.
> **Answer:** Last summer we went to my cousin's farm.

We <u>done</u> all kinds of things there. We <u>eat</u> raspberries. My Uncle Ned <u>growed</u>. We <u>swum</u> in the creek. We <u>drunk</u> cider that my Aunt Julianne had made. Mom <u>drived</u> the tractor. I had never <u>rode</u> on a hay wagon before. We <u>seen</u> baby lambs being born and <u>sung</u> songs around a campfire at night. My younger brother, however, got <u>stinged</u> by a hornet.

Verbs: Past and Past Participle Forms

EXERCISE A: Write the verbs in parentheses that correctly complete the sentences.

> **Example:** Some talent scouts (came, come) to our school.
> **Answer:** came

1. They (chose, had chose) our school from all the rest.
2. They had (flew, flown) from Hollywood.
3. They were (drawn, drew) to our school by its reputation.
4. Many people have (spoke, spoken) of our theater troupe.
5. We wondered if we would be (chose, chosen) to be in a movie.
6. My friend Lillian (sang, sung) a song she had (written, wrote).
7. Donny told some stories that the Scouts hadn't (knew, known).
8. After the Scouts had (went, gone), our hearts were not (broke, broken).
9. We were confident that we hadn't (blew, blown) our chance for stardom.
10. We (knew, known) that tomorrow was another day.

EXERCISE B: Write the correct form of the verb in each sentence. Label each form correctly.

> **Example:** We (eat) dinner at a new seafood restaurant last night.
> **Answer:** ate (past)

1. We (go) there because we had read about it in the newspaper.
2. We (hear) from our friends that it was very unusual.
3. Each waiter (wear) a different fish costume.
4. An undersea mural was (draw) on the wall.
5. The waiter never (bring) us a menu.
6. Instead he (sing) about the house specialties.
7. We each (choose) something different.
8. Each time they delivered a dinner they (ring) a ship's bell.
9. They (give) each of us a balloon as we left.
10. Have you ever (see) such a place?

EXERCISE C: Write a sentence for each verb.

> **Example:** keep (past participle)
> **Answer:** Edith <u>had kept</u> the secret longer than anyone expected.

1. steal (past)
2. lead (past)
3. fly (past participle)
4. think (past participle)
5. wear (past participle)

Pronoun Problems

Pronouns: Awkward or Indefinite Antecedents

EXERCISE A: Write whether each sentence is *correct* or *incorrect* in its use of pronouns.

> **Example:** In some communities, they elect a supervisor instead of a mayor.
> **Answer:** incorrect

1. When it's cold outside, you feel like staying indoors and drinking hot cocoa.
2. Lucy and Dina went to a concert to celebrate her thirteenth birthday.
3. Everyone on the nominating committee had already made his or her speech.
4. Before Ed wrote that letter to his uncle, he didn't know the real story.
5. They didn't admit Hawaii as a state until 1959.

EXERCISE B: Rewrite each sentence, correcting any awkward or unclear use of pronouns.

> **Example:** Ophelia told my friend that she had to make a decision right away.
> **Answer:** Ophelia told my friend, "I have to make a decision right away."

1. They do a lot of coal mining where I come from.
2. If a member of our family has something important to discuss, he is allowed to call a family meeting.
3. He threw the vase at the window and almost broke it.
4. One of our pet rabbits caught their paw in a trap.
5. If Cathy decides to run against Jessica for class president, she won't stand a chance of winning.

EXERCISE C: Revise each sentence in two different ways to correct any awkward or indefinite use of pronouns.

> **Example:**   A teacher should always try to be truthful with her students.
> **Possible Answers:** A teacher should always try to be truthful with his or her students.
>
>   Teachers should always try to be truthful with their students.

1. No one in our group remembered to bring their toothbrush.
2. Until Ann became friends with Rose, she didn't understand the true meaning of friendship.
3. After World War II, they began moving to the suburbs in great numbers.
4. For every person who seems to understand my poetry, you find a dozen people who are completely mystified.

Pronouns: Other Pronoun Problems

EXERCISE A: Write whether each sentence is *correct* or *incorrect* in its use of pronouns.

> **Example:** Fred likes going to the library because you can borrow tapes.
> **Answer:** incorrect

1. My sister won't take piano lessons because you have to practice every day.
2. The story was very complex, but in time it could be understood.
3. They decided to study for the test at Margo's house, which was a good idea.
4. If our team wants to win, you have to try your best at all times.
5. John liked reading about cars, which he got out of the library.

EXERCISE B: Rewrite each sentence, correcting any vague or improper pronoun references.

> **Example:** Every time I start my homework, the telephone rings and you have to answer it.
> **Answer:** Every time I start my homework, the telephone rings and I have to answer it.

1. William forgot his lines in the play, which puzzled everyone.
2. My advice to anyone who plays tennis is that you have to do warm-up exercises before you start.
3. My brother set the table and offered to make the salad, which he had never done before.
4. None of us liked the new coach at first, but you realized after the first few games that she had done a terrific job.
5. As we read the mystery, you realized that the suspect hadn't committed the crime.

EXERCISE C: Complete each sentence. Include a pronoun in the words you add, but be careful to avoid vague or improper pronoun references.

> **Example:** Paula grows radishes in her garden, _____ learned at summer camp.
> **Answer:** Paula grows radishes in her garden, a skill that she learned at summer camp.

1. The children were as patient as they could be, but _____ tired of waiting.
2. If your nose runs, your throat is scratchy, and your muscles ache, _____.
3. The poem is very long and the test is on Monday; _____.
4. I enjoy playing the violin, but _____ without practicing every day.
5. Chad loves to fence, _____ perfected while practicing with his instructor.

Problems with Modifiers

Misplaced Modifiers

EXERCISE A: Write the letter of the sentence in each pair that is correct. Then identify its modifying phrase or clause.

> **Example:** a. The toy display caught the eye of shoppers in the store window.
>
> b. The toy display in the store window caught the eye of shoppers.
> **Answer:** b   in the store window

1. a. We saw the bears dancing through our binoculars.
   b. Through our binoculars we saw the bears dancing.
2. a. A bear was on a bicycle with a top hat.
   b. A bear with a top hat was on a bicycle.
3. a. The bear that I liked best wore a bow tie.
   b. The bear wore a bow tie that I liked best.
4. a. In the shop were many stuffed bears that you could buy.
   b. There were many stuffed bears in the shop that you could buy.

EXERCISE B: Rewrite the sentences, placing modifiers as close as possible to the words that they modify.

> **Example:** He searched for ancient ruins with old maps.
> **Answer:** He searched with old maps for ancient ruins.

1. The ruin rose above the sea with its tower intact.
2. The map crumbled into pieces that he had been reading.
3. An assistant pointed out a boa constrictor without fear.
4. He thinks that the orginal inhabitants in his mind were a gentle people.

EXERCISE C: Use each modifying phrase or clause in a sentence. Be careful to place it close to the word that it modifies.

> **Example:** without much hope
> **Answer:** <u>Without much hope</u> I cast my line into the water.

1. that no one could dislike
2. under the elevated train tracks
3. that felt as smooth as silk
4. into a crowded room
5. with a shiny yellow top

Dangling Modifiers

EXERCISE A: Write the letter of the sentence in each pair that is correct. Then identify its modifying verbal phrase or clause.

 Example: a. Lying on the floor, she saw the crystal.

   b. Lying on the floor, the crystal was in view.
 Answer: b Lying on the floor

1. a. Dropped from a great height, the crystal ball lay in pieces.
   b. The crystal ball lay in pieces dropped from a great height.
2. a. To repair it, we would need a glass-making kit.
   b. To repair it, a glass-making kit would be needed.
3. a. My aunt called the police horrified at the sight.
   b. Horrified at the sight, my aunt called the police.
4. a. After arriving with sirens blaring, clues were hunted for by the police.
   b. After arriving with sirens blaring, the police hunted for clues.

EXERCISE B: Rewrite the sentences, placing modifiers as close as possible to the words that they modify.

 Example: Casting off from the dock, our fishing trip began.
 Answer: Casting off from the dock, we began our fishing trip.

1. While waiting on the dock, a boatful of tourists waved to us.
2. To fish for marlin, strength and endurance are needed.
3. Steadying my pole, a flying fish distracted me.
4. Amazed by the experience, promises were made to try this again soon.

EXERCISE C: Use each modifying phrase or clause in a sentence. Be careful to place it close to the word that it modifies.

 Example: after recording our statement
 Answer: After recording our statement, the police officer led us upstairs.

1. fleeing from the tiger
2. to avoid harmful bacteria
3. shocked by the rap song
4. laughing bitterly
5. to determine my size

Problems with Possessives

Using Possessive Forms Correctly

EXERCISE A: Write the word in parentheses that correctly completes each sentence.

> **Example:** (Their's, Theirs) is the only opinion that matters.
> **Answer:** <u>Theirs</u>

1. Did your dog get (it's, its) shots yet?
2. The (queen's, queens) crown was encrusted with rubies.
3. Those (boy's, boys') reports were handed in late.
4. That is the girl (who's, whose) face I saw in my dream.
5. John (Keats's, Keats') poems are among the most beautiful ever written.

EXERCISE B: Rewrite each sentence, correcting any missing or misplaced apostrophes. If a sentence needs no changes, write *Correct*.

> **Example:** Someones' project hasn't been turned in yet.
> **Answer:** Someone's project hasn't been turned in yet.

1. Those author's opinions are clearly expressed in their books.
2. The radio is his, but the tapes are all her's.
3. It's about time that you admitted you're mistake!
4. My three cousins' teachers are all named Smith!
5. The two actresses performances were magnificent.

EXERCISE C: Write the possessive form of each word. Then write a sentence using each possessive form.

> **Example:** teachers
> **Answer:** <u>teachers'</u>; The teachers' meeting was on Tuesday.

1. country
2. who
3. women
4. cactus
5. it
6. anybody
7. buses
8. she
9. Carlos
10. doctors

Missing Commas

Missing Commas

EXERCISE A: Rewrite the sentences, adding any missing commas. If a sentence needs no changes, write *Correct*.

> **Example:** New York Tokyo and Mexico City are very large cities.
> **Answer:** New York, Tokyo, and Mexico City are very large cities.

1. They crossed the yard entered the house and climbed the stairs.
2. The explorers steered their boat down the long winding river.
3. Their favorite old-time comedians include the Marx Brothers the Three Stooges and Abbott and Costello.
4. The crafty old fox eluded the howling hounds.
5. We knew that those brave honest reliable Scouts would save the day.

EXERCISE B: Rewrite the paragraph, adding or removing commas as needed.

> **Example:** The club meets Mondays Wednesdays and Fridays.
> **Answer:** The club meets Mondays, Wednesdays, and Fridays.

Jason, Wendy and Wanda, organized the computer club. We talked about choosing a computer, deciding when to update and selecting software. Our members shared many interesting opinions at the meeting. Noreen brought in a huge ancient rusty calculator to show the group. Computers can be used for word processing mathematics and, of course, playing games. The computer we use has a color monitor, a keyboard, two disk drives, and a mouse. "Space Race," an arcade-type game is our favorite. Players have to track the alien ships through cyberspace explore strange places and solve all kinds of mind-boggling puzzles along the way.

EXERCISE C: Write a sentence using each of these groups. Add commas where needed.

> **Example:** onions ketchup and relish
> **Answer:** Do you want onions, ketchup, and relish on your hot dog?

1. coffee tea or milk
2. sweet sticky
3. quarters nickels and dimes
4. yes no or maybe
5. furry little
6. men's women's and children's
7. boiling hot
8. small quiet but courageous
9. tall skinny
10. my best friend since fourth grade

Answer Key

Problem Solver

Run-on Sentences

Run-on Sentences, EXERCISE A
Answers will vary; possible answers are given.
1. I like to swim in the ocean, for the waves are awesome.
2. My dad collects shells on the beach; last year he found a conch.
3. My brother likes to build castles in the sand. He made one with towers on the wall.
4. My mom always brings a book; she sits under a big umbrella and reads all day.
5. Lacy loves to surf. She can stay in the water for hours.

Run-on Sentences, EXERCISE B
Answers will vary; possible answers are given.
1. Correct
2. Adrienne sings in the school chorus, and she hopes to have a career as a performer.
3. Judith runs at least a mile every day; she is one of the fastest runners on the cross-country team.
4. Aaron delivers newspapers. Edward skates and Nora paints.
5. Ashley takes violin lessons, but Forrest practices soccer.

Run-on Sentences, EXERCISE C
Answers will vary; possible answers are given.
   California condors are vultures. They have huge wings, and so they can soar over long distances in search of food. Condors are a threatened species; they may become extinct. People have captured them and want to try breeding them. Later they will be able to return the birds to their natural habitat.

Sentence Fragments

Sentence Fragments, EXERCISE A
Answers will vary; possible answers are given.
1. The advertisements are promising thrills and excitement.
2. The sign says, "Expect danger and suspense minute after minute."
3. Ads warn of frightening monsters beyond your imagination.
4. The brave research scientist, working against all odds, is the movie's hero.
5. This movie comes with a surprise ending, too!

Sentence Fragments, EXERCISE B
Answers will vary; possible answers are given.
1. Pioneer women and their families <u>crossed the prairie.</u>
2. Following the trail for hundreds of miles, <u>the wagon train headed west.</u>
3. <u>The pioneers</u> made a temporary camp above the banks of the Yellowstone.
4. A friendly clan of Cheyenne <u>gave them food</u>.
5. Their leader, a thoughtful but careful man, <u>was cautious about leaving the pioneer camp</u>.
6. <u>The pioneers acted</u> as if they had been rescued from disaster.
7. <u>The Cheyennes lived by</u> hunting and trapping wild animals.
8. Correct
9. The return of good weather <u>meant that it was time to get back on the trail</u>.
10. <u>The pioneers were restless</u> until they were able to be on their way again.

Sentence Fragments, EXERCISE C
Answers will vary; possible answers are given.

   Mount Rushmore, an unusual national monument to some famous Americans, <u>was built by a sculptor named Gutzon Borglum</u>. <u>The monument is</u> located in the Black Hills of South Dakota. <u>The artist</u> carved in the side of a mountain the faces of George Washington, Thomas Jefferson, Theodore Roosevelt, and Abraham Lincoln. <u>The sculpting</u> took more than fifteen years to complete.

Subject-Verb Agreement

Subject-Verb Agreement: Compound Subjects, EXERCISE A
1. is
2. has
3. Is
4. prevent
5. are

Subject-Verb Agreement: Compound Subjects, EXERCISE B
1. Correct
2. Some grapes or an orange <u>is</u> waiting to be eaten for a snack.
3. Macaroni and cheese <u>makes</u> a good meal on a cold day.
4. Each postcard and photograph <u>reminds</u> me of my summer vacation.
5. Many a painter and poet <u>was</u> inspired by love.

Subject-Verb Agreement: Compound Subjects, EXERCISE C
Answers will vary; possible answers are given.
1. The principal and the council president run the nomination assembly.
2. Many a hand or voice is raised to nominate a candidate.
3. Pamela and Jamal write four names for each office.
4. Neither the candidates nor their campaign managers talk together very much.

Subject-Verb Agreement: Other Agreement Problems, EXERCISE A
1. are
2. are
3. creates
4. appear
5. are

Subject-Verb Agreement: Other Agreement Problems, EXERCISE B
1. songs, come
2. reasons are
3. beat, means
4. collection, features
5. singer, makes

Subject-Verb Agreement: Other Agreement Problems, EXERCISE C
1. With a computer <u>come</u> many advantages.
2. Often, many drafts of a paper <u>are</u> necessary.
3. Ease of revision, as well as speed, <u>has</u> long been a key to successful software.
4. There <u>are</u> some helpful books about word processing.
5. Any of the aides in the media center <u>has</u> enough computer experience to help you.

Verb Forms

Verbs: Irregular Forms, EXERCISE A
1. seen
2. told
3. taken
4. flew
5. gone
6. knew
7. ridden
8. did
9. bought
10. heard

Verbs: Irregular Forms, EXERCISE B
1. came
2. spoken
3. broken
4. caught
5. began

Verbs: Irregular Forms, EXERCISE C
We <u>did</u> all kinds of things there. We <u>ate</u> raspberries that my Uncle Ned <u>had grown</u>. We <u>swam</u> in the creek. We <u>drank</u> cider that my Aunt Julianne had made. Mom <u>drove</u> the tractor. I had never <u>ridden</u> on a hay wagon before. We <u>saw</u> baby lambs being born and <u>sang</u> songs around a campfire at night. My younger brother, however, got <u>stung</u> by a hornet.

Verbs: Past and Past Participle Forms, EXERCISE A
1. chose
2. flown
3. drawn
4. spoken
5. chosen
6. sang, written
7. known
8. gone, broken
9. blown
10. knew

Verbs: Past and Past Participle Forms, EXERCISE B
1. went (past)
2. had heard (past participle)/heard (past)
3. wore (past)
4. drawn (past participle)
5. brought (past)
6. sang (past)
7. chose (past)
8. rang (past)
9. gave (past)
10. seen (past participle)

Verbs: Past and Past Participle Forms, EXERCISE C
Answers will vary; possible answers are given.
1. The evil wizard <u>stole</u> the king's gold.
2. The trail <u>led</u> to the wizard's cave.
3. A plane <u>had flown</u> across the sky.
4. The wizard <u>had thought</u> that no one would follow him.
5. He <u>had worn</u> that magic cape for years.

Pronoun Problems

Pronouns: Awkward or Indefinite Antecedents, EXERCISE A
1. incorrect
2. incorrect
3. correct
4. incorrect
5. incorrect

Pronouns: Awkward or Indefinite Antecedents, EXERCISE B
Answers will vary; possible answers are given. Corrections are underlined.
1. <u>A lot of coal mining is done</u> where I come from.
2. If a member of our family has something important to discuss, <u>he or she</u> is allowed to call a family meeting.
3. <u>The window almost broke when he threw the vase at it.</u>
4. One of our pet rabbits caught <u>its</u> paw in a trap.
5. If Cathy decides to run against Jessica for class president, <u>Jessica</u> won't stand a chance of winning.

Pronouns: Awkward or Indefinite Antecedents, EXERCISE C
Answers will vary; possible answers are given.
1. No one in our group remembered to bring his or her toothbrush.
   The members of our group all forgot to bring their toothbrushes.
2. Until Ann became friends with Rose, Ann didn't understand the true meaning of friendship.
   Rose didn't understand the true meaning of friendship until she became friends with Ann.
3. After World War II, people began moving to the suburbs in great numbers.
   Great numbers of people began moving to the suburbs after World War II.
4. For every person who seems to understand my poetry, I find a dozen people who are completely mystified.
   For every person who seems to understand my poetry, a dozen people who are completely mystified can be found.

Pronouns: Other Pronoun Problems, EXERCISE A
1. incorrect
2. correct
3. incorrect
4. incorrect
5. incorrect

Pronouns: Other Pronoun Problems, EXERCISE B
Answers will vary; possible answers are given.
1. When William forgot his lines in the play, everyone was puzzled.
2. My advice to anyone who plays tennis is to do warm-up exercises before starting.
3. My brother set the table and offered to make the salad—two chores that he had never done before.
4. None of us liked the new coach at first, but we realized after the first few games that she had done a terrific job.
5. As we read the mystery, we realized that the suspect hadn't committed the crime.

Pronouns: Other Pronoun Problems, EXERCISE C
Answers will vary; possible answers are given. Additions are underlined.
1. The children were as patient as they could be, but <u>they got</u> tired of waiting.
2. If your nose runs, your throat is scratchy, and your muscles ache, <u>you might be coming down with the flu</u>.
3. The poem is very long and the test is on Monday; thus, <u>memorizing it is a challenge</u>.
4. I enjoy playing the violin, but <u>a person can't get better</u> without practicing every day.
5. Chad loves to fence, <u>a sport that he</u> perfected while practicing with his instructor.

Problems with Modifiers

Misplaced Modifiers, EXERCISE A
1. b, through our binoculars
2. b, with a top hat
3. a, that I liked best
4. a, that you could buy

Misplaced Modifiers, EXERCISE B
Answers may vary slightly; possible answers are given.
1. With its tower intact, the ruin rose above the sea.
2. The map that he had been reading crumbled into pieces.
3. Without fear, an assistant pointed out a boa constrictor.
4. In his mind, he thinks that the orginal inhabitants were a gentle people.

Misplaced Modifiers, EXERCISE C
Answers will vary; possible answers are given.
1. This was a play <u>that no one could dislike</u>.
2. He worked in a restaurant <u>under the elevated train tracks</u>.
3. Mom wore a fabric <u>that felt as smooth as silk</u>.
4. She led them <u>into a crowded room</u> filled with musicians.
5. I once had a toy taxi <u>with a shiny yellow top</u>.

Dangling Modifiers, EXERCISE A
1. a, dropped from a great height
2. a, to repair it
3. b, horrified at the sight
4. b, after arriving with sirens blaring

Dangling Modifiers, EXERCISE B
Answers may vary; possible answers are given.
1. While waiting on the dock, we saw a boatful of tourists wave to us.
2. To fish for marlin, one needs strength and endurance.
3. Steadying my pole, I was distracted by a flying fish.
4. Amazed by the experience, we promised to try this again soon.

Dangling Modifiers, EXERCISE C
Answers will vary; possible answers are given.
1. Fleeing from the tiger, the goats sprang across a creek.
2. To avoid harmful bacteria, you should not drink that water.
3. Shocked by the rap song, Mrs. Daugherty called the radio station.
4. Laughing bitterly, Mr. Xu described his day.
5. To determine my size, I used a measuring tape.

Problems with Possessives

Using Possessive Forms Correctly, EXERCISE A
1. its
2. queen's
3. boys'
4. whose
5. Keats's

Using Possessive Forms Correctly, EXERCISE B
1. Those authors' opinions are clearly expressed in their books.
2. The radio is his, but the tapes are all hers.
3. It's about time that you admitted your mistake!
4. Correct
5. The two actresses' performances were magnificent.

Using Possessive Forms Correctly, EXERCISE C
Answers will vary; possible answers are given.
1. country's; My country's flag is red, white, and blue.
2. whose; Whose book is this?
3. women's; The women's clothes are on the second floor.
4. cactus's; They were scratched by the cactus's needles.
5. its; The cat hurt its tail.
6. anybody's; Is anybody's homework finished?
7. buses; The buses' mechanics were on strike.
8. her; She read her poem to the class.
9. Carlos's; Carlos's mother has a cold.
10. doctors; The doctors' schedules have been changed.

Missing Commas

Missing Commas, EXERCISE A
1. They crossed the yard, entered the house, and climbed the stairs.
2. The explorers steered their boat down the long, winding river.
3. Their favorite old-time comedians include the Marx Brothers, the Three Stooges, and Abbott and Costello.
4. Correct
5. We knew that those brave, honest, reliable Scouts would save the day.

Missing Commas, EXERCISE B
Jason, Wendy, and Wanda organized the computer club. We talked about choosing a computer, deciding when to update, and selecting software. Our members shared many interesting opinions at the meeting. Noreen brought in a huge, ancient, rusty calculator to show the group. Computers can be used for word processing, mathematics, and, of course, playing games. The computer we use has a color monitor, a keyboard, two disk drives, and a mouse. "Space Race," an arcade-type game, is our favorite. Players have to track the alien ships through cyberspace, explore strange places, and solve all kinds of mind-boggling puzzles along the way.

Missing Commas, EXERCISE C
Answers will vary; possible answers are given.
1. The flight attendant offered us <u>coffee, tea, or milk</u>.
2. The <u>sweet, sticky</u> cotton candy was delicious.
3. We took rolls of <u>quarters, nickels, and dimes</u> to the bank.
4. Our choices in the survey were <u>yes, no, or maybe</u>.
5. We played with the <u>furry little</u> kitten.
6. The store sold <u>men's, women's, and children's</u> clothing.
7. They poured some of the <u>boiling hot</u> liquid into each cup.
8. <u>Small, quiet, but courageous</u>, the little girl set forth on her journey.
9. A <u>tall, skinny</u> stranger entered the room.
10. Becky, <u>my best friend since fourth grade</u>, lives across the street.

Grammar, Usage, and Mechanics

Abbreviations

Writing Abbreviations Correctly

EXERCISE A: Find the word or words in each sentence that can be abbreviated. Write the word and its abbreviation.

> **Example:** Our school held an assembly to hear Representative Cornells's speech.
> **Answer:** Representative—Rep.

1. Cornell represents a district from New Hampshire.
2. As a student, she volunteered for work with the United Nations.
3. The speaker's podium was about one meter high.
4. Our assembly on Thursday began at 3:00 in the afternoon.
5. The meeting was organized by Professor Martin Goldman and Doctor R.C. Rand.

EXERCISE B: Write the abbreviation for each of the following. Write the Postal Service abbreviations for state names.

> **Example:** President; California
> **Answer:** Pres.; CA

1. Major
2. Mountain
3. Wednesday
4. gram
5. inches
6. Missouri
7. kilometer
8. February
9. Central Intelligence Agency
10. Tennessee

EXERCISE C: Rewrite the shipping list, replacing names, titles, and other words with the correct abbreviations.

> **Example:** Mister Percy R Chen, Esquire
> **Answer:** <u>Mr.</u> Percy <u>R.</u> Chen, <u>Esq.</u>

Order:
1. 1 4-pound box of oranges
   2 4-ounce coffee cakes

2. 1 6-kilogram country ham
   NOTE: MUST ARRIVE BY
   WEDNESDAY, OCTOBER 12

Ship To:
Doctor Rachel L Adams
12 North Water Drive, Apartment 3-C
Weston, Vermont 05161
Attorney Carlos Rivera, Junior
273 Basin Boulevard East
Houston, Texas 77215

Addresses

Writing Addresses Correctly

EXERCISE A: Rewrite the addresses. Use commas, numerals, and abbreviations correctly.

    Example: Eleven Main Street
               Redwood City Calif. 94062
    Answer: 11 Main Street
              Redwood City, <u>CA</u> 94062

1. 81 Fifty-fifth Ave.
   Apartment Twelve-A
2. One Hundred Irving Street
   Akron OH 44313
3. They live in Gresham Township Baltimore County.
4. Deliver the materials to me at 86 Pinto St. Unity, ME 04285.

EXERCISE B: Rewrite each item, using commas, numerals, and abbreviations correctly. Then rewrite each address as it would appear in a paragraph in the body of a letter.

    Example: Eighteen Oak Crest Rd.
               Ithaca N.Y. 14850
    Answer: <u>18</u> Oak Crest Rd.
              Ithaca, <u>NY</u> 14850

1. Fourteen Day St.
   Fayette AL 35555
2. Forest Hills
   Queens County NY
3. Forty-five James Ave.
   Ogden UT 84401
4. 12 Elm St., Apartment Six
   Hickory NC 28601

EXERCISE C: Rewrite the letter, writing all addresses correctly.

269 Sixty-fifth Avenue
Ames IA 50010
May 29, 1995

Hartford Minerals
Thirty-one Lloyd St., Suite Twenty-two B
Hartford CT 06101

    Dear Hartford Minerals:

    Please note our change of shipping address to Ten Cypress St. Indianapolis IN 46222. Thank you.

Sincerely,

Ed Haines

Adjectives

Identifying Adjectives and Their Functions

EXERCISE A: Write each adjective that appears in parentheses and the noun or pronoun that each adjective modifies.

> **Example:** I am (eager) about (this) visit to Washington.
> **Answer:** eager—I   this—visit

1. Washington has (many) (natural) resources.
2. Forests provide (the) (largest) source of income.
3. The (fir) trees, (tall) and (majestic), stretch for miles.
4. (Sixty) kinds of minerals are (state) treasures.
5. (Large) sections of (this) state have (few) people.
6. (Many) farms are quite (small).
7. Washington has (many) (fine) (natural) harbors.
8. (That) (well-known) park has (rainy) forests.

EXERCISE B: Write the adjective in the sentences and the noun that each adjective modifies. Then write whether the adjective tells *which one*, *how many*, or *what kind*. (There are 20 adjectives in all.)

> **Example:** All snakes are legless animals.
> **Answer:** All—snakes (how many)   legless—animals (what kind)

1. Most snakes seem to have a glassy stare.
2. Few kinds are harmful to people.
3. The colubrid family of snakes lives mainly in deserts and tropical forests.
4. Boas have some lizardlike features.
5. Coral snakes have multicolored rings.
6. The tails of young rattlesnakes have one button, round and shiny.
7. This little-known sidewinder leaves unusual tracks.

EXERCISE C: Write a sentence about each topic given. Include at least two adjectives in each sentence, not counting articles. Underline each adjective.

> **Example:** the first day of school
> **Answer:**   The halls, <u>silent</u> all summer, were now <u>noisy</u>.

1. Getting up in the morning
2. The weather on the way to school
3. Your first class of the day
4. Lunch in the cafeteria
5. Talking with your friends after school

Identifying and Using Proper Adjectives

EXERCISE A: Write the proper adjectives in the sentences.

> **Example:** In *Pacific Crossing*, by Gary Soto, two Chicano boys go to Japan for the summer.
> **Answer:** *Pacific*   Chicano

1. The billboards along the freeway in Tokyo include English words.
2. Lincoln Mendoza, a character in the book, stays with an Asian family.
3. Mitsuo Ono tells Lincoln about the Buddhist religion.
4. Lincoln tells Mitsuo about Mexican food.
5. Lincoln grows fond of his Japanese family.

EXERCISE B: Write each proper adjective and the noun that it modifies.

> **Example:** Mom likes Brazilian coffee and Chinese tea.
> **Answer:** Brazilian—coffee; Chinese—tea

1. The Kentuckian stables are famous for their racing horses.
2. Mr. Kaplan is a well-known American scholar.
3. His wife works for a British company in the clothing business.
4. The German students enjoyed the Canadian film.
5. He wondered if his car would survive a Midwestern winter.

EXERCISE C: Form a proper adjective about each topic and use it in a sentence. Underline each proper adjective in your sentences.

> **Example:** the name of your state
> **Answer:** Each Fourth of July, my friends and I march in the <u>Hawaiian</u> parade.

1. your nationality
2. your ethnic background
3. the name of your city or town
4. an ethnic food
5. a language you know

Identifying and Using Demonstrative and Indefinite Adjectives

EXERCISE A: Write the underlined demonstrative or indefinite adjectives in the sentences. Label each one as *demonstrative* or *indefinite*. Then write the word that each modifies. (There are ten in all.)

> **Example:** <u>Many</u> students entered the science fair <u>this</u> year.
> **Answer:** Many (indefinite) students   this (demonstrative) year

1. Models of the solar system or of molecules were entered by <u>some</u> students.
2. The DNA model on <u>that</u> table is particularly well made.
3. <u>These</u> plants have grown on a diet of <u>several</u> nutrients.
4. <u>This</u> chart gives the symptoms of <u>certain</u> types of cancer.
5. Of course, <u>no</u> science fair would be complete without a working volcano!
6. <u>Every</u> visitor wants to try <u>those</u> hands-on experiments in the back.
7. Certainly, <u>much</u> fuss will be made about the winners of the fair.

EXERCISE B: Complete the sentences with appropriate demonstrative and indefinite adjectives. Label each choice as *demonstrative* or *indefinite*.

> **Example:** Leah was looking for _____ book about the Civil War.
> **Answer:** Leah was looking for <u>another</u> book about the Civil War. (indefinite)

1. _____ letters from Union and Confederate soldiers are quite moving.
2. _____ book ought to contain a _____ little-known facts.
3. You'll find good information in _____ articles about the Battle of Shiloh.
4. You'll get _____ help from the magazine, however.
5. You might watch _____ video documentaries and take notes on them.
6. I wonder if _____ people today realize how tragic _____ years were.
7. _____ fighters of _____ war have passed away, but their stories remain.

EXERCISE C: Use the demonstrative and indefinite adjectives below to write eight sentences about a family activity. (Two sentences contain two adjectives each.)

> **Example:** several
> **Answer:** We'll need <u>several</u> rags to clean out the garage.

1. this
2. another
3. those
4. every
5. that
6. no
7. these, some
8. most, few

Comparing with Adjectives

EXERCISE A: Complete each item so that it shows the positive, comparative, and superlative form of the adjective.

> **Example:** _____, more suspicious, _____
> **Answer:** <u>suspicious</u>, more suspicious, <u>most suspicious</u>

1. tall, _____, _____
2. _____, _____, tiniest
3. _____, more colorful, _____
4. smooth, _____, _____
5. _____, _____, best
6. _____, bolder, _____
7. _____, worse, _____
8. _____, _____, most frantic
9. little, _____, _____
10. far-fetched, _____, _____

EXERCISE B: Rewrite the sentences, using the correct form of the adjective in parentheses. Label each choice as *positive*, *comparative*, or *superlative*.

> **Example:** The woodpecker was (noisy) than any we had ever heard before.
> **Answer:** The woodpecker was (noisier; comparative) than any we had ever heard before.

1. Last week, Pete hit the (spectacular) home run of the year.
2. Kathleen is (worried) than I am about our upcoming camping trip.
3. That's the (refreshing) breeze I've felt all day!
4. Are you (jealous) that I got (much) attention than you did?
5. Of all the cheerleaders, Loni comes up with the (creative) routines.
6. I feel (calm) right now, but I'll feel even (good) when this is over!
7. After the intermission, the band played (lively) tunes than they had offered before, and the audience responded with (enthusiastic) applause, than at the beginning of the performance.

EXERCISE C: Write two sentences based on each sentence below. Use the comparative and superlative forms of the adjectives in parentheses.

> **Example:** Travis told us some (surprising) news.
> **Answer:** It was (more surprising) than the news he brought us last week.
>
> In fact, it was the (most surprising) news we'd had all year.

1. It was about the (old) farmhouse on Kendall Pike.
2. (Mysterious) sounds had been heard there on Saturday night.
3. At first, I paid this announcement (little) attention.
4. As Ben supplied details, however, I felt (sure).

Using Adjectives Correctly

EXERCISE A: Write whether each item is *correct* or *incorrect* in its use of adjectives.

> **Example:** the most energetic lion of the two at the zoo
> **Answer:** incorrect

1. the most playfulest polar bear of the three
2. the sleepiest tiger I have ever seen
3. the friendliest pot-bellied pig of the two
4. the most gracefullest otter in the entire group
5. the more protective mother elephant of the pair

EXERCISE B: Rewrite the sentences, correcting any errors in the use of adjectives. If a sentence needs no changes, write *Correct.*

> **Example:** This is the more desirable of the three lakeside lots.
> **Answer:** This is the <u>most desirable</u> of the three lakeside lots.

1. That's the most saddest story you've ever told.
2. This wallpaper design is most interesting than that one.
3. The fever was worser in the morning than at night.
4. You are the most agreeablest friend I have.
5. After studying the two maps, she picked the most detailed one.
6. The most wonderful idea has occurred to me!
7. The friends grew more closer every day.
8. Would the relish tray or the fruit salad be easiest for you to bring?
9. Do you throw better with your right hand or your left?
10. Of the two sisters, Carla is the most sharp-tongued.

EXERCISE C: Rewrite the passage of dialogue, correcting its five errors in adjective usage.

AUDRA: John Ford may have been the more successful filmmaker in the world.
ELIZA: I know. His Westerns were the most popularest movies of all time. His stars had the more broader appeal across age groups of any filmmaker.
AUDRA: John Ford may have been successfuller than Alfred Hitchcock.
ELIZA: Of all Hitchcock's movies, I think *North by Northwest* is the more respected.

Developing Your Style: Using Precise Adjectives

EXERCISE A: Choose the more vivid adjective in parentheses. Rewrite each phrase.

> **Example:** a (bright, blazing) sun below the equator
> **Answer:** a <u>blazing</u> sun below the equator

1. a (cloudless, perfect) sky
2. a (wet, glistening) dewdrop
3. the (noisy, deafening) waterfall
4. a (terrible, putrid) skunk odor
5. a (tired, footsore) hiker
6. a (vibrant, pretty) red
7. the (strange, haunted) house
8. a (nice, mellow) voice
9. a (great, spectacular) view
10. a(n) (endless, long) wait

EXERCISE B: Rewrite each sentence, using a vivid adjective in place of the underlined word.

> **Example:** We found some <u>old</u> tools in the shed.
> **Answer:** We found some rustic tools in the shed.

1. Some tools had <u>strange</u> shapes.
2. The wood handles were wet and <u>smelly</u>.
3. A <u>long</u> trail of dirt led to the door.
4. Outside, the color of the shed looked <u>bad</u>.
5. We could hear <u>noisy</u> starlings nearby.

EXERCISE C: Rewrite the following passage by using more vivid adjectives. Replace at least ten less precise adjectives.

> **Example:** Wearing her winter coat, Joan felt uncomfortable in the bus.
> **Answer:** Wearing her winter coat, Joan felt <u>feverish</u> in the bus.

At the busy terminal, the weary commuters hustled to board their crowded buses. Joan spotted a shiny bus at the end of the long platform. Holding a ticket in her closed fist, she walked with a slow step toward the bus. With the lights off, it appeared strange inside. Suddenly, a nice bus driver asked Joan if she were lost. She showed him her worn ticket. "Oh, that's your bus over there," he said in a pleasant voice. He was pointing to the bus with the bright headlights and noisy engine.

Developing Your Style: Avoiding Overuse of Adjectives

EXERCISE A: In one sentence in each pair, the use of an adjective appears strained and artificial. Write the letter of the sentence that gives a clearer image by using a precise and vivid noun or verb.

> **Example:** a. The special lens magnified the actual size of the object.
>
> b. The special lens caused to make larger the actual size of the object.
>
> **Answer:** a

1. a. Without a microscope, there is low visible-like evidence of bacteria on the slide.
   b. Without a microscope, there is low visibility of bacteria on the slide.
2. a. Bacteria multiply by splitting apart.
   b. Bacteria increase a given number of times by splitting apart.
3. a. Certain bacteria cause poor conditions of health.
   b. Certain bacteria cause diseases.
4. a. Diseases can ravage people, animals, and plants.
   b. Diseases can cause great damage to people, animals, and plants.

EXERCISE B: Rewrite each sentence, using the choice in parentheses that is more vivid or precise.

> **Example:** The (important role, importance) of computers is immeasurable.
> **Answer:** The <u>importance</u> of computers is immeasurable.

1. A computer's (retentive ability, memory) is enhanced by microchips.
2. Computers (process, prepare by a special method) the information.
3. They also (solve, find the correct answers to) complicated problems.
4. Mom and Dad recently (purchased, made a money transaction for) a home computer.
5. We (observed with proper ceremony, celebrated) the purchase.

EXERCISE C: Rewrite each sentence, replacing the group of words containing a weak or awkward adjective with a more vivid noun or verb.

> **Example:** Which animal can use clever tactics against a fox?
> **Answer:** Which animal can <u>outwit</u> a fox?

1. Do coyotes live up to their reputed character?
2. The coyote can be found on the prairie-like areas of western North America.
3. It makes a loud, howling-type noise at night.
4. The coyote can use deceitful ways to trick its enemies.
5. Does the coyote's clever behavior match the fox's slyness?

Adverbs

Identifying Adverbs That Modify Verbs

EXERCISE A: Write each adverb and the verb that it modifies.

> **Example:** The rancher expertly shears the wool off the alpaca.
> **Answer:**   expertly shears

1. First the workers dye the wool.
2. They pull the wool fibers carefully to make yarn.
3. The weaver often uses different colors of yarn.
4. Clothes made of alpaca wool sell everywhere.
5. An alpaca sweater lasts forever.

EXERCISE B: Write each adverb in the sentences. Then write the question that each adverb answers: *Where? When? In what manner?* or *To what extent?*

> **Example:** Uncle Roy visits us often.
> **Answer:**   often When?

1. For a minute I almost believed her.
2. Now I understand the problem.
3. The dog must stay outside.
4. Then Ana stopped and looked thoughtfully at us.
5. I think the guinea pig rather likes you.
6. You may leave the note here on the table.
7. Someone told me today that you spoke beautifully.
8. I believe that no one has seen him since.

EXERCISE C: Write the adverb or adverbs in each sentence. Then rewrite the sentence, using a different adverb to take the place of the original one.

> **Example:** The customer complained loudly to the waiter.
> **Answer:**   loudly   The customer complained <u>vigorously</u> to the waiter.

1. The waiter walked to the table speedily.
2. Then he clumsily handed the menu to the diner.
3. The glass of water nearly fell, but the diner caught it quickly.
4. When dinner arrived late, the diner rose briskly.
5. Soon the manager appeared and nervously apologized to the diner.
6. A new plate of food appeared quickly.

Identifying Adverbs That Modify Adjectives and Other Adverbs

EXERCISE A: Write each underlined adverb and the word that it modifies. Then write whether the modified word is an *adjective* or an *adverb*.

> **Example:** The Olympic Games are <u>very</u> popular.
> **Answer:** very popular (adjective)

1. Olympic Games were held <u>every</u> four years.
2. In ancient Greece, the contests were staged <u>rather</u> simply.
3. Modern Games are <u>much</u> more competitive.
4. In 1994, Bonnie Blair speed-skated <u>extremely</u> well for the U.S.
5. Blair's performances in Norway were <u>truly</u> amazing.

EXERCISE B: Each sentence contains two adverbs that modify adjectives and/or other adverbs. Write each adverb and the adjective or other adverb that it modifies.

> **Example:** Jake's cat, Mittens, is rather old and quite heavy.
> **Answer:** rather old, quite heavy

1. Mittens is like a slightly spoiled but absolutely adorable child.
2. The cat moves relatively slowly and sleeps almost hourly.
3. Her litter box is always fresh and uncommonly clean.
4. Her rather large eyes give Mittens an amusingly puzzled look.

EXERCISE C: Each sentence contains an adverb that modifies an adjective or another adverb. Write the adverb; then rewrite the sentence, replacing the adverb with an original one.

> **Example:** He reminded me of a cheerfully busy beaver.
> **Answer:** cheerfully   He reminded me of an <u>enthusiastically</u> busy beaver.

1. The student scored extremely high marks on his reports.
2. He approached his work most vigorously.
3. Other students did not work especially hard.
4. Their reports were usually inaccurate.
5. The teacher was highly outraged.
6. The sorely inadequate facts were unacceptable.
7. She concluded, somewhat angrily, that changes were necessary.
8. She asked the singularly clever student to display his work.
9. She ordered the others to do their research rather thoroughly.
10. Are the students slightly nervous about their new assignment?

Distinguishing Adverbs from Adjectives and Prepositions

EXERCISE A: Write whether the underlined word in each sentence is an *adverb*, an *adjective*, or a *preposition*.

> **Example:** The paper blew <u>out</u> the window.
> **Answer:** preposition

1. Please put the cat <u>out</u> before you go to bed.
2. Sometimes his brother drives too <u>fast</u>.
3. Rod's a <u>fast</u> runner, but he lost the race.
4. Oh, the papers blew <u>off</u> the desk!
5. Everyone has an <u>off</u> day once in a while.
6. I think the aspirin is wearing <u>off</u>.
7. Put <u>on</u> your coat; then go home.
8. I hit the "<u>on</u>" switch and entered the room.
9. He jumped back as the car sped <u>by</u>.
10. On this team, Devon, everyone plays <u>by</u> the rules.

EXERCISE B: Find the word that each pair of sentences has in common. For each sentence, write whether the word is an *adverb*, an *adjective*, or a *preposition*.

> **Example:** I will wait inside./Look inside your backpack.
> **Answer:** inside—adverb, preposition

1. Since Tuesday the jar has stood empty./Where has he been since?
2. We heard them through an open window./The train has gone through already.
3. Heather arrived early for the party./Six o'clock is a very early wake-up call!
4. Two balloons sailed up into the sky./Our farmhouse is up this hill.

EXERCISE C: Write ten sentences, using each word as directed in parentheses.

> **Example:** outside (adverb)
> **Answer:** The boys went <u>outside</u> to play.

1. outside (adjective)
2. outside (preposition)
3. on (preposition)
4. on (adverb)
5. right (adjective)
6. right (adverb)
7. under (preposition)
8. under (adverb)
9. below (adverb)
10. below (preposition)

Comparing with Adverbs

EXERCISE A: Write the comparative and superlative degrees of each adverb.

> **Example:** frequently
> **Answer:** more frequently, most frequently

1. softly
2. high
3. nearly
4. badly
5. casually
6. soon
7. habitually
8. far
9. well
10. little

EXERCISE B: Write whether the underlined word or words in each sentence are used in the comparative or superlative degree.

> **Example:** Comedians tell jokes <u>best</u>.
> **Answer:** superlative

1. A professional comic tells jokes <u>better</u> than an amateur.
2. Some comedians imitate famous people <u>most convincingly</u>.
3. Tonight this stand-up comic performed <u>worst</u> of all.
4. She talked <u>faster</u> this time.
5. The audience drifted <u>further</u> away by the minute.
6. The comic laughed <u>louder</u> than anyone in the audience.
7. Didn't she perform <u>best</u> at the beginning of the show?
8. The last part of the show passed <u>more slowly</u> than the first.
9. Of all the acts, this comic's ended <u>most promptly</u>.
10. Next time, I think that the comic should try <u>harder</u>.

EXERCISE C: Write the form of the adverb in parentheses that correctly completes each sentence. Then label the degree of the adverb.

> **Example:** The next highway exit was two miles (farther, farthest) away.
> **Answer:** farther (comparative)

1. Of all days, it rained (harder, hardest) today.
2. My father drove (more cautiously, most cautiously) than before.
3. We left the house (earlier, earliest) than last time.
4. Which of all the roads could we travel (more safely, most safely)?
5. Of all the drivers I know, Dad does (better, best) in foul weather.

Using Adverbs Correctly

EXERCISE A: Write whether each of the following groups of words is *correct* or *incorrect* in its use of adverbs.

> **Example:** the game was real exciting
> **Answer:** incorrect

1. the entire team played good
2. no one couldn't stop watching
3. no one in the bleachers felt bad
4. that coach won't get no help
5. I can't scarcely read the score
6. she looked badly at halftime
7. the score is sure close
8. a win is no great surprise
9. hardly never have we lost
10. this game is as well as it gets

EXERCISE B: Rewrite the sentences, completing each with the correct word or phrase in parentheses.

> **Example:** Haven't you _____ heard of Thomas Stevens? (never, ever)
> **Answer:** Haven't you <u>ever</u> heard of Thomas Stevens?

1. Probably no one you know has had an adventure _____ like his. (anything, nothing)
2. Stevens was _____ to take a trip around the world on his bicycle, so he left San Franciso in 1884. (all ready, already)
3. Unpaved roads and mountainous terrain made Stevens's trip _____ uncomfortable at times. (real, very)
4. Hardly _____ who read the newspaper failed to follow his journey around the globe or applaud him for a job done so _____. (anyone, no one; good, well)

EXERCISE C: Rewrite the following passage of dialogue, correcting its five errors in adverb usage.

> **Example:** RAVI: I can't think of no ideas for the school talent show.
> **Answer:** RAVI: I can't think of <u>any</u> ideas for the school talent show.

CARA: Nothing won't keep me out of the talent show this year. I'm going to sing good enough to win in the vocal category! In fact, I've all ready started rehearsing! Can you play a musical instrument?

RAVI: I can play the clarinet, but not too good. I'm not badly on the guitar, though.

Developing Your Style: Adverbs

EXERCISE A: Write the adverb or adverbs in each sentence. Then write another adverb that could be used instead.

> **Example:** The horseman galloped rapidly down the roadway.
> **Answer:** rapidly   fearlessly

1. The rider drew unexpectedly to a halt.
2. He glanced nervously around the clearing.
3. An arrow swiftly sailed through the air.
4. A note was tied securely to the arrow.
5. He hurriedly read the note and departed.

EXERCISE B: Add one or two adverbs to make each sentence more interesting. Do not use the same adverb twice.

> **Example:** The water slapped against the posts of the dock.
> **Answer:** The water slapped <u>quietly</u> but <u>steadily</u> against the posts of the dock.

1. Andy baited his hook.
2. He cast the line halfway across the lake.
3. A large fish nibbled on the bait.
4. Andy gave the fish some line.
5. The fish swam toward the dock.
6. The fish jerked the cork under the water.
7. Andy reeled in the line.
8. He removed the hook from the bass's mouth.
9. The landed bass was large.
10. It flopped off the pier and into the water.

EXERCISE C: Write five sentences about what you like to do on summer days, using the adverbs provided.

> **Example:** loudly
> **Answer:** I always yell <u>loudly</u> at baseball games.

1. lazily
2. eagerly
3. unusually
4. frequently
5. contentedly

Apostrophes

Using Apostrophes in Possessives and Contractions

EXERCISE A: Write each item, adding apostrophes where necessary. If no apostrophe is needed, write *Correct*.

    Example: Georges   the mens department
    Answers: George's   the men's department

1. Benjamins novel
2. a poets rhyme
3. everybodys favorite singer
4. two months work
5. three writers poetry
6. you would
7. do not
8. hers
9. they are
10. Sam will

EXERCISE B: Write the word from the choice in parentheses that correctly completes each sentence.

    Example: The screenplay (contest's, contests) deadline is tomorrow.
    Answer: contest's

1. The judging (panel's, panels') decision is final.
2. Natalie (hasn't, has'nt) submitted her manuscript yet.
3. She hopes that (hers', hers) will be the winning entry.
4. (She'll, Shell) have to wait about two months for the results.
5. Her story begins with a young boy who (won't, wont) talk to anyone.
6. At the (movies', movie's) end, the boy finally utters (his, his') first line.
7. Natalie asked for two (teacher's, teachers') comments on her screenplay.
8. She knows that her final draft (would'nt, wouldn't) be as good without these (supporter's, supporters') help.

EXERCISE C: Rewrite the paragraph, correcting any errors in the use of apostrophes.

    Example: The three friends couldnt agree about Jennifers party.
    Answer: The three friends <u>couldn't</u> agree about <u>Jennifer's</u> party.

Julia thought that shed like to make a surprise party, but Nancy wasn't going along with the idea. She believes that nobodys ever happy about being surprised. Still, Nancys sister thought that Jennifer would enjoy all the fuss. The friend's problem wasnt resolved until the next days meeting. Jennifer had guessed her pal's plan and did'nt hesitate to talk to them about it. She said, "I dont mind a surprise party, so long as there arent too many people there."

Other Uses of Apostrophes

EXERCISE A: Rewrite each item, adding apostrophes where necessary.

   Example: too many you *knows* in that speech
   Answer: too many you *know's* in that speech

1. dot your *is* and cross your *ts*
2. count by *10s*
3. *7s* that look like *zs*
4. a glut of *!s*
5. so many *verys* in that poem
6. "Blowin in the Wind"
7. three *5s* in her telephone number
8. use *&s*, not *+s*
9. The speaker drops all initial *hs*.
10. "Lend me an elping and," he'll say.

EXERCISE B: Rewrite each sentence, adding apostrophes, where needed.

   Example: He had strung all the sentences together with *ands*.
   Answer: He had strung all the sentences together with *and's*.

1. The storyteller presented "Dancin and Prancin with the Lady of the Moon."
2. He said that he'd heard enough *once upon a times* and *happily ever afters* to last a lifetime.
3. He asked his audience, "Have you been mindin your *ps* and *qs*?"
4. The moral of his tale was "If *ifs* and *ands* were pots and pans, there'd be no need for tinkers."
5. You'd better get em to come here quickly.

EXERCISE C: Rewrite each sentence, adding apostrophes where needed. If a sentence needs no change, write *Correct*.

   Example: The boys grew weary of their mom's continual *maybes*.
   Answer: The boys grew weary of their mom's continual *maybe's*.

1. Hal always makes *As* and *Bs*; getting *Cs* would crush him.
2. When do you change the *ys* to *is*?
3. The room resounded with *nos* when she asked if we wanted a test.
4. "I was zoomin down the road, feelin the wind round my helmet".
5. There are two *ns* and two *ss* in *unnecessary*.
6. Does the answer have two *3's* in it?
7. Using too many *!s* can actually reduce the impact of your writing.
8. Television first become part of popular culture in the 1950's.
9. Jimmy asked, "Can you ear me when I say ello?"
10. I heard more *yeah's* in that telephone conversation than I thought possible.

Appositives

Identifying and Punctuating Appositives

EXERCISE A: Write the appositive word or phrase in each sentence. Then write the word that it renames.

>   **Example:** Mr. Williams, the librarian, showed us where to find books about Sojourner Truth.
>   **Answer:**   the librarian, Mr. Williams

1. Taisha took out a book about Harriet Tubman, an African-American hero.
2. My best friend Yvonne likes to read about famous athletes.
3. She chose a book about Henry Aaron, the great baseball player.
4. Has Samantha found any books by Jean Fritz, her favorite author?
5. Steven picked out a book about the American general Robert E. Lee.

EXERCISE B: Complete each sentence with an appositive or appositive phrase. Add commas where needed. Then write the word that each appositive names.

>   **Example:** Our neighbor _____ helped us build these bookcases.
>   **Answer:**   Our neighbor, a carpenter, helped us build these bookcases. (neighbor)

1. Mr. Grant _____ wants to see me this afternoon.
2. Would you take these books to Mrs. Willis _____ ?
3. My mother _____ should take a look at that cut.
4. We took the bus to Baseline Road _____ .
5. The poet _____ is one of my favorite writers.

EXERCISE C: Combine each pair of sentences by using an appositive. Write the new sentence, using commas correctly.

>   **Example:** Glass is one of the most useful materials
>
>   Glass is made from common materials.
>   **Answer:**   Glass, one of the most useful materials, is made from common materials.

1. Corning Glass Works has developed more than 100,000 kinds of glass. The Corning Glass Works is a company that makes glass.
2. Safety glass is made of layers of glass and plastic. Safety glass is a substance used for car windshields.
3. The first glass objects were made thousands of years ago. They were the creations of unknown artisans.
4. Venice is a city in Italy. Venice was a center for manufacturing glass.
5. Louis Tiffany created many beautiful objects from glass. Louis Tiffany was an American designer.

Name _____ Class _____ Date _____

Developing Your Style: Appositives

EXERCISE A: Write each sentence, inserting commas where needed. If no commas are needed, write *Correct*.

> **Example:** Arthur Conan Doyle a British physician is best known as a writer.
> **Answer:** Arthur Conan Doyle, a British physician, is best known as a writer.

1. Arthur Conan Doyle created the character Sherlock Holmes.
2. Sherlock Holmes a brilliant detective can solve any mystery.
3. Dr. Watson a good friend assists Holmes in solving his cases.
4. The character of Holmes was based on a real person Dr. Joseph Bell.
5. Holmes's trademark a curved pipe is familiar to most people.

EXERCISE B: Combine each pair of sentences by using an appositive or an appositive phrase. Use commas where needed.

> **Example:** Gary Paulsen writes about sports.
>
> Gary Paulsen is an author from Minnesota.
> **Answer:** Gary Paulsen, an author from Minnesota, writes about sports.

1. Gary Paulsen wrote *Dogsong* in 1984.
   Dogsong is a book about the Iditarod Sled Dog Race.
2. The Iditarod is run from Anchorage to Nome, Alaska.
   The Iditarod is a thousand-mile race.
3. *Dogsong* won an important award from the American Library Association. This award was the Newbery Honor Book.
4. Another book reveals Paulsen's love of water sports.
   This book is *The Voyage of the Frog*.
5. *The Voyage of the Frog* is based on an event in Paulsen's own life. *The Voyage of the Frog* is the story of a boy lost at sea.

EXERCISE C: Imagine that you are a detective. Write sentences about a case you are solving, using each of the phrases or proper nouns as appositives. Use commas where needed.

> **Example:** the gardener
> **Answer:** Mr. Green, the gardener, led me to the scene of the crime.

1. Penelope Peacock
2. cyanide
3. a muddy footprint
4. a smudged fingerprint
5. the cook

Capitalization

Capitalizing Names and Titles of People

EXERCISE A: Rewrite each item, using capital letters where needed.

> **Example:** sherlock holmes
> **Answer:** <u>S</u>herlock <u>H</u>olmes

1. dr. watson
2. sir arthur
3. frankenstein's monster
4. emily dickinson's poems
5. Yesterday i read a sonnet by shakespeare.
6. langston hughes
7. james thurber's walter mitty
8. t.s. eliot
9. ms. dorothy parker
10. You're right, lord wembley!

EXERCISE B: Rewrite each sentence, using a capital letter where needed.

> **Example:** mr saunders told me a joke last night.
> **Answer:** <u>M</u>r. <u>S</u>aunders told me a joke last night.

1. i told mrs. whittaker what i'd heard.
2. Hey, dad, have you heard the joke yet?
3. After dr. ruiz read the joke, she told it to sally and chelsea.
4. sally and chelsea sent the joke to mr. t.j. goodman, who publishes *Ha-Ha* magazine.
5. mr. goodman asked Ms. ellen parnell to illustrate the joke.

EXERCISE C: Rewrite each sentence, correcting any mistakes in capitalization. If a sentence needs no changes, write *Correct*.

> **Example:** Could you lend me that book, mrs. warren?
> **Answer:** Could you lend me that book, <u>M</u>rs. <u>W</u>arren?

1. *Little Women* is a novel by louisa may alcott.
2. It tells about the march Family.
3. There are four sisters: meg, jo, beth, and amy.
4. mrs. march's first name is marmee.
5. They live next to mr. lawrence and his son, theodore.
6. theodore's nickname is laurie.
7. A tutor is in love with jo.
8. Toward the end of the book, Meg has two children named Daisy and Demi.
9. Who is your favorite character, mom?
10. Mother likes meg, but i think that aunt march and john brooke are also very interesting characters.

Capitalizing Name of Places

EXERCISE A: Rewrite each item, using capital letters where needed.

> **Example:** the indian ocean
> **Answer:** the Indian Ocean

1. the ohio river
2. park avenue
3. san joaquin valley
4. albuquerque, new mexico
5. the sahara desert
6. prince edward island
7. yellowstone national park
8. mediterranean sea
9. people's republic of china
10. a european country

EXERCISE B: Rewrite each sentence, using capital letters where needed.

> **Example:** The pacific ocean can be seen from california's beaches.
> **Answer:** The Pacific Ocean can be seen from California's beaches.

1. The continent of north america includes the countries of canada, the united states, and mexico.
2. The region called the great plains extends from the canadian provinces of alberta, saskatchewan, and monitoba through the central united states into northern texas.
3. The middle west includes the states of illinois, indiana, iowa, kansas, michigan, minnesota, missouri, nebraska, ohio, and wisconsin.
4. The mississippi river flows from minnesota to louisiana, where it empties into the gulf of mexico.

EXERCISE C: Rewrite this part of a letter, correcting the twenty mistakes in capitalization.

> **Example:** In paris we walked along the champs Élysées.
> **Answer:** In Paris we walked along the Champs Élysées.

Greetings from great britain! Our trip has been wonderful. We arrived at gatwick airport last Sunday. We took a train to victoria station and then the underground to our hotel in earl's court road. The sites in london were marvelous, especially kensington gardens and the thames river. We traveled North to york, which is on the north sea. Tomorrow we will reach edinburgh, scotland.

Capitalizing Other Names

EXERCISE A: Rewrite each item, using capital letters where needed.

> **Example:** the empire state building
> **Answer:** the <u>E</u>mpire <u>S</u>tate <u>B</u>uilding

1. before world war I
2. buckingham palace
3. *the sound of music*
4. speaking in italian
5. "the pit and the pendulum"
6. african-american art
7. the bible
8. the new york stock exchange
9. after the great depression
10. drive a pontiac *bonneville*

EXERCISE B: Rewrite each sentence, using capital letters where needed.

> **Example:** Have you read *alice's adventures in wonderland?*
> **Answer:** Have you read *<u>A</u>lice's <u>A</u>dventures in <u>W</u>onderland?*

1. Can you imagine driving in a *model T* ford?
2. How tall is the chrysler building, Ginny?
3. Can you speak portuguese?
4. Will you take american history 101 next year?
5. Have you ever visited mount rushmore?
6. When did the battle between the *monitor* and the *merrimack* take place?
7. Was the battle of yorktown part of the revolutionary war?
8. In which countries do many people practice buddhism?
9. Have you ever seen *the hunchback of notre dame?*
10. Can you remember the lyrics to "the star-spangled banner"?

EXERCISE C: Complete each sentence. Follow any instructions in parentheses. Remember to capitalize each name correctly.

> **Example:** My favorite poem is "_____."
> **Answer:** My favorite poem is "<u>My Last Duchess</u>."

1. My favorite movie is _____. (Underline or italicize the name of the movie.)
2. One song that really gets on my nerves is "_____."
3. I think that the landmark that best represents the United States is _____.
4. I would like to join _____ someday. (Name an organization.)
5. If I could travel backward in time, I would like to see _____. (Write the name of a historic event.)

Using Capitals to Mark Beginnings of Sentences and Direct Quotations

EXERCISE A: Rewrite each item, using a capital letter where needed.

> **Example:** our community pool is open. let's go swimming.
> **Answer:** Our community pool is open. Let's go swimming.

1. swimming is my favorite sport, but I do not like diving.
2. marie said to Lena, "you and I could go to the pool this afternoon."
3. lena said, "what a good idea! we can practice our synchronized swimming routine."
4. the lifeguard called them over. the two partners left the pool.
5. will we find deck chairs in the sun?

EXERCISE B: Rewrite each sentence, correcting any mistakes in capitalization. If a sentence needs no changes, write *Correct*.

> **Example:** adobe bricks are usually made from clay, water, and a little straw.
> **Answer:** Adobe bricks are usually made from clay, water, and a little straw.

1. Julio said, "many houses in Mexico are built of adobe."
2. "Yes," agreed his mother. "our family grew up in an adobe house."
3. Julio wanted to build an adobe house; he talked to his uncle.
4. "Well," said Uncle Raimundo, "this climate is not appropriate for adobe. when they get damp, adobe bricks will crumble."
5. "oh, well," said Julio, "if I can't live in an adobe house, I'm glad I got to see one in person."

EXERCISE C: Rewrite each paragraph, using capital letters where needed.

> **Example:** my report is about *The Prince and the Pauper.*
> **Answer:** My report is about *The Prince and the Pauper.*

1. humorous author Mark Twain wrote *The Prince and the Pauper* in 1882. it is an entertaining tale of reversed identities. the prince of England, Edward, and a London street beggar named Tom Canty exchange places. their adventures take them into parts of the world that they had never before encountered.
2. "my favorite book is *The Prince and the Pauper,*" said Christa. "it is everything a novel should be. it's funny, exciting, and perceptive. if you enjoy reading this book, you will also like *A Connecticut Yankee in King Arthur's Court.*"

Using Capitals to Mark Other Beginnings

EXERCISE A: Rewrite each sentence, using a capital letter where needed.

   Example: The first line of the sonnet is "shall I compare thee to a summer's day?"
   Answer: The first line of the sonnet is "Shall I compare thee to a summer's day?"

1. The next line is "thou art more lovely and more temperate."
2. The final couplet is "so long as men can breathe, or eyes can see,/so long lives this, and this gives life to thee."
3. Delia wrote "dear mom and dad" at the top of the card.
4. The first entry in Ike's outline was "I. the South Pole."
5. Beneath that came "a. the southern end of Earth's axis."

EXERCISE B: Rewrite each item, using capital letters where needed.

   Example: to whom it may concern:
   Answer: To Whom It May Concern:

1. "here a star, and there a star,/some lose their way!" (Emily Dickinson)
2. dear sir or madam:
3. dear editor of the *cleveland plain dealer*,
4. dearest melanie,
5. I. the attack on Pearl Harbor
   a. took place on Dec. 7, 1941
   b. naval base attacked by Japanese
   c. war declared the next day

EXERCISE C: Rewrite each item, correcting any mistakes in capitalization. If an item needs no changes, write *Correct*.

   Example: dear aunt nancy and uncle pete,
   Answer: Dear Aunt Nancy and Uncle Pete,

1. "Dark brown is the river,/golden is the sand . . ." (Robert Louis Stevenson)
2. Dearest senator:
3. Dear Supervisor of Consumer Affairs:
4. II. discovery of buoyancy
   a. bathtub experiment
   b. volume can be measured by displacement of water

Clauses

Identifying and Using Main and Subordinate Clauses

EXERCISE A: Write whether each group of words is a *phrase*, a *main clause*, or a *subordinate clause*.

> **Example:** since bumper stickers on cars are more popular than ever
> **Answer:** subordinate clause

1. some bumper stickers are political in nature
2. on the back bumper of the car
3. because it is visible to the other driver
4. no two stickers are alike
5. that have no bumper stickers

EXERCISE B: Write whether each group of words in parentheses is a *main clause* or a *subordinate clause*. If a group of words is a main clause, use it to write a sentence with a new subordinate clause.

> **Example:** If you know the answer, (you should not miss it on the test).
> **Answer:** main clause
>
> <u>Because the answer is obvious,</u> you should not miss it on the test.

1. Before you begin, (I want to go over some things).
2. The instructions will become clear (if you read them carefully).
3. If you need to sharpen your pencils, (do it now).
4. (Place your papers on my desk) when you have finished.
5. (While I have your attention), I want to wish you good luck!

EXERCISE C: Use the subordinate clause in each sentence to write an original sentence.

> **Example:** Because jellyfish sting, you should avoid them in the water.
> **Answer:** Because jellyfish sting, <u>Tod didn't go near them</u>.

1. When we visited the marine museum, we heard a lecture about lobsters.
2. Since one shark has been there for years, it is now quite large.
3. Although horseshoe crabs are not really crabs, they do look primitive.
4. Wherever we went, we saw fascinating sea creatures.
5. We took one last look at the electric eels before we left.

Identifying and Using Adjective Clauses

EXERCISE A: Write the adjective clause in each sentence.

> **Example:** The woman who spoke to you just now is Mayor Weston.
> **Answer:**   who spoke to you just now

1. The monster that scared everyone disappeared at the end of the movie.
2. No one enjoys talking to a person who interrupts all the time.
3. Grandpa traveled on trains, which many people once rode.
4. Carl Sandburg, who won many awards, is my favorite poet.
5. Russ is the student whose essay took first prize.

EXERCISE B: Write each adjective clause and the noun that it modifies.

> **Example:** This plant, which has red blossoms, is a cactus.
> **Answer:**   which has red blossoms   plant

1. Synonyms are words that have similar meanings.
2. The poet who wrote "Jabberwocky" was Lewis Carroll.
3. A dog that is well behaved makes a good companion.
4. Chicago, which is sixty miles from here, faces Lake Michigan.
5. Soccer is a sport that has become very popular.
6. Mr. Riley is a coach whom everyone likes.
7. Dogs that help the blind are carefully trained.
8. Are these the children whose mother has just arrived?
9. Aurore Dupin, who wrote under the name of George Sand, became famous.
10. Can you hear the music that is coming from downstairs?

EXERCISE C: Create five complete sentences by adding words to each adjective clause. Write the new sentences.

> **Example:** who just made a report
> **Answer:**   The student <u>who just made a report</u> is Nick.

1. who is always smiling
2. whose flight was delayed
3. that Su Lin and Martin admired
4. which many people like
5. whom the police had suspected

Distinguishing Between Restrictive and Nonrestrictive Clauses

EXERCISE A: Write whether each underlined clause is *restrictive* or *nonrestrictive*.

> **Example:** This poet, <u>who died in 1928</u>, is well beloved.
> **Answer:** nonrestrictive

1. Elinor Wylie, <u>whom I admire</u>, wrote poems and novels.
2. The style <u>that she preferred</u> was the historical novel.
3. "Velvet Shoes," <u>which Wylie published quite early</u>, is a favorite of mine.
4. The poets <u>whom I most enjoy</u> use unusual imagery.
5. Wylie, <u>who borrowed her style from an earlier era</u>, always seems fresh and surprising.

EXERCISE B: Write the adjective clause in each sentence. Then identify it as *restrictive* or *nonrestrictive*.

> **Example:** People who know him call him hilarious.
> **Answer:** who know him   restrictive

1. My uncle, who seems quite shy, is very amusing.
2. His style, which can surprise you, is deadpan.
3. He constantly cracks jokes that bewilder strangers.
4. Those who understand him fall down laughing.
5. The people whom he most amazes are my parents.
6. They cannot understand Uncle Bob, whom I adore.
7. A man whose looks are so ordinary can get away with a lot.
8. Bob enjoys the fact that folks expect him to be dull.
9. He cracks jokes that leave me howling.
10. My parents, whose patience is limited, miss the point.

EXERCISE C: Rewrite each sentence, adding a comma or commas to any nonrestrictive clause. If a sentence does not need one or more commas, write *Correct*.

> **Example:** Danielle's train which was late finally arrived.
> **Answer:** Danielle's train, which was late, finally arrived.

1. Danielle comes from Marseilles which is in southern France.
2. Marseilles is a city that is known for its port.
3. My city which has a port as well may seem similar.
4. One thing that I will show Danielle is the aquarium.
5. My cousin Emily who works there will give us a behind-the-scenes tour.

Identifying and Using Adverb Clauses

EXERCISE A: Write the subordinating conjunction in each underlined adverb clause.

> **Example:** <u>After he attended college</u>, Joe applied to medical school.
> **Answer:** After

1. <u>Before Joe was in high school</u>, his first love was medicine.
2. He studied science and math <u>so that he might prepare himself</u>.
3. He interviewed doctors and nurses <u>wherever he went</u>.
4. <u>When he broke his arm</u>, Joe interviewed his doctor about her profession.

EXERCISE B: Write the adverb clause in each sentence. Then write whether it tells *when, why, how,* or *under what condition* about the underlined verb.

> **Example:** As soon as the bell rings, I <u>will ask</u> him.
> **Answer:** As soon as the bell rings   when

1. They <u>changed</u> their clothes so that they would be comfortable.
2. The family <u>sang</u> when they rode along the highway.
3. Before spring comes, I <u>will plant</u> a vegetable garden.
4. Because her family <u>speaks</u> Russian at home, Alena <u>speaks</u> it well, too.
5. You <u>could make</u> friends if you would speak up.
6. I <u>will turn</u> the hamburgers while you slice the tomatoes.
7. Lorenzo <u>acts</u> as if we had never met.
8. After the games were over, everyone <u>enjoyed</u> a picnic.
9. I <u>am writing</u> about Helen Keller because I admire her.
10. Until you finish eating, <u>remain</u> at the table.

EXERCISE C: Choose an adverb clause from the list below to expand each sentence. Use commas as needed.

- until he laughed
- because he was happy
- as soon as he heard
- while he waited
- if he wished to do so

> **Example:** He looked ordinary.
> **Answer:** He looked ordinary <u>until he laughed</u>.

1. Jason chuckled.
2. Jason would stand on his head
3. Jason paced in a circle.
4. Jason tapped his toes.

Using Clauses Correctly

EXERCISE A: For each sentence, write *Correct* if the main clause contains the main idea. Write *faulty subordination* if the main idea is misplaced in the subordinate clause. Then rewrite only the correct main clause.

> **Example:** Because John wants a dog, he never had a pet.
> **Answer:** faulty subordination   John wants a dog

1. He could choose any dog at the pound although John chose the terrier.
2. Before John made his decision, the terrier wagged its tail at him.
3. He had had any questions if his doubts were now gone.
4. The time came to leave when John took his new pet home.
5. Because the dog was not yet housebroken, John put newspapers on the kitchen floor.

EXERCISE B: Rewrite the sentences that have faulty subordination, correcting the error. If a sentence does not contain this error, write *Correct*.

> **Example:** When we will be at home, the new refrigerator arrives.
> **Answer:** We will be at home when the new refrigerator arrives.

1. Gina can't leave the house until the store delivers the package.
2. Unless she will be late for her appointment, the package is delivered on time.
3. If she will accept it, the new refrigerator is not damaged.
4. Before she signs a release form, Gina will inspect the appliance.
5. If she can call her mother at work, there is a problem.

EXERCISE C: Rewrite each sentence to correct faulty subordination.

> **Example:** You are finished with your homework if you can watch TV.
> **Answer:** You can watch TV if you are finished with your homework.

1. Although you should study, you don't have homework.
2. You are a speed reader unless it will take you hours.
3. If you would be quite literate, you could read a book each week.
4. The book is nonfiction because it may take you more time.
5. You write your own book when you can make it any length.

Developing Your Style: Clauses

EXERCISE A: Combine a main clause from the first column with a subordinate clause from the second column to create a vivid, informative sentence. Write the new sentences.

Example: use a dictionary if you need to check the spelling of a word
Answer: If you need to check the spelling of a word, use a dictionary.

I	II
1. supervisors train new editors	if you look it up in a dictionary
2. the new edition is longer	because it has more words
3. some old words were dropped	before they added foreign foods
4. you'll find the meaning	who may be inexperienced
5. they called restaurant owners	when new words were added

EXERCISE B: Replace the weak phrasing in parentheses with a vivid subordinate clause. Write the new sentences, adding commas and subordinate conjunctions correctly.

Example: You respond to this survey, (and then) you'll receive a gift.
Answer: If you respond to this survey, the company will send you a gift.

1. You send in your answers, (and then) we'll print your responses.
2. You print your name and address, (or else) we won't know who you are.
3. You may send us a fax, (but then) we'd prefer a mailed entry.
4. The deadline is next week, (and so) you have no time to lose.
5. There are no guarantees, (and yet) you can be a winner!

EXERCISE C: Write ten vivid sentences using one of the clauses below in each one.

Example: because of the change of seasons
Answer: The weather varies greatly in the Northeast <u>because of the change of seasons</u>.

1. I like the wintertime
2. although we had a harsh winter
3. we had to borrow a sled
4. since I can't ski
5. indoor sports are fun, too
6. springtime is best
7. if I could choose any sport
8. since we moved here
9. unless the weather gets too hot
10. this storm broke all records

Colons

Using Colons Correctly

EXERCISE A: Rewrite each item, adding colons where needed.

> **Example:** 330 P.M.
> **Answer:** 3:30 P.M.

1. 130 P.M.
2. Dear Mr. Morrison
3. Caution Open Door Slowly
4. 1100 A.M.
5. To Whom It May Concern

EXERCISE B: Rewrite the sentences, adding colons where needed.

> **Example:** We grew these vegetables corn, beans, and squash.
> **Answer:** We grew these vegetables: corn, beans, and squash.

1. Sift together the following the cornmeal, the flour, and the salt.
2. The train leaves at 315 P.M. and arrives at 402 P.M.
3. The sign read, "Caution Wet Floor."
4. Use these methods to prepare the fish broiling, baking, or grilling.
5. In Florida we saw several kinds of citrus trees lemon, orange, lime, and grapefruit.

EXERCISE C: Rewrite the letter, adding colons where needed.

> **Example:** The following items will be needed for registration a birth certificate, a health record, and a report card.
> **Answer:** The following items will be needed for registration: a birth certificate, a health record, and a report card.

Dear Student

Welcome to Pleasant Valley Middle School! During your first visit, plan to do the following locate your classrooms, meet your new teachers, and look at your new textbooks. Your daily schedule will be as follows classes from 830 A.M. to 1130 A.M.; lunch from 1145 to 1215; and classes from 1230 P.M. to 300 P.M. Remember that at Pleasant Valley, we have one simple rule treat others as you would like to be treated.

Commas

Using Commas with Coordinating Conjunctions

EXERCISE A: Rewrite each sentence, adding the missing comma.

> **Example:** I haven't sent her an invitation nor will I.
> **Answer:**   I haven't sent her an invitation, nor will I.

1. Carmen is my best friend and she knows it.
2. Everyone likes going to parties yet no one likes to plan them.
3. Receiving presents is wonderful but giving them is even better.
4. Can you come or will you be busy that night?
5. Roger didn't show up nor did he offer me a good explanation.

EXERCISE B: Expand on each sentence so that it becomes a compound sentence. Be sure to use commas correctly.

> **Example:** Liana bought the food _____.
> **Answer:**   Liana bought the food, but Nathan and I did the cooking.

1. The tapes belong to Li and Sun _____.
2. The littler children began to cry _____.
3. The storyteller talked on and on _____.
4. Shall we order Chinese food _____?
5. Maritza would not look at anyone _____.
6. Dad made a pasta salad _____.
7. Many birds had flown south _____.
8. I had set the alarm _____.
9. Darrell was fond of his sister _____.
10. Shall we read a story _____?

EXERCISE C: Rewrite each pair of sentences, using a coordinating conjunction. Change punctuation and capitalization as needed.

> **Example:** Everyone wants a good grade. No one is willing to work for it.
> **Answer:**   Everyone wants a good grade, but no one is willing to work for it.

1. Dogs make good pets. I prefer cats.
2. Do you want to go out tonight? Would you rather stay home?
3. I like the new girl. I'll tell her so.
4. French is a beautiful language. I think I'd rather learn Spanish.
5. I have not broken the club rules. Will I.

Using Commas with Adjectives

EXERCISE A: Copy the adjectives in parentheses, adding commas where needed.

> **Example:** The (cold icy) country of Denmark is the setting for this ancient story.
> **Answer:** cold, icy

1. Hrothgar, the king of Denmark, built a feast hall of (massive thick) timbers.
2. Near the feast hall was a (cold murky) inlet of the sea.
3. A (fierce huge diabolical) monster of incredible strength lived in a cave beneath its waters.
4. Grendel made (numerous vicious) attacks on Hrothgar's warriors.
5. Soon Hrothgar's (bold fearless) nephew, Beowulf, slew Grendel.

EXERCISE B: Rewrite the sentences, adding commas where needed. If a sentence needs no commas, write *Correct.*

1. The clouds seemed caught upon the majestic proud mountaintop.
2. A cooling refreshing breeze touched their sweaty faces.
3. Those three tiny bones carry the sound waves from the outer ear.
4. Many brave men fell here in battle.
5. A sleek swift quarterhorse was his mount.
6. Did the rough wiry cow ponies put in a long day?
7. The dark dusty drab basement didn't seem much of a place to study.
8. Corinne comforted the sobbing shaking child with a soft sweet lullaby.
9. We need an intelligent outgoing level-headed candidate for senator.

EXERCISE C: Complete each sentence, adding at least two adjectives. Be sure to use commas correctly.

> **Example:** He needed the _____ climate of the Southwest.
> **Answer:** He needed the <u>warm, dry, unpolluted</u> climate of the Southwest.

1. A _____ lump was forming in her throat.
2. With a _____ salute, the lieutenant greeted the colonel.
3. Wearing your seat belt is a _____ habit to learn.
4. They heard _____ laughter from the top of the stairs.
5. A _____ shadow appeared on the wall.

Using Commas with Subordinating Conjunctions

EXERCISE A: Rewrite each sentence, adding the missing comma.

> **Example:** Whenever I get hungry I try to have a carrot.
> **Answer:** Whenever I get hungry, I try to have a carrot.

1. While you're up would you bring me something from the kitchen?
2. If you had a choice would you rather have a cookie or an apple?
3. Although I like junk food I'd rather have a home-cooked meal.
4. Whatever we have for dinner my brother always wants something else.
5. Until you've tried my recipe you don't know how good okra can be.

EXERCISE B: Rewrite each sentence, adding a comma or commas as needed. If a sentence needs no changes, write *Correct.*

> **Example:** Because you're my friend I won't reveal your secret.
> **Answer:** Because you're my friend, I won't reveal your secret.

1. Before you answer the question be sure you know the facts.
2. After all we've been through together how can you treat me this way?
3. Unless you have something more to say you should leave now.
4. So that there's no misunderstanding later, let's put our agreement in writing.
5. While you're in town I hope you'll pay us a visit.

EXERCISE C: Expand on each sentence to create a complex sentence. Be sure to use commas correctly.

> **Example:** Although I've always been good at English _____.
> **Answer:** Although I've always been good at English, <u>I may fail this test</u>.

1. Until I started junior high school _____.
2. Whether you like Mr. Decker or not _____.
3. Because I want to do well _____.
4. After school today _____.
5. Whenever we have midterms _____.
6. As I told you before _____.
7. Unless I'm mistaken _____.
8. When I think about it _____.
9. Since I took that exam _____.
10. _____ if I don't do well in this class.

Using Commas with Introductory Words and Phrases

EXERCISE A: Rewrite each sentence, adding commas where needed.

    Example: Born in 1875 Mary McLeod Bethune had a difficult childhood.
    Answer: Born in 1875, Mary McLeod Bethune had a difficult childhood.

1. As the fifteenth child of former slaves Bethune often had no money.
2. During that time in South Carolina most African Americans had no schools.
3. At the invitation of a teacher Mary attended a newly established school.
4. Excelling as a student she won a scholarship to college.
5. With the help of wealthy businesspeople Bethune later founded a college in Florida.

EXERCISE B: Rewrite each sentence, moving a phrase or phrases to the beginning of the sentence. Add commas where needed.

    Example: We found the package in the middle of the afternoon.
    Answer: In the middle of the afternoon, we found the package.

1. The teacher frowned at us annoyed by our antics.
2. How do we know she can be trusted on the other hand?
3. We decided to open the box puzzled by its contents.
4. The information is correct according to the news on the radio.
5. The dog had tiny black eyes under its mop of hair.

EXERCISE C: Write ten sentences about what you do after school, beginning each with one of the following introductory phrases. Add commas where needed.

    Example: At the end of the period
    Answer: At the end of the period, the bell finally rang.

1. Cramming books into my backpack
2. Waiting for the bus
3. Near the front of the bus
4. Starving for a snack
5. On the way to a friend's house
6. Working on our homework
7. Satisfied with our progress
8. By the end of the afternoon
9. After helping with the dishes
10. Tired from my studies

Using Commas with Interrupters

EXERCISE A: Rewrite each sentence, adding commas where needed.

> **Example:** Gwendolyn Brooks is in my opinion a great poet.
> **Answer:** Gwendolyn Brooks is, in my opinion, a great poet.

1. Brooks winner of a Pulitzer prize grew up in Chicago.
2. She has served moreover as a consultant to the Library of Congress.
3. Her poetry which draws from African-American experiences can be harsh and yet moving.
4. A number of poets I believe had their roots in Chicago.
5. Carl Sandburg who wrote the poem "Chicago" is one of the most famous.

EXERCISE B: Rewrite the sentences, correcting errors in comma usage. If a sentence needs no commas, write *Correct*.

> **Example:** The Hungarian goulash by the way has an unusual flavor.
> **Answer:** The Hungarian goulash, by the way, has an unusual flavor.

1. The meal in general was quite delicious.
2. The bread an old family recipe contains two packages of yeast.
3. It rose as you can imagine over the edges of the pan.
4. We were meanwhile chopping vegetables for the goulash.
5. You wonder I suppose about the seasoning in the goulash.
6. The vegetables that we had scorched were thrown away.
7. Those black specks which look like pepper may be something else.
8. The bread on the other hand seems perfect.
9. Its crust for example is a golden brown.
10. We bought the dessert an apple cobbler at the bakery.

EXERCISE C: Rewrite each sentence, inserting the information in parentheses in a position other than the beginning. Use commas where needed.

> **Example:** Yesterday I cooked supper. (by the way)
> **Answer:** Yesterday, by the way, I cooked supper.

1. The meal was pretty simple. (to tell the truth)
2. My specialty begins with a good quality of meat. (hamburgers)
3. Sometimes I will add chopped onions to the meat. (if I have the time)
4. The salad doesn't take long to make. (torn lettuce and raw vegetables)
5. Be sure to clean up afterward! (of course)

Using Commas in Series

EXERCISE A: Rewrite the sentences, adding commas where needed.

Example: Frank Lloyd Wright designed homes public buildings and churches.
Answer: Frank Lloyd Wright designed homes, public buildings, and churches.

1. An architect designs buildings selects materials and supervises construction.
2. The architect should consider where the structure will be built what the purpose of the building will be and how much the construction will cost.
3. Wright's designs combine rough stone stained glass and natural wood.
4. Admirers find his designs exciting bold and original.
5. Tourists see his work at the Guggenheim Museum Taliesin West and Fallingwater.

EXERCISE B: Rewrite the sentences, adding or deleting commas as needed. If commas are used incorrectly, correct the sentence.

Example: Cars are made of glass metal and plastic.
Answer: Cars are made of glass, metal, and plastic.

1. Tired dirty and hungry, the hikers arrived at their campsite.
2. The Spanish test covered grammar, poetry, and, vocabulary.
3. We walked over the bridge through the field and around the hill.
4. The breakfast specials were fried, eggs, oatmeal and griddle, cakes.
5. When it is your turn, Jan, throw the dice move your piece on the board read the instructions on the card and do as the card says.

EXERCISE C: Write five sentences, following the directions given. Be sure to use commas correctly.

Example: Write a sentence containing three nouns in a series.
Answer: She ate <u>toast, juice, and cereal</u> for breakfast.

1. Write a sentence containing three pronouns in a series.
2. Write a sentence containing three prepositional phrases in a series.
3. Write a sentence containing three clauses in a series.
4. Write a sentence containing three adjectives in a series.
5. Write a sentence containing three verbs in a series.

Using Commas with Direct Quotations

EXERCISE A: Write five sentences, following the directions given. Be sure to use commas correctly.

> **Example:** "We'll be at Loch Ness soon" Sean promised.
> **Answer:** "We'll be at Loch Ness soon‚" Sean promised.

1. Marnie asked "Do you think we'll see the monster?"
2. "It first appeared in the sixth century" the guide claimed.
3. "According to legend" he continued "St. Columba was the first to see it."
4. "Well" Marnie commented "scientists haven't been able to find the creature."
5. Marnie suddenly shouted "Something is stirring up the water!"

EXERCISE B: Rewrite the sentences, adding or deleting commas as needed. If a sentence needs no changes, write *Correct*.

> **Example:** "This is an old legend of the Inuit Indians" said my grandmother.
> **Answer:** "This is an old legend of the Inuit Indians‚" said my grandmother.

1. "Many years ago" she began "there was no daylight in the land."
2. "Where can we get light?‚" the Inuit asked.
3. The Crow said, that daylight could be found in the far north.
4. "Please fly there and bring us some daylight" the chief pleaded.
5. Crow agreed that this was a good idea and immediately obeyed.
6. "I can become a piece of dust" he thought "and hide in a baby's ear."
7. "Ask for some daylight to play with" Crow whispered to the baby.
8. "Father" the baby asked "may I have a ball of daylight to play with?"
9. "Of course" replied his father.
10. Crow decided "I'll resume my bird shape now, snatch the ball with my beak, and carry it home!"

EXERCISE C: Rewrite each indirect quotation as a direct quotation. Be sure to use commas correctly.

> **Example:** My brother asks when we are going to see some mountains.
> **Answer:** My brother asks‚ "When are we going to see some mountains?"

1. Mom asks how far it is to Gatlinburg.
2. My sister Jane wonders when we are going to eat.
3. Dad comments that the highest point in the park is Clingman's Dome.
4. Suddenly Dad exclaims that the car needs gas!
5. Jane glumly remarks that there are no service stations in the park.

Other Uses of Commas

EXERCISE A: Rewrite the items, adding commas where needed.

Example: 21680 miles
Answer: 21,680 miles

1. September 20 1953
2. Los Angeles CA 90038
3. Very truly yours
4. 3356 kilometers
5. $71590.60
6. 14583 employees
7. Dear Mr. and Mrs. Tranh
8. 56650 acres
9. 1515263 miles
10. 1920000 square feet

EXERCISE B: Rewrite the items, adding commas where needed.

Example: The Sears Tower in Chicago is 1454 feet tall.
Answer: The Sears Tower in Chicago is 1,454 feet tall.

1. Dear Ramona
2. On June 11 1994 I visited the Empire State Building.
3. It is 1250 feet tall 100 feet shorter than the World Trade Center.
4. The building weighs 365000 tons.
5. Write me at 57 Bank Street New York New York 10014.

EXERCISE C: Rewrite the letter, inserting commas in the ten places where needed.

Dear Rosa

We got back from Disney World yesterday! Did you know that it covers more than 27400 acres? When Walt Disney died on December 15 1966 he had just begun building his "Magic Kingdom" in Orlando. Our vacation cost $1236.15 this year.

Luisa wrote me last week. Her mom loves her new job. The company she works for has 17500 employees. Luisa's new address is 392 First Avenue Glencoe IL 60022. Luisa's sixteenth birthday is on July 1 1994. Don't forget!

Your friend

Graciela

Using Comma Sense

EXERCISE A: Read each sentence and notice the placement of the comma. Then answer the question after the sentence.

> **Example:** When the car stops, in the driveway the children continue playing.
>
> Are the children in the driveway, or is the car in the driveway?
>
> **Answer:** The children are in the driveway.

1. When the car stops in the driveway, the children continue playing.
   Are the children in the driveway, or is the car in the driveway?
2. As the children come to the car, near the curb there is a funny sound.
   Where is the funny sound?
3. As the children come to the car near the curb, there is a funny sound.
   Where is the car?
4. Finishing his soft drink with a gulp, Pedro begins explaining the sound. Does Pedro finish the drink with a gulp, or begin explaining with a gulp?

EXERCISE B: Read each sentence. Then rewrite the sentence, using commas to show the meaning suggested in parentheses.

> **Example:** Peter my pet rabbit got lost recently. (Peter is your pet rabbit.)
> **Answer:** Peter, my pet rabbit, got lost recently.

1. When Peter disappeared for an hour no one noticed. (Peter disappeared for an hour.)
2. When Peter disappeared for an hour no one noticed. (No one noticed for an hour.)
3. After we searched under the truck in the barn we finally found him. (The truck is in the barn.)
4. After we searched under the truck in the barn we finally found him. (We found him in the barn.)

EXERCISE C: Rewrite the paragraph, inserting commas where needed. Remember to use your "comma sense" in making decisions.

> **Example:** Perhaps Jasmine my cousin will visit us this weekend.
> **Answer:** Perhaps Jasmine, my cousin, will visit us this weekend.

Because of the bad weather everywhere in the North many people are taking vacations. When Jasmine called us from Pennsylvania there was a cry of surprise. Throwing some clothes into a suitcase with the dog she jumped into her car. Before we even thought she was heading south!

Commonly Confused or Misused Words

Commonly Confused or Misused Words I

EXERCISE A: Write the word in parentheses that correctly completes each sentence.

> **Example:** Florence Nightingale was sixteen years old when she _____ to study nursing.
> (choose/chose)
> **Answer:** chose

1. Nightingale had _____ shown an early interest in nursing. (all ready/already)
2. Her parents refused to _____ her money to study nursing at a hospital in Paris, but she was able to train there, anyway. (borrow/lend/loan)
3. Nightingale later studied in Germany to _____ her Paris training. (compliment/complement)
4. Army doctors did not always listen to Nightingale's _____. (advice/advise)
5. Still, her ideas had a great _____ on nursing today. (affect/effect)

EXERCISE B: Write whether each underlined word is *correct* or *incorrect* in its usage. If it is used incorrectly, write the correct word.

> **Example:** Ostriches live on the African <u>dessert</u>.
> **Answer:** incorrect, desert

1. <u>Accept</u> for the extinct moa, ostriches are the tallest birds in the world.
2. <u>Beside</u> eating plants, ostriches like to snack on lizards and turtles.
3. Ostrich hens lay <u>alot</u> of eggs.
4. The father ostrich stands <u>beside</u> the eggs and guards them.
5. Is it <u>alright</u> to wear ostrich feathers?

EXERCISE C: Rewrite each sentence in which the underlined word is used incorrectly. If the underlined word is used correctly, write *Correct*.

> **Example:** I asked my parents to <u>loan</u> me five dollars for the field trip.
> **Answer:** I asked my parents to lend me five dollars for the field trip.

1. Our class <u>chose</u> to go to the museum.
2. I wanted to go very <u>bad</u>.
3. <u>Less</u> kids were going than originally had signed up for the trip.
4. Our teachers <u>excepted</u> an invitation to eat lunch with the museum director.
5. He said that it was quite a <u>complement</u> to our class.

Commonly Confused or Misused Words II

EXERCISE A: Write the word that correctly completes each sentence.

> **Example:** The spiritual says, "(Leave/Let) my people go."
> **Answer:** Let

1. We traveled to (hear/here) the Jubilee Singers.
2. I liked the first (peace/piece) of music in particular.
3. It sounded (as/as if/like) thousands were singing.
4. The (principal/principle) soloist was a tenor.
5. They sang the music of times (passed/past).

EXERCISE B: If the underlined word is used correctly, write *Correct*. If it is not, rewrite the sentence correctly.

> **Example:** Can you <u>learn</u> my dog to behave?
> **Answer:** Can you teach my dog to behave?

1. <u>Its</u> time to sign up for a dog-training class.
2. My puppy is not doing <u>good</u> at home.
3. He runs around <u>like</u> a mad dog.
4. I managed to teach him to <u>lay</u> down on command.
5. However, I cannot allow him to run <u>lose</u> outside.

EXERCISE C: Write a sentence for each of these words. Let your sentences show that you know the difference between the words in each pair.

> **Example:** leave/let
> **Answer:** Please <u>leave</u> the flowers alone.
>
> Please <u>let</u> me water the flowers.

1. loose/lose
2. good/well
3. hear/here
4. lay/lie
5. passed/past
6. principal/principle
7. peace/piece
8. its/it's
9. learn/teach
10. as if/like

Commonly Confused or Misused Words III

EXERCISE A: Write the word that correctly completes each sentence.

> **Example:** (Irregardless/Regardless) of his position, I admire his mind.
> **Answer:** Regardless

1. My invitation was on creamy (stationary/stationery).
2. It mentioned a guest (who's/whose) name is famous.
3. I will attend (weather/whether) it rains or snows.
4. Suppose I (set/sit) at the great man's table!
5. Would you (real/really) do that?

EXERCISE B: If the underlined word is used correctly, write *Correct.* If it is not, rewrite the sentence correctly.

> **Example:** We can expect a <u>raise</u> in temperature.
> **Answer:** We can expect a rise in temperature.

1. A <u>stationery</u> front is resting directly overhead.
2. It is simply <u>too</u> hot for polite behavior.
3. <u>Your</u> bound to hear people ask, "Hot enough for you?"
4. Is there any question more annoying <u>then</u> that?
5. Ignore them, <u>irregardless</u> of their persistence.

EXERCISE C: Write a sentence for each of these words. Let your sentences show that you know the difference between the words in each pair.

> **Example:** who's/whose
> **Answer:** Tell me <u>who's</u> coming to dinner.
>
> Tell me <u>whose</u> guest will sit next to Aunt Martha.

1. real/really
2. sit/set
3. stationary/stationery
4. weather/whether
5. too/two
6. than/then
7. their/there
8. raise/rise
9. your/you're
10. who/whom

Conjunctions

Identifying and Using Coordinating Conjunctions

EXERCISE A: Write the coordinating conjunctions in the sentences.

> **Example:** I enjoy books and TV programs about nature.
> **Answer:** and

1. I recently watched a program about frogs and toads.
2. Frogs are adapted to living on land or water.
3. To survive, frogs need water or some other kind of moisture.
4. In the North African desert, an area that is dry and arid, one type of frog survives well.
5. Many of these amphibians are dying all over the world, yet no one knows just why.

EXERCISE B: Complete the sentences, using appropriate coordinating conjunctions.

> **Example:** Canoes _____ rowboats can be rented at the pier.
> **Answer:** Canoes <u>and</u> rowboats can be rented at the pier.

1. Are those birds crows _____ wrens?
2. Artie _____ Fran finished the race, tired _____ proud.
3. I must leave soon, _____ you'll have to take over.
4. We pushed _____ prodded the cow, _____ it would not move.
5. Derek jumped _____ shuddered, _____ the lightning had startled him.

EXERCISE C: Write five sentences about a real or imaginary vacation. Use coordinating conjunctions to connect nouns, verbs, adjectives, prepositional phrases, and main clauses. (You may add to this list, and you may use more than one conjunction in a sentence.) Try to use all seven coordinating conjunctions—*and, but, or, nor, for, so,* and *yet*—in the sentences that you write.

> **Example:** My friends <u>and</u> I could ride the surf <u>or</u> visit volcanoes in Hawaii.
>
> We wanted to go to Diamondhead, <u>for</u> we longed to tell our friends we had been there.
>
> Dad wanted to stay on Oahu, <u>but</u> Mom convinced him to visit Maui.
>
> Unfortunately, my sister didn't want to go to Maui, <u>nor</u> to any other island.
>
> She was in a sullen mood, <u>yet</u> she perked up when we invited her to come snorkeling, <u>so</u> there must be some truth in the saying, "If at first you don't succeed, try, try again."

Identifying and Using Correlative Conjunctions

EXERCISE A: Write the correlative conjunction in each sentence.

> **Example:** Spencer took the twins not only to lunch but also to the playground.
> **Answer:** not only . . . but also

1. Both Penny and Pat asked Spencer, their uncle, where to start.
2. "You can either go on the slide or climb the jungle gym," he suggested.
3. Of course, neither Pat nor Penny wanted to slide.
4. As the moments passed, the twins grew not only more demanding but also more determined.
5. As he returned the twins to their mother, Spencer was both pleased and relieved that he did not yet have children of his own!

EXERCISE B: Complete the sentences, using appropriate correlative conjunctions.

> **Example:** _____ alligators _____ crocodiles can be dangerous.
> **Answer:** <u>Both</u> alligators <u>and</u> crocodiles can be dangerous.

1. The crocodile is _____ as heavy _____ as slow as the alligator.
2. Both reptiles are well suited _____ for walking _____ for swimming.
3. However, _____ the alligator _____ the crocodile walks as much as it swims.
4. Since _____ their eyes _____ their nostrils are higher than the rest of their heads, both beasts can watch for prey while floating in the water.
5. Would you dare to get close to _____ an alligator _____ a crocodile?

EXERCISE C: Use correlative conjunctions to add information to the sentences. (Some correlative conjunctions will change the meaning of a sentence.) Change other words as needed. Be sure to place the correlative conjunctions correctly.

> **Example:** The thief was quick.
> **Answer:** The thief was <u>neither</u> quick <u>nor</u> quiet.

1. We will fly to California.
2. Marianne came to visit me.
3. I played my radio.
4. Good writing will be clear.
5. We told Phil about the movie.
6. Nails are in the toolbox.
7. Did the children sing?
8. A new car can be expensive.
9. The music was very sweet.
10. Archaeology really interests me.

Identifying and Using Subordinating Conjunctions

EXERCISE A: Write the subordinating conjunction in each sentence.

Example: When my relatives discuss music, different opinions emerge.
Answer: When

1. We listen to different kinds of music because we all have particular tastes.
2. Since Lara likes a smooth beat, cool jazz is her favorite.
3. Mom likes jazz, although she prefers "Top 40" country music.
4. Wherever she goes, Aunt Bonnie listens to Broadway musicals.
5. If you like classical music, you should meet my opera-singing grandfather!

EXERCISE B: Combine each pair of sentences, using the subordinating conjunction in parentheses. Be sure to use commas correctly.

Example: I need money. I've started walking dogs. (because)
Answer: <u>Because</u> I need money, I've started walking dogs.

1. I got used to the routine. I began to enjoy the work. (once)
2. My schedule varies. I try to walk at least three dogs a day. (although)
3. We make quite a picture. We walk along. (as)
4. Usually, the dogs take me. They want to walk. (where)
5. The dogs are nice. They behave themselves. (when)
6. I started this job. I've made about thirty dollars. (since)
7. All goes well. I'll reach my goal in another five or six weeks. (if)
8. I'll be able to go shopping. I've earned the cash. (because)
9. I finish the job, but I spend my money. I'll consider my options. (after, before)
10. I try to save part of it. I earn money. (When)

EXERCISE C: Create five complex sentences by choosing a clause from the left-hand column and a clause from the right-hand column. Write the letter of the correct choice on the line and then rewrite the sentence. Be sure to use commas correctly.

Example: 1. If you need advice.   a. Try talking to a relative.
Answer: <u>a.</u> If you need advice, try talking to a relative.

____ 1. When I had a problem last week   a. I finally went to my sister.
____ 2. Although I was shy about asking   b. because she's a good listener.
____ 3. She's easy to talk to   c. after we spoke about them.
____ 4. As I talked to her   d. I couldn't think of a solution.
____ 5. The issues became clear   e. she asked me some questions.

Identifying and Using Conjunctive Adverbs

EXERCISE A: Write the conjunctive adverb in each sentence.

Example: J. J. and I go to different schools; consequently, our interests sometimes clash.
Answer: consequently

1. J. J. cheers for the Bulldogs; however, I root for the Falcons.
2. Our basketball teams are fierce competitors; furthermore, both our schools have award-winning debate teams.
3. We want to stay friends; therefore, we leave our rivalries at school.
4. He may come to some of my games; I also may go to some of his.
5. We're different in many ways; nevertheless, our friendship is strong.

EXERCISE B: Rewrite each sentence. Add an appropriate conjunctive adverb; insert commas where needed.

Example: Australia is a land of rare natural sights; _____ it is home to some unusual animals.
Answer: Australia is a land of rare natural sights; <u>furthermore</u>, it is home to some unusual animals.

1. Australia has beautiful beaches; _____ it also has scorching deserts.
2. Ayers Rock is in the middle of one desert; _____ tourists must brave the heat to visit it.
3. Western Australia is mostly desert; _____ sheep graze there.
4. Kangaroos are a delight to tourists; koalas _____ are popular.
5. Despite its cuddly image, the koala has sharp, curved claws; _____ tourists should be careful around these Australian "teddy bears."

EXERCISE C: Use a conjunctive adverb to combine each pair of sentences. Be sure to use commas correctly.

Example: Sue has a talent for machines. She didn't want to use a computer.
Answer: Sue has a talent for machines; <u>nevertheless</u>, she didn't want to use a computer.

1. She needed to write faster. Sue decided to learn word processing.
2. She had used a computer. She read the manual.
3. The instructions seemed clear. She couldn't get the machine to double-space.
4. Sue hit the *I* key by itself. She pressed it and *Control* at the same time.
5. The combination opened the *Help* function. Sue found the instructions she needed.

Using Conjunctions Correctly

EXERCISE A: Write the conjunction in each item. Then write whether each item is *correct* or *incorrect* in its use of conjunctions.

Example: The Himalayas form India's north border and cover the country of Nepal.
Answer: and (correct)

1. The name *Himalayas* means "House of Snow," or "Snowy Range."
2. Much of the Himalayas is unexplored; the reason is because they're so high.
3. But all parts of the Himalayas are high.
4. A famous "animal" of the Himalayas is the Abominable Snowman, or Yeti.
5. Does this creature really exist, like some people say?

EXERCISE B: Rewrite the sentences, correcting any misuse of conjunctions.

Example: A dictionary gives the definition of a word. And it also gives its pronunciation.
Answer: A dictionary gives the definition of a word; it also gives its pronunciation.

1. But sometimes a definition may be difficult to understand.
2. So the dictionary may use the word in a sentence.
3. The reason is because using a word in a sentence often makes its meaning clearer.
4. You might consider a thesaurus, like many students do.
5. And it's fun just to skim the pages of a dictionary or a thesaurus.

EXERCISE C: Rewrite the paragraph, correcting all misused conjunctions.

Daisy had to take her cats to the veterinarian. Bibs and Thomas needed vaccinations. And Hartley needed vitamins. Daisy called the three, but they seemed to know Daisy's purpose. So the two males hid under the bed. But Bibs couldn't find a hiding place. She raced around the house like she were a miniature tornado. Daisy finally caught her; the reason was because Bibs ran into a corner. Then Daisy went after the other two. She could wear herself out getting under the bed. Or she could outwit them. Daisy coaxed Thomas out with a cat treat. But Hartley stayed where he was, like he knew that Daisy was trying to trick him. So, as she walked to the front door, Daisy talked about the good time that the others would have. And Hartley, fooled by the sound of her voice, was at the door before Daisy got there.

Developing Your Style: Conjunctions

EXERCISE A: Write the conjunction from each clause. Then write the relationship that each conjunction expresses—*addition, contradiction, cause/effect,* or *time.*

> **Example:** although he didn't expect to win
> **Answer:** although   contradiction

1. she also drives a bus
2. consequently, he always got *A*'s
3. when you went away
4. furthermore, it was made well
5. therefore, the roof must be replaced
6. because the tortoise kept going
7. while they were at the movies
8. however, he went to sleep immediately
9. after it had stopped snowing
10. but she performed anyway

EXERCISE B: Rewrite each item. Either combine sentences, using the conjunction in parentheses, or replace *and* with the conjunction in parentheses. (Hint: If the conjunction begins with a capital letter, write it at the beginning of the revised sentence.)

> **Example:** The sun was setting. The girls continued their hike. (nevertheless)
> **Answer:** The sun was setting; nevertheless, the girls continued their hike.

1. It got darker and the girls turned back toward camp. (As)
2. They walked faster. They sighted camp as darkness fell. (consequently)
3. The fire had been out for many hours. The girls built a new one. (Because)
4. The fire crackled merrily and the girls enjoyed its light and warmth. (Once)
5. The firelight was soon gone. The dark night seemed friendly. (however)

EXERCISE C: Replace *and* or connect the sentence pairs with a conjunction from the parentheses. Be sure that your choice expresses the correct relationship between the two sentences.

> **Example:** The crisis is serious <u>and</u> people who waste water will be fined. (thus, but)
> **Answer:** The crisis is serious; thus, people who waste water will be fined.

1. The lawn is brown. There has been a water shortage. (although, because)
2. It hasn't rained and the level at the reservoir is down. (however, consequently)
3. People can't fill their swimming pools, either. Nobody has complained. (thus, but)
4. Water has been rationed. Many continue to waste water. (nevertheless, also)
5. I watch water running down the street. The waste upsets me. (as, but)

Contractions

Identifying and Forming Contractions

EXERCISE A: Write the words that are combined in each contraction.

> **Example:** could've
> **Answer:** could have

1. isn't
2. we'll
3. we'd
4. they've
5. doesn't
6. I'm
7. won't
8. that's
9. you're
10. Mary's

EXERCISE B: Write the contraction that can be used in place of each underlined word.

> **Example:** Splashdown <u>is not</u> until this afternoon.
> **Answer:** isn't

1. The space shuttle <u>has not</u> landed yet.
2. The shuttle <u>could have</u> landed earlier, but the weather <u>was not</u> favorable.
3. <u>Where is</u> the shuttle going to land?
4. The astronauts <u>did not</u> achieve every one of their goals, but <u>they are</u> still quite pleased with the mission.
5. <u>They will</u> broadcast a live message at noon today.

EXERCISE C: Write the word in parentheses that correctly completes each sentence.

> **Example:** They judge (won't, wont) permit cameras in the courtroom.
> **Answer:** won't

1. The trial (isn't, is'nt) over yet.
2. The jury (can not, can't) reach a verdict.
3. Do you think (they'll, theyll) decide today?
4. (I'am, I'm) glad that I (don't, do'nt) have to make that decision!
5. (We're, Were) going to hear the verdict today.
6. (I'll, Ill) be interested to hear the jury's decision.
7. (Wheres, Where's) the defendant?
8. The defendant (hasn't, has'nt) been found guilty.
9. (Its, It's) hard to describe the feeling in the courtroom.
10. I think that the judge (should've, should of) allowed cameras.

Distinguishing Between Possessive Pronouns and Contractions

EXERCISE A: Match each term in the left-hand column with its definition in the right-hand column. Write the correct letter on the blank line.

Example: 1. they're   a. they are
Answer: <u>a.</u>

___ 1. whose   a. it is
___ 2. your   b. you are
___ 3. who's   c. belonging to whom
___ 4. it's   d. who is
___ 5. you're   e. belonging to you

EXERCISE B: Write the word in parentheses that correctly completes each sentence.

Example: (There's, Theirs) been a mix-up with our newspapers.
Answer: There's

1. (Your, You're) paper was delivered to the Santanas.
2. (Theirs, There's) was delivered to the Thompsons.
3. (They're, Their) on vacation, so (they're, their) paper delivery is supposed to be stopped.
4. Do you know (who's, whose) supposed to get this paper?
5. (It's, Its) been a very long morning!

EXERCISE C: Rewrite each sentence, correcting any confused possessive pronouns and contractions. If a sentence needs no changes, write *Correct*.

Example: I found they're lost dog.
Answer: I found <u>their</u> lost dog.

1. Who's dog is this?
2. Is this you're dog?
3. No, it's the Gordons' dog.
4. I can tell because I recognize it's markings.
5. They're house is three blocks away.
6. You're certain to get a reward for finding they're dog.
7. Look, theirs Mrs. Gordon!
8. She says that the dog isn't there's!
9. Who's going to tell me whose dog I found?
10. If you can't find the owners, maybe its you're dog now!

Dashes

Using Dashes Correctly

EXERCISE A: Rewrite each of the following sentences, inserting dashes where appropriate.

> **Example:** H.G. Wells the initials stand for Herbert George was born in 1866.
> **Answer:** H.G. Wells—the initials stand for Herbert George—was born in 1866.

1. Wells wrote numerous books nearly one hundred, in fact.
2. Many of his books for example, *The Time Machine* became science-fiction classics.
3. Wells's future world has two social classes the Morlocks and the Eloi.
4. The Morlocks they live underground do all the work.
5. The Eloi they live on the earth's surface simply enjoy life.

EXERCISE B: Rewrite the sentences, inserting dashes where appropriate. If a sentence needs no dashes, write *Correct*.

> **Example:** Scott Joplin played several instruments piano, banjo, and guitar.
> **Answer:** Scott Joplin played several instruments—piano, banjo, and guitar.

1. Texarkana, Texas its name comes from the letters of three adjoining states was the hometown of Scott Joplin.
2. Joplin's talents as a pianist earned him the nickname "the king of ragtime."
3. Ragtime music its name comes from the expression "ragged time" had its origins in the complex rhythms of African music.
4. In 1976 Joplin's ragtime opera won an award the Pulitzer Prize!
5. Had he been alive, he might have started to say, "Well, it's about ti!"

EXERCISE C: Combine the information in each pair of sentences into one sentence, using dashes where appropriate.

> **Example:** Edward Ellington was a famous African-American jazz musician. Most people know him as "Duke."
> **Answer:** Edward Ellington—most people know him as "Duke"—was a famous African-American jazz musician.

1. Duke Ellington and Scott Joplin played the same type of instrument. Duke Ellington and Scott Joplin played the piano.
2. Jazz developed from the music of enslaved Africans. No one is sure where the actual name came from.

Dates

Writing Dates Correctly

EXERCISE A: Rewrite each date correctly. If no changes are needed, write *Correct*.

> **Example:** december 1, 1994
> **Answer:** <u>December 1, 1994</u>

1. tuesday, March 16
2. September 11 1550
3. the twentieth century
4. the 1920s
5. June 12, 1955
6. the 1800's
7. labor day
8. Thanksgiving, 1996
9. the fourth of july
10. Friday May 27 1994

EXERCISE B: Rewrite the sentences, correcting errors in dates.

> **Example:** I was born on October 5 1983.
> **Answer:** I was born on October 5, 1983.

1. My little brother was born the day after christmas.
2. That made december 26 1986 a very important day in our house.
3. Last year, Dad's birthday came on a saturday; Grandpa's birthday fell on the friday before.
4. The two of them had a big party with music from the 1940's—a great way to start the Winter!
5. I think monday is the best day for a holiday!

EXERCISE C: Complete each sentence with the information designated in parentheses. Be sure to write all dates correctly.

> **Example:** My birthday is (month/day/year).
> **Answer:** My birthday is <u>January 23, 1982</u>.

1. My best friend's birthday is (month/day/year).
2. When (season) comes, we can go to the beach!
3. My favorite holiday is (holiday); this year, it falls on a (day of week).
4. The music that I like best comes from the (decade).
5. On (month/day/year) the Declaration of Independence was signed.

Double Negatives

Avoiding Double Negatives

EXERCISE A: Correct each sentence that contains two negative words when only one is needed. Rewrite the sentence.

> **Example:** She doesn't have no gloves.
> **Answer:** She <u>doesn't have any</u> gloves.
>
> *or*
>
> She <u>has no</u> gloves.

1. Carlene didn't get no straws for us.
2. I haven't never seen a mountain range, have you?
3. Judy never wrote us nothing about her engagement.
4. The President hadn't answered none of the questions.
5. I never told nobody about the hiding place.

EXERCISE B: Some of the following sentences contain double negatives. Correct the incorrect uses of negatives in two ways. If a sentence needs no changes, write *Correct*.

> **Example:** There wasn't no room left.
> **Answer:** There wasn't any room left.
>
> *or*
>
> There was no room left.

1. These railroad tracks haven't had no use in years.
2. She couldn't give an answer to that question.
3. Sharon had grown so tall she could hardly squeeze into her clothes.
4. His shoulder pads didn't hardly help on that tackle.
5. My favorite red shoes haven't got no marks on them.

EXERCISE C: Complete each sentence, with an appropriate word. Be careful to avoid double negatives.

> **Example:** _____ before had it been so cold in the month of May.
> **Answer:** <u>Never</u> before had it been so cold in the month of May.

1. By May 20, scarcely _____ plants or shrubs had bloomed.
2. We _____ see green leaves on the trees anywhere.
3. _____ about this springtime weather seemed normal.
4. Farmers couldn't plant _____ crops until the beginning of June.
5. They had _____ enough time to plant before summer arrived.

Ellipses

Using Ellipsis Points Correctly

EXERCISE A: For each sentence, tell whether ellipses are used to indicate a *pause*, an *omission within a sentence*, or an *omission between sentences*.

> **Example:** Audubon wrote well. . . . His "Hunting Tales" are still often quoted.
> **Answer:** omission between sentences

1. According to this, "*Birds of America* . . . was published early in Audubon's career."
2. Jan asked, "Um . . . was Audubon English?"
3. The author says, "Little is known about Audubon's childhood. . . . Even his real name is debatable."
4. "Nevertheless, few . . . can dispute his importance to our understanding of our own natural heritage."

EXERCISE B: If ellipses are used correctly, write *Correct*. If they are not, rewrite the sentence correctly.

> **Example:** Well . . . I. . . . I don't know what to say.
> **Answer:** Well . . . I . . . I don't know what to say.

1. "The more we love. . . . the less we flatter," Molière once wrote.
2. I am honored. . . . thrilled to be here.
3. This award . . . is truly magnificent!
4. As my friend said, "I am humble . . . This is great."

EXERCISE C: Rewrite each item. In 1 and 2, use ellipsis points to show omission of the underlined words. In 3 and 4, use ellipsis points to indicate the pauses marked by each blank line.

> **Example:** The ellipsis <u>is often used to indicate omission and</u> resembles a series of dots.
> **Answer:** The ellipsis . . . resembles a series of dots.

1. The period, <u>as you know,</u> is a single dot.
2. A colon is a pair of dots. <u>Do not mistake it for a semicolon.</u> It is used in front of lists.
3. The ellipsis_____ what can I say about it?
4. It _____ well _____ it is rarely used.

Exclamation Points

Using Exclamation Points Correctly

EXERCISE A: Rewrite each item, adding the necessary exclamaton points to show strong emotion.

>   **Example:** How I loved your story, Laura
>   **Answer:**   How I loved your story, Laura!

1. What an amazing plot it had
2. I couldn't believe it when the house caught on fire
3. Whew What a relief that Cara survived
4. Wow What an ending
5. "Fire Fire" they exclaimed hurriedly.

EXERCISE B: Rewrite each item, adding exclamation points or periods where needed.

>   **Example:** Oh, you startled me I'm glad you've come
>   **Answer:**   Oh, you startled me! I'm glad you've come.

1. We're trying to decide what to do I've got it
2. We'll build a snow-dinosaur What a blast
3. Whew This is hard work
4. How great it will look when it's finished
5. It's finished at last Hooray

EXERCISE C: Rewrite the passage of dialogue, adding appropriate end marks—periods, questions marks, and exclamation points.

>   **Example:** MANNY: Dad, wake up The smoke alarm is sounding
>   **Answer:**   MANNY: Dad, wake up! The smoke alarm is sounding!

DAD:	The smoke alarm Get out of the house—now
MANNY:	You, too, Dad I can smell the smoke
DAD:	Ready, Son Let's run for it
MANNY:	Whew We made it
DAD:	I'm so glad we're both out Let's get to our neighbor's phone

Gender

Using Gender References Correctly

EXERCISE A: Write the pronoun in the correct gender to complete each sentence.

> **Example:** Jerome and _____ sister Anne went on a cruise to watch whales.
> **Answer:** his

1. Anne had been eager to see the whales, and _____ saw them right away.
2. In fact, three whales surfaced near the ship an hour after _____ had left shore.
3. The biggest whale slapped the water with _____ tail and then dived, drenching some crew members.
4. Like _____ sister, Jerome was excited at seeing the whales.
5. Each of the passengers had the time of _____ life.

EXERCISE B: Write whether the missing pronoun should be neuter, masculine, or feminine. Then write an appropriate pronoun to complete the sentence.

> **Example:** When the storm approached, each of us scurried to _____ home.
> **Answer:** masculine and feminine—his or her

1. A person may think that _____ won't be hit by lightning.
2. People look at the odds of being struck and think that _____ is unlikely.
3. However, when lightning does strike, _____ can kill a person easily.
4. Do you remember Benjamin Franklin and how _____ flew a kite in a storm.
5. Lightning struck _____ kite and followed the string down to a key.
6. Franklin touched the key and got a shock from _____.
7. Franklin was lucky that the lightning did not kill _____!
8. _____ was lucky, but the people who are killed by lightning each year are not.
9. Probably none of them ever imagined that _____ would be struck.
10. No one should be out in a thunderstorm because lightning could strike _____.

EXERCISE C: Rewrite the paragraph, correcting errors in gender agreement.

You probably think that Mother Goose was not real, but many scholars believe that he actually lived. However, each has his own opinion of exactly who they think Mother Goose really was. Some claim that she was the Queen of Sheba; others, that she was Queen Bertha, the wife of the famous medieval king Charlemagne. Some scholars argue that they know she was Elizabeth Goose of colonial Boston. No one can prove their theory, but everyone likes to think that her opinion is right.

Hypens

Using Hyphens Correctly

EXERCISE A: Rewrite each item that requires a hyphen. If an item does not require a hyphen, write *Correct*.

    Example: seventy six trombones
    Answer: seventy-six trombones

1. the ex President
2. a well known singer
3. pro British forces
4. one third of the land
5. Ask the hotel manager to come inside.
6. two thirds vote
7. self defense
8. a cleverly designed plan
9. my sister in law
10. The report was well organized.

EXERCISE B: Rewrite the following sentences, adding hyphens where needed. For each underlined word, indicate how it could be hyphenated at the end of a line.

    Example: The self centered actor took the stage.
    Answer: The self-centered actor took the stage./self-centered

1. His <u>report</u> seemed long winded to us.
2. The mayor elect was <u>seated</u> in the audience.
3. A well-liked comedian <u>introduced</u> the acts.
4. The theme was a recreation of our town's <u>founding</u>.
5. Forty five <u>children</u> performed in the show.
6. One <u>high spirited</u> child read a poem.
7. <u>Dancers</u> in pre Civil War dress pranced around.
8. Did you <u>grumble</u> that the show seemed un American?
9. Our <u>great aunt</u> should see this depiction!
10. To call this unpatriotic is a half baked <u>notion</u>.

EXERCISE C: Rewrite the following paragraph, adding hyphens where needed. As you write, hyphenate long words that fall at the ends of lines.

    Example: I need self control to stick to a healthful diet.
    Answer: I need self-control to stick to a healthful diet.

    Grandma claims to be all knowing when it comes to diet and nutrition. She has a post Depression mentality about the need to eat one quarter cup of carrots a day. If it were up to her, we'd eat ninety two cups of carrots each year! I don't mean it as a put down, but I honestly think that Grandma behaves as though she's my mother in law.

Nouns

Identifying and Using Common and Proper Nouns

EXERCISE A: Write whether each noun is *common* or *proper*.

> **Example:** Coretta Scott King
> **Answer:** proper

1. Nebraska
2. painter
3. Paris
4. "The Tell-Tale Heart"
5. poetry
6. Rock River
7. principal
8. Declaration of Independence
9. national anthem
10. East St. Louis

EXERCISE B: For each common noun, write a *C* and a corresponding proper noun. For each proper noun, write a *P* and a corresponding common noun.

> **Example:** Alaska   lake
> **Answer:**   P, state   C, Great Salt Lake

1. river
2. Cadillac
3. street
4. Philadelphia
5. president
6. Africa
7. athlete
8. song
9. Thanksgiving
10. Mexico

EXERCISE C: Write and label each noun *P* (proper) or *C* (common). Then rewrite the sentence, replacing each noun with one of your own choice. (There are 20 nouns in all.)

> **Example:** Wade received a diploma last June.
> **Answer:**   Wade, P   diploma, C   June, P
>
> Mariana received a telegram last March.

1. Alaska is a beautiful state.
2. Ned took two sweaters and some socks to the cashier.
3. On Labor Day, the family camped at Indian Island Park.
4. The announcement on Wednesday was met with great excitement.
5. The United Nations plays an active role in the fight against hunger.
6. Annette, my cousin, sings "Yankee Doodle Dandy" every Independence Day.

Identifying and Using Collective Nouns

EXERCISE A: Write the collective noun in each group.

> **Example:** smile team activity
> **Answer:** team

1. cow	time	herd
2. faculty	student	teacher
3. collection	witness	leader
4. angel	mob	strangeness
5. congress	capital	senator
6. truth	princess	club
7. ostrich	audience	jingle
8. fox	wolf	pack
9. squadron	clock	antique
10. group	member	purpose

EXERCISE B: Write the ten collective nouns in the paragraph.

> **Example:** This year, our school held a spring carnival.
> **Answer:** school

The faculty helped run the carnival, which was organized by a committee of students and teachers. A large crowd showed up, including many prominent leaders of the community. Members of the cheerleading squad performed some amazing stunts while the varsity basketball team entertained the enthusiastic throng. Our band played beautifully throughout the afternoon, and the audience cheered loudly to express its appreciation. Even the flock of seagulls that flew overhead seemed to be adding their raucous voices in approval!

EXERCISE C: Write ten sentences, using the collective nouns below.

> **Example:** panel
> **Answer:** The <u>panel</u> discussed the latest Mideast crisis.

1. flock
2. quartet
3. audience
4. herd
5. Congress
6. squad
7. mob
8. Drama Club
9. troop
10. Boston Philharmonic

Identifying and Using Concrete and Abstract Nouns

EXERCISE A: Write whether each noun is *concrete* or *abstract*.

Example: love
Answer: abstract

1. happiness
2. carrots
3. string
4. feeling
5. truth
6. face
7. regret
8. horse
9. patriotism
10. fingernail

11. loneliness
12. jury
13. chair
14. friendship
15. attitude
16. hope
17. guitar
18. tragedy
19. salt
20. representation

EXERCISE B: Write the concrete noun in each pair.

Example: justice, judge
Answer: judge

1. democracy, senator
2. joy, smile
3. sleepiness, bed
4. love, mother
5. tombstone, death
6. poverty, rags
7. health, medicine
8. snapshot, photography
9. fun, toys
10. book, curiosity

EXERCISE C: Write whether each noun is *concrete* or *abstract*. Then write a sentence that uses both nouns in each item.

Example: hope, heart
Answer: hope, abstract heart, concrete   Her <u>heart</u> was filled with <u>hope</u>.

1. intelligence, book
2. circus, happiness
3. sorrow, tree
4. generosity, toys
5. patriotism, flag
6. lilacs, delight
7. fear, monster
8. democracy, president
9. cat, sleepiness
10. cousin, Islam

Spelling Plural Nouns Correctly

EXERCISE A: Write the correct plural form for each noun.

> **Example:** horse
> **Answer:** horses

1. house
2. mouse
3. fox
4. baby
5. child
6. landlady
7. bush
8. monkey
9. class
10. echo

11. wife
12. sister-in-law
13. tomato
14. series
15. crisis
16. woman
17. knife
18. belief
19. duty
20. bacterium

EXERCISE B: Write the correct plural of each noun.

> **Example:** mosquito
> **Answer:** mosquitoes

1. ox
2. box
3. brother-in-law
4. man
5. speech
6. thief
7. donkey
8. sheep
9. tooth
10. piano

EXERCISE C: Rewrite the sentences, changing each singular noun to a plural noun. Make any other necessary changes.

> **Example:** The wolf was howling.
> **Answer:** The <u>wolves</u> <u>were</u> howling.

1. Please return the library book to the proper shelf.
2. It was hard to tell the hero from the villain.
3. The cat landed on its foot.
4. A flock of goose flew overhead.
5. We bought a new fish for our aquarium.
6. I'm afraid that the dish boke when it fell.
7. Please pass the mashed potato and the broccoli.
8. Has the leaf turned color yet?
9. They visited a large city on their trip.
10. We studied the journey of the European explorer.

Developing Your Style: Choosing Specific, Concrete Nouns

EXERCISE A: From each group of nouns, write the noun that is the least specific or concrete. Next to it, write a noun (common or proper) that is related in meaning but is more specific and concrete.

> **Example:** sparrow   strawberry   instrument
> **Answer:** instrument   trumpet

1. horse   ocean   dictionary
2. game   Columbus   hatchet
3. saxophone   ruby   animal
4. peach   worker   lightbulb
5. crystal   zebra   politician
6. country   clock   penny
7. unicorn   clothing   popcorn
8. vehicle   window   courtroom
9. helmet   rhubarb   color
10. battery   emotion   stapler

EXERCISE B: Rewrite the sentences, replacing each underlined noun or noun phrase with one that is more specific and concrete.

> **Example:** <u>Birds</u> are very interesting creatures.
> **Answer:** Pigeons are very interesting creatures.

1. We saw a wonderful <u>performer</u> at the <u>event</u>.
2. Last <u>holiday</u>, I got a <u>present</u>.
3. The story was about people from a <u>planet</u> who visit Earth in a <u>vehicle</u>.
4. Is that <u>your relative</u> eating <u>food</u>?
5. The technician fixed our <u>appliance</u> with a <u>tool</u>.

EXERCISE C: Rewrite the paragraph, replacing each underlined word or phrase with a specific, concrete noun or noun phrase.

> **Example:** In a <u>season</u>, my family always goes to <u>a place</u>.
> **Answer:** In the summer, my family always goes to Wisconsin.

   My <u>relatives</u> live on a farm, and I can hardly wait to visit each year. <u>My sibling</u> and I climb into the back seat of our <u>vehicle</u> as my <u>parent</u> sits impatiently behind the wheel. Then we're off, zooming past <u>scenery</u> and <u>more scenery</u> as we travel across the <u>place</u>. Sometimes we play <u>a game</u> as we travel. We know we've arrived when we hear the <u>sound</u> of <u>animals</u> from the barn, which is painted <u>a color</u>. We unload our <u>objects</u> and take them inside. In the evening, <u>somebody</u> gives us lots of <u>food</u> and <u>other food</u> to eat and <u>a beverage</u> to drink. Then we listen to <u>somebody</u> play <u>something</u> on the <u>instrument</u>, and my heart is filled with an <u>emotion</u>.

Numerals

Ways of Writing Cardinals and Ordinals

EXERCISE A: Rewrite the sentences, changing each numeral to a number word.

> **Example:** All 7 children stood in a line.
> **Answer:** All <u>seven</u> children stood in a line.

1. At that time, school began at 8 o'clock.
2. The children attended school 6 days a week.
3. On the 7th day, they often worked in the fields.
4. 45 children learned in a single room.
5. When they reached 9th grade, they graduated.

EXERCISE B: Rewrite each number word as a numeral and each numeral as a number word. Identify each item as *cardinal* or *ordinal*.

> **Example:** 19th
> **Answer:** nineteenth   ordinal

1. 860
2. twenty-seven
3. 43rd
4. 212
5. 710th
6. 38
7. 92nd
8. 1,500
9. fifty-first
10. 3,409

EXERCISE C: Rewrite the sentences, correcting errors in the use of numbers. If a sentence contains no errors, write *Correct*.

> **Example:** Aunt Dawn was born in 1952.
> **Answer:** Correct

1. My aunt showed me 5 old photographs.
2. 3 of them showed my parents.
3. In the 3rd photograph, I was a baby.
4. I certainly was no more than two years old.
5. We went into the attic around 7 o'clock.
6. At ten o'clock, we were still talking.
7. She told me stories of 3 hundred different relatives.
8. At least fifty of them were truly strange.
9. 18 of my relatives lived on a farm.
10. The 19th member of that family worked on Wall Street.

Using Numerals Correctly

EXERCISE A: Rewrite each item, using numerals correctly.

Example: Fourteen ninety-two
Answer: 1492

1. one thirty A.M.
2. sixteen eleven
3. A. The Land of Oz
   one.   South
   two.   North
4. Twelve hundred Main Street
5. I sold five bow ties, 29 neckties, and forty-five hair ribbons.

EXERCISE B: Rewrite the outline excerpt, using numerals correctly.

Example: Poodle from Ninety-two Lemon Street
Answer: Poodle from 92 Lemon Street

Report of March 12, 1994

I.   Missing animals
A. Collie from Fourteen Jazz Street
B. Beagles from Nine Hundred Creole Lane
   one.   Called in at ten A.M.
   two.   Called in at three P.M.
II. Found animals
A. Report on two terriers and 120 cats
B. Collie from Jazz Street found at Twelve Pine Place

EXERCISE C: Rewrite the letter, making any necessary corrections.

Eighteen Stewart Avenue
Apartment Ten-B
June 26, nineteen ninety-five

Dear Jack,

I hope you can attend our Independence Day Party on Saturday from three P.M. till evening. We had a great time in 1993, and I'm sure this party will be 5 times better. We plan to (1) eat barbecued chicken, (2) play softball, and (three) dance to the music of a seven-piece band. Of course we will also have a display of eighty-five zillion fireworks! I've invited five relatives, sixteen of my closest friends, and around 250 neighbors!

Your friend,

Diana

Parentheses

Using Parentheses Correctly

EXERCISE A: Rewrite the sentences, adding parentheses where needed.

> **Example:** Going to school is at least, in my humble opinion a career tool.
> **Answer:** Going to school is <u>(at least, in my humble opinion)</u> a career tool.

1. There are two things I like about school: 1 vocational training and 2 playing basketball in gym class.
2. Most of the kids I know feel the same way about school as I do. I'm obviously not talking about "Brains" Applegate, the class genius.
3. Our gym teacher a man who obviously doesn't understand kids says I have to improve my skills.
4. Still, when we moved to this town only a month ago, come to think of it, I couldn't really play basketball, and I didn't know anythng about woodworking.

EXERCISE B: Rewrite the sentences, replacing commas with parentheses where needed. (Not every comma can be replaced.)

> **Example:** Ms. Woodbridge, definitely one of my all-time favorite teachers, is teaching us about Greek and Roman mythology.
> **Answer:** Ms. Woodbridge <u>(definitely one of my all-time favorite teachers)</u> is teaching us about Greek and Roman mythology.

1. The Greek god Apollo, the son of Zeus and Leto, is often depicted driving a chariot across the sky.
2. Poseidon, the god of the sea, is usually shown wearing a crown, carrying a trident, and riding in a chariot drawn by dolphins.
3. Aphrodite, known to the Romans as Venus, was said to have risen from the sea.
4. Some people think, although I can't understand why, that studying mythology is boring.

EXERCISE C: Rewrite the sentences, inserting parentheses where needed. Change capitalization and punctuation wherever appropriate.

> **Example:** The National Audubon Society, which was named for the artist John James Audubon, is the oldest conservation organization in North America.
> **Answer:** The National Audubon Society <u>(which was named for the artist John James Audubon)</u> is the oldest conservation organization in North America.

1. Watching and feeding birds, something I've enjoyed doing for years, is a wonderful hobby.
2. Many birds, pigeons and sparrows, for example, are commonly found in urban areas.
3. In about 1850, the house sparrow was first introduced to North America. It was in Brooklyn, New York, to be exact.
4. If you decide to feed the birds, and it really is a lot of fun, you should continue feeding them throughout the winter and into the early spring.

Periods

Using Periods at the Ends of Sentences and Direct Quotations

EXERCISE A: Rewrite these sentences, adding periods where needed.

> **Example:** Raynell said, "I'm trying to write a poem"
> **Answer:**   Raynell said, "I'm trying to write a poem."

1. Kyle said, "Maybe you should think about a performance poem"
2. As the name suggests, a performance poet is also an actor"
3. Some performance poets use live jazz, strobe lights, or even alarm clocks as they present their work
4. "I'll do it," Raynell agreed "Later, though, I want you to help me rehearse"
5. "First, I must read to my little sister," Kyle noted

EXERCISE B: Rewrite these sentences, adding periods where needed.

> **Example:** Ralph Waldo Emerson was a philosopher, essayist, and poet
> **Answer:**   Ralph Waldo Emerson was a philosopher, essayist, and poet.

1. One of Emerson's best-known poems is "Concord Hymn"
2. It was written for the dedication of a memorial in Concord, Massachusetts
3. Poems for special occasions are called, naturally, "occasional poetry"
4. On April 19, 1775, colonial farmers at Concord battled British soldiers
5. Their clash signaled the "official" beginning of the Revolutionary War
6. Emerson called it "the shot heard 'round the world"
7. In 1837, a monument was erected at the site; it was dedicated on July Fourth
8. "Concord Hymn" was sung to a hymn tune known as "Old Hundredth"
9. "That tune is still used in churches today"
10. "It is not uncommon for one hymn tune to be used for several hymns," she added

EXERCISE C: Rewrite each paragraph, adding periods where needed.

   1. In music class, Mr. Charles explained that all drums are beaten "Well, he noted, "there is one exception—the friction drum" He showed us a picture of a drum with a hole through its skin Then he said, "By pulling a string or stick through the hole, the musician produces the desired sound" Mr. Charles also told us that the "talking drums" of Africa help people communicate

   2. Mr. Charles then said, "Let's take a closer look at drums in orchestras" He explained that every orchestra includes a set of kettledrums "Of course," he explained, "you may know kettledrums by their Italian name—timpani" Mr. Charles added, "Some 'orchestras' in Asia consist entirely of different kinds of drums The drums, which are lacquered, are beautiful to see as well as hear"

Other Uses of Periods

EXERCISE A: Rewrite each item, adding periods where needed.

Example: $1206 (twelve dollars and six cents)
Answer: $12.06

1. Dr Dolores E Hernandez
2. B G Singh, PhD
3. Prof J R R Tolkien
4. the Rev Mary T Jefferson
5. $470 (four dollars and seventy cents)
6. 165 (sixteen and five tenths)
7. 165 (one and sixty-five hundredths)
8. $2022 (twenty dollars and twenty-two cents)
9. $22200 (two hundred twenty-two dollars and no cents)
10. 38083 (thirty-eight and eighty-three thousandths)

EXERCISE B: Rewrite each sentence, adding periods where needed.

Example: $1007 is a little more than my goal of ten dollars.
Answer: $10.07 is a little more than my goal of ten dollars.

1. Half of seven dollars is $350, isn't it?
2. In 1867, William H Seward arranged the purchase of Alaska.
3. The memorial service was arranged by Capt Ron Hayes and M R Bryant.
4. At a height of 140 meters, the bookcase was just right for Hassan's room.
5. *The War of the Worlds* was written by H G Wells, not Robert A Heinlein.

EXERCISE C: Rewrite the sentences. Add or delete periods as needed.

Example: The book I have to read for class is 34 centimeters thick.
Answer: The book I have to read for class is 3.4 centimeters thick.

1. *The Way to Rainy Mountain,* by N Scott Momaday, mixes history and legend.
2. If we split our twelve-dollar debt three ways, we'll each owe $400.
3. A 198-kilometer race is just a little shorter than twenty kilometers.
4. With those dark glasses, Terri, you look like a C.I.A. spy!
5. I need ten dollars, but I'm a little short; could you lend me $115?

Phrases

Identifying and Using Types of Phrases

EXERCISE A: Identify each underlined phrase as a *prepositional phrase*, a *participial phrase*, a *gerund phrase*, an *infinitive phrase*, or an *appositive phrase*.

> **Example:** Last week, I borrowed a book <u>from the library</u>.
> **Answer:** prepositional phrase

1. The story was about a courageous dog that was devoted <u>to his young master</u>.
2. The dog, <u>a mutt named Rex</u>, was very intelligent.
3. One day, the boy fell <u>off a raft</u> and almost drowned.
4. <u>Saving his master</u> was the dog's only concern.
5. <u>Jumping in the water</u>, the dog swam <u>to rescue the boy</u>.
6. The boy, <u>a clever lad of twelve</u>, grabbed <u>onto the dog's collar</u>.
7. <u>Swimming mightily</u>, the boy and the dog made their way to safety—<u>the shore</u>.

EXERCISE B: Identify each underlined phrase as a *prepositional*, *participial*, *gerund*, *infinitive* or *appositive phrase*. Write whether each phrase acts as an *adjective*, an *adverb*, or a *noun*.

> **Example:** The new stadium <u>in Jefferson county</u> opened this spring.
> **Answer:** prepositional, adjective

1. We bought tickets <u>to see the ballgame</u>, which began <u>at one o'clock</u>.
2. <u>Squinting at the catcher</u>, the pitcher shook his head.
3. <u>Playing baseball</u> was all he'd ever wanted <u>to do</u>.
4. The center fielder, <u>a gawky left-hander</u>, made a lunge <u>for the ball</u>.
5. The batter ran <u>like the wind</u> toward home plate.
6. <u>Sliding home</u>, he made <u>winning the game</u> a certainty.

EXERCISE C: Identify each underlined phrase. Then rewrite the sentence, using another phrase of the same type.

> **Example:** My father works <u>in the emergency room</u> <u>of a busy hospital</u>.
> **Answer:** prepositional, prepositional; My father works <u>at home</u> <u>on a computer</u>.

1. My parents like <u>to sleep late</u> <u>on the weekends</u>.
2. <u>Traveling to work</u> takes them about half an hour.
3. I go to school <u>on a large yellow bus</u> every morning.
4. My math teacher, <u>a tall, gray-haired man</u>, enjoys <u>coaching soccer</u>.
5. <u>Traveling by car</u>, Mom reaches her job downtown.
6. Her job involves accounting and <u>answering the phone</u>.
7. My sister, <u>a junior in high school</u>, is hoping <u>to find a summer job</u>.

Using Commas with Phrases

EXERCISE A: Rewrite the sentences, adding commas where needed. If a sentence needs no comma or commas, write *Correct*.

> **Example:** Shining brightly in the sky the sun warmed the earth below.
> **Answer:**   Shining brightly in the sky, the sun warmed the earth below.

1. Having handed in our permission slips we went outside to wait for the bus.
2. Saundria wanted to sit with her friend Johanna.
3. At the head of the line our teacher decided to do a quick head count.
4. After counting several times she realized that somebody was missing.
5. The man driving the bus waited patiently.

EXERCISE B: Rewrite the sentences, adding or removing commas as required.

> **Example:** Staying home with the flu I had plenty of time to read.
> **Answer:**   Staying home with the flu, I had plenty of time to read.

1. Feeling ill, is never a pleasant experience.
2. My mother a very sympathetic person offered to borrow books for me.
3. Leaving work early she went straight to the library.
4. The librarian, working that afternoon, was glad to be of assistance.
5. In the fiction section in the "New Titles" rack she choose some novels for me.

EXERCISE C: Rewrite the paragraph, adding commas where needed.

> **Example:** Reading, the new mystery novel Samantha lost track of the time.
> **Answer:**   Reading the new mystery novel, Samantha lost track of the time.

   Being an early riser, Samantha decided to read a chapter of her book before breakfast. Turning the pages quietly she tried not to wake either of her sisters. In her bed across the room her older sister slept soundly. Miriam a sophomore in high school often spent hours on her homework. Their sister Emily also shared the room. Emily clutching a teddy bear to her chest was in the third grade. Her teacher Ms. Douglas also had been Samantha and Miriam's teacher. The girl holding the book glanced at the clock. Noticing it was late she carefully marked her place. Just then, Miriam's alarm clock went off startling the two sleeping sisters.

Using Phrases Correctly

EXERCISE A: Rewrite each sentence to correct any dangling or misplaced modifiers. If the words do not form a complete sentence, write *not a sentence*.

> **Example:** Chewing contentedly on a bone, I brushed my dog's shaggy coat.
> **Answer:** <u>As my dog chewed</u> contentedly on a bone, I brushed his shaggy coat.

1. Eating my dinner last night, there was a knock at the door.
2. To find out the truth no matter what?
3. The farmer milked the cow in her new overalls.
4. Looking desperately for a reason not to go.
5. Visiting the zoo, the monkeys are my favorite attraction.

EXERCISE B: Rewrite the sentences to correct errors in the usage of phrases. Add a subject and predicate to complete any incomplete sentences.

> **Example:** Sitting in the sun on a beautiful summer day.
> **Answer:** Sitting in the sun on a beautiful summer day, <u>I read</u>.

1. Drinking lemonade, the glass slipped out of his hand.
2. Standing silently in the doorway.
3. Divers carried the treasure from the sunken ship with strong arms.
4. To win the game.
5. Sitting by the window.

EXERCISE C: Rewrite the paragraph, completing any incomplete sentences and correcting any errors in the usage of phrases.

> **Example:** At the age of eight, my father gave me my first camera.
> **Answer:** My father gave me my first camera when I was eight years old.

To be a good photographer, patience is required. Learning the art of photography, books can be very helpful. Browsing in the photography section in bookstores and libraries. Having sharp angles and interesting shadows, some people like photographing buildings and other urban structures. Heading outdoors with my camera, nature is my favorite subject. Bursting with enthusiasm, flowers and wildlife seem to demand my attention. To breathe the fresh, clean air. Hanging from a tree limb, I once saw a gray squirrel. Unfortunately, while focusing my camera, the squirrel ran away. I could have taken a better picture of the squirrel with a tripod.

Developing Your Style: Phrases

EXERCISE A: Rewrite each sentence, using a phrase to answer the question in parentheses.

>   **Example:** Felicia wrote a story (when or where?).
>   **Answer:** Felicia wrote a story <u>in English class</u>.

1. Felicia, (who is she?), wrote a story.
2. The story is about a girl (doing what?).
3. (To do what?) the girl goes (where?).
4. (What or how?), she decides (to do what?) (how, where, when, or why?).
5. (When?), the girl learns that (what?).

EXERCISE B: Make each sentence more interesting by completing it with an appropriate phrase or with phrases.

>   **Example:** _____, some boys and girls _____ started a club.
>   **Answer:** <u>Hoping to help people in need</u>, some boys and girls <u>in our community</u> started a club.

1. _____, the club met _____.
2. The original members _____ made plans _____.
3. _____, new members joined the club.
4. Club members took a trip _____ _____.
5. _____, they learned something _____.
6. _____ was the club's greatest accomplishment.
7. _____ was another achievement.
8. Some of the members _____ decided _____.
9. Barry, _____, and Kenny, _____, thought of a way _____ _____.
10. _____, some parents came up with the idea _____ _____.

EXERCISE C: Rewrite the paragraph, adding phrases to make the sentences more varied and interesting. Be sure to use commas where needed.

>   **Example:** The cat wandered.
>   **Answer:** <u>Waking up early</u>, the cat <u>with white paws</u> wandered <u>around the city</u>.

The cat was surprised. She saw a boy. The boy stopped. He took the cat home. The cat explored the house. She heard a noise. A large dog was barking. The cat ran away. She knew she was lost. The cat found her way home, but she never forgot the boy.

Possessive Forms

Identifying and Forming Possessive Nouns and Pronouns

EXERCISE A: Write the possessive nouns and pronouns in each sentence.

> **Example:** My mother is her mother's sister.
> **Answer:** My, her, mother's

1. Our family is much larger than Jack's family.
2. His brothers are their friends' second cousins.
3. My family's history can be traced back many generations.
4. This book tells our story in my grandmother's own words.

EXERCISE B: Write the possessive nouns and pronouns that correctly complete the sentences.

> **Example:** That (doctors', doctor's) assistant handed her the stethoscope.
> **Answer:** doctor's

1. The students were given (they're, their) assignments.
2. The hotel clerk mixed up all the (guests, guests') keys.
3. Are you sure this room is (our's, ours)?
4. The (potato's, potatoes) peel is full of vitamins.
5. That (girl's, girls') study habits are good; I wish (my, mine) were better.
6. Are those papers (your's, yours), or are they (Michelle, Michelle's)?
7. She said the cat was (hers, her's), but that she didn't know (it's, its) name.

EXERCISE C: Rewrite each sentence, correcting errors in the use of possessive nouns or pronouns. If a sentence contains no errors, write *Correct*.

> **Example:** The cups are their's, but the plates are Kims.
> **Answer:** The cups are <u>theirs</u>, but the plates are <u>Kim's</u>.

1. The day was our's to spend any way we chose.
2. Your friends borrowed my friends' bicycles.
3. My two older sister's boyfriends are twin brothers!
4. The old maple shed it's leaves as the weather turned chilly.
5. The children's game ended when they're mother called them.

Using Possessive Forms Correctly

EXERCISE A: Write the choice in parentheses that correctly completes each sentence.

> **Example:** The horse hurt (its, it's) hoof.
> **Answer:** its

1. Can she prove that the ticket is (her's, hers)?
2. That's the girl (who's whose) money was stolen.
3. (Sam's and Laura's, Sam and Laura's) new baby sister is adorable!
4. That's (they're, their) excuse, and (they're, their) stuck with it.

EXERCISE B: Write whether each underlined word or phrase is *correct* or *incorrect* in its usage. If it is incorrect, write the correct word or phrase.

> **Example:** <u>Who's</u> homework is this?
> **Answer:** incorrect, Whose

1. If the radio is <u>there's</u>, please return it to them.
2. <u>Your's</u> is the one with the red stripe on the side.
3. <u>Theirs</u> no one here who can help you right now.
4. That's not my camera; <u>it's</u> his.
5. <u>Her's</u> was the only essay that made any sense.
6. Find out <u>whose</u> footprints those are and we'll find out <u>who's</u> been here.
7. <u>Robert and Jana's</u> projects are the two best entries in the contest.
8. If <u>they're</u> feelings were hurt, I think you should apologize.
9. My guinea pig needs <u>it's</u> nails clipped.
10. We can't use those ideas because they aren't <u>our's</u>.

EXERCISE C: Rewrite each sentence, correcting any errors in pronoun use. If the sentence is correct, write *Correct*.

> **Example:** These books are mine, and those books are their's.
> **Answer:** These books are mine, and those books are <u>theirs</u>.

1. I was looking for my coat, but I think I took your's by mistake.
2. Do you know who's turn it is?
3. I'd like to help you, but theirs nothing I can do.
4. If it's not too much trouble, could you bring me some water?
5. We gave them a set of his' and her' towels for their anniversary.
6. That cat looks like our's, but its really theirs.

Developing Your Style: Streamlining Sentences with Possessive Forms

EXERCISE A: Rewrite the sentences. Revise the underlined phrase in each sentence, shortening it by using possessive forms.

    Example: Jack London's books are <u>favorites of many readers</u>.
    Answer: Jack London's books are many readers' favorites.

1. Jack London was one of <u>the most popular writers in America</u>.
2. <u>The first home of Jack London</u> was in Oakland, California.
3. London grew up along <u>the rough-and-tumble waterfront of that city</u>.
4. It's no wonder that <u>the first jobs he had</u> were connected with the sea.
5. He worked as a <u>seaman of a ship</u> and in other jobs around the waterfront.

EXERCISE B: Rewrite the sentences, using possessive forms to shorten them.

    Example: The shelves of the main library contain more than 8 million items.
    Answer: The <u>main library's shelves</u> contain more than 8 million items.

1. Brian and Ana went to the library of their school.
2. The research project of Brian and Ana was the history of libraries.
3. About 5,500 years ago, ancient scholars learned to record the ideas of people.
4. One of the great discoveries of the Egyptians was papyrus, a kind of paper.
5. The libraries of today are simply more advanced storage systems.

EXERCISE C: Revise the paragraph, using possessive forms to shorten it.

    Example: The cuckoo is a bird that never builds a nest that it owns.
    Answer: The cuckoo is a bird that never builds <u>its own nest</u>.

    The people of New Guinea tell a story to explain the strange behavior of the cuckoo. In the story, the son of the forest god had died. The god was sad and asked the animals to sing for him. The animals sang until they became tired and stopped. Finally, the only animal who could still be heard was the cuckoo. She sang the song of her until the god told her to stop. He was so happy with the singing that he told her she would never have to build a nest or care for her eggs again; other birds would do that for her. So to this day, the cuckoo lays eggs in the nests of other birds.

Prepositions

Identifying and Using Prepositions and Prepositional Phrases

EXERCISE A: Write the ten prepositional phrases in the following sentences; underline the preposition in each one.

Example: Do you know anything about the life of Louisa May Alcott?
Answer: <u>about</u> the life <u>of</u> Louisa May Alcott

1. Alcott wrote *Little Women,* one of America's most popular novels.
2. Through this story, the reader becomes acquainted with Jo March.
3. The March family was like the Alcott family in many ways.
4. Louisa May Alcott was born on November 29, 1832.
5. Because the family often lived under a financial burden, Alcott wrote for money.
6. After *Little Women,* Alcott wrote *Jo's Boys* along with *Little Men.*

EXERCISE B: Write the preposition in each sentence. Rewrite the sentence, using a different preposition; then underline the new prepositional phrase.

Example: I saw your friend at the game.
Answer: at   I saw your friend <u>before the game</u>.

1. Rachel left her bicycle outside the garage.
2. The rock sank beneath the waves.
3. Because of his bad cold, Emilio can't sing tonight.
4. Deanna waited quietly in front of the supermarket.
5. Do you mean that the work won't be finished until next week?

EXERCISE C: Use the ten prepositional phrases to write original sentences. Underline each phrase in the finished sentences and write whether it functions as an *adjective* or as an *adverb*.

Example: without my coat
Answer: I felt quite chilly <u>without my coat</u>. (adverb)

1. behind the bookcase
2. like mine
3. to Mr. and Mrs. Ramirez
4. during the snowstorm
5. at 10:00 P.M.
6. near Duane's house
7. in spite of our plans
8. on top of the stove
9. with the checkered shirt
10. against the back door

Using Prepositions Correctly

EXERCISE A: Write whether each sentence is *correct* or *incorrect* in its use of prepositions.

> **Example:** I am writing a science paper on Jupiter, but I'm not sure where to get my information at.
> **Answer:** incorrect

1. Some scientists think that Jupiter's Great Red Spot is like a hurricane.
2. Other scientists' theories are different than that.
3. Where could I get more information from?
4. An encyclopedia is where I was thinking of looking in.
5. Can you think of anywhere else I should look at?

EXERCISE B: Rewrite the sentences, using prepositions correctly.

> **Example:** Last summer I visited the Baltimore Aquarium, where there were sharks and many other fish that I'd only dreamed about.
> **Answer:** Last summer I visited the Baltimore Aquarium, where there were sharks and many other fish <u>about which</u> I had only dreamed.

1. My brother's opinions about what to see first were different than mine.
2. We got separated, and I wasn't sure where he had gone to.
3. I finally found him and asked him where he'd been at.
4. He showed me an exhibit with fish that were very different than those that you see around here.

EXERCISE C: Rewrite the paragraph, correcting its five errors in the usage of prepositions.

> **Example:** When I go to the fair, the carousel is what I look for.
> **Answer:** When I go to the fair, I look for the carousel.

The rides are the first things we go to. We walk around to choose what rides to go on. The roller coaster is what I'm looking for. It's different to any other roller coaster that I've ever ridden. We'll get a map so that we'll know where we're at.

Developing Your Style: Using Prepositional Phrases in Transitions

EXERCISE A: Combine a simple sentence from the left-hand column with a prepositional phrase from the right-hand column to create a sentence that contains a transitional phrase. Write the letter of each correct answer on the line below.

> **Example:** 1. We went to the mall   a. after the game.
> **Answer:** <u>a</u>

  ___ 1. Sara shrieked with delight   a. around the corner.
  ___ 2. The weary dog took a nap   b. during the debate.
  ___ 3. Joshua entered his new school   c. upon seeing the present.
  ___ 4. Beth waits for her bus   d. beneath the oak tree.
  ___ 5. Both teams expressed their views   e. with much anxiety.

EXERCISE B: Write a complete sentence using each prepositional phrase as a transition.

> **Example:** behind the door
> **Answer:** <u>Behind the door</u>, Craig hid from his sister.

1. above the clouds
2. down the street
3. like a rocket
4. toward the road
5. until midnight
6. together with his sister
7. without hesitation
8. during the discussion
9. for many years
10. after the rain

EXERCISE C: Rewrite the paragraph. Combine sentences or make other revisions so that you will have at least ten prepositional phrases serving as transitions.

> **Example:** I ate breakfast. I went to the park.
> **Answer:** <u>After breakfast</u>, I went to the park.

The championship soccer game was held today. The Hawks took on the Force. The Hawks scored three goals in the first quarter. The Force became rattled by this quick score. Their offensive players moved slowly. They were across the field. Their defensive players stood. They were near the goal. The coach called a time-out. He told his players to forget the score. The team came alive after the time-out. They regained their confidence. They kept in position. They did that for the remainder of the game. The Force answered with two goals. That was before halftime. Then came the second half, throughout which their momentum continued. The Force tied the game. Only five minutes were left. They scored the winning goal at the one minute mark.

Developing Your Style: Avoiding Prepositional Phrases in Strings

EXERCISE A: Write the letter of the sentence in each pair that successfully avoids using strings of prepositional phrases.

Example: a. Along the wooded trail, we hiked.

b. Along the trail through the woods, we hiked.

Answer: a

1. a. The plane zoomed through the clouds toward the sunshine of Florida.
   b. The plane zoomed through the clouds toward the Florida sunshine.
2. a. The anguished dog barked for some water.
   b. The thirsty dog barked with much anguish for some water in his bowl.
3. a. The sister of Hayley sang in the musicale this spring at our school.
   b. Hayley's sister sang in our school's spring musicale.
4. a. Mariposa's brother rode his motorcycle cross-country last summer.
   b. The brother of Mariposa rode his motorcycle across the country in the heat of the summer last year.

EXERCISE B: Rewrite each sentence to revise its string of prepositional phrases.

Example: I was born on the fifth day of July in the year 1982.
Answer: I was born on July 5, 1982.

1. The van is equipped with a television above the window of the passenger.
2. During the dance in the cafeteria of the high school, the lights suddenly went out.
3. Underneath the bed in the room up the stairs, you will find the cat.
4. Dan exercised for twenty minutes without stopping for a break.

EXERCISE C: Rewrite the dialogue, revising at least five strings of prepositional phrases.

Example: ROBIN: Did you go to the carnival around the block from the library?
Answer: ROBIN: Did you go to the carnival near the library?

ADAM: Yes! I went last night with some friends from the band of the high school. We
          played games in the midway along the center portion of the carnival.
ROBIN: I will go tonight, but I intend to spend all evening on the rides with my friends.
ADAM: The only ride I enjoy is the Ferris wheel. I love looking out at the city from it. It
          makes me feel like a bird on the wing in flight among the clouds!
ROBIN: My favorite ride is the roller coaster. I love zooming around the curves like a
          racer in a competition of the luge.

Pronouns

Identifying and Using Personal Pronouns

EXERCISE A: Write the ten personal pronouns in the sentences. After each pronoun, write its identification: *first person*, *second person*, or *third person*.

> **Example:** What is your favorite book?
> **Answer:** your, second person

1. My favorite book? It is *A Tale of Two Cities*.
2. I enjoy the way the author blends history and fiction.
3. Charles Dickens wrote his story about the French Revolution.
4. The book contains a famous opening line: "It was the best of times; it was the worst of times."
5. Madame Defarge brings her knitting to every execution.
6. The hero dies for the person he loves. What would you have done in his place?

EXERCISE B: Identify each pronoun in parentheses as *first person*, *second person*, or *third person* and as *singular* or *plural*.

> **Example:** What has Emily done to (her) hair?
> **Answer:** her, third person singular

1. After the form is completed, send it back to (them).
2. Whatever happened to (our) plan for a holiday party?
3. Andrea says that (she) will be moving away in July.
4. (I) will be glad when this hot weather is over, won't (you)?

EXERCISE C: Write the personal pronoun that matches the description in parentheses.

> **Example:** What are (second person singular) reading about?
> **Answer:** you

1. (First person singular) recently visited Texas.
2. Did (second person singular) know that Texas used to be an independent country?
3. (Third person singular) was independent from 1836 until 1845.
4. Many famous Texans were at the battle of the Alamo, and all of (third person plural) died.

Identifying and Using Interrogative Pronouns

EXERCISE A: Write the interrogative pronoun in each sentence.

Example: To whom did Shari address the letter?
Answer: whom

1. Which of the puppies did you decide to take?
2. For whom is this message intended?
3. What is that noise all about?
4. Who wants to have a second helping of chili?
5. Whose was the bike in the yard?

EXERCISE B: Write the interrogative pronoun in each sentence. Write the antecedent of the pronoun, if one exists.

Example: Who was that masked man?
Answer: Who, man

1. From whom did the school teams get that nickname?
2. Which of these paintings do you prefer?
3. Whose was the idea about painting this room black?
4. To what do I owe the honor of this visit?
5. Who is the person in the middle of that group?

EXERCISE C: Write a question that each sentence can answer. Use an interrogative pronoun in each sentence.

Example: *The Jazz Singer* was the first talking movie.
Answer: <u>Which</u> was the first talking movie: *The Jazz Singer* or *The Wizard of Oz*?

1. The star of *The Jazz Singer* was Al Jolson.
2. The first movie to win an Academy Award was *Wings*.
3. It starred *Richard Arlen and Clara Bow*.
4. *Alfred Hitchcock* directed many terrifying movies.
5. It was George Lucas's vision that became *Star Wars*.
6. Of *the three Star Wars* films, I like *Return of the Jedi* most.
7. *A St. Bernard* is the title character in the *Beethoven* movies.
8. Disney's *Beauty and the Beast* was dedicated to *Howard Ashman*.
9. *Gone With the Wind* was named Best Picture of 1939.
10. *Hattie McDaniel* was the first African American to win an Academy Award.

Identifying and Using Relative Pronouns

EXERCISE A: Write the relative pronoun in each sentence.

> **Example:** Amelia Earhart is a pilot whom I admire.
> **Answer:** whom

1. Amelia Earhart is an aviator whose adventures are well known.
2. With whom did she learn how to fly?
3. Leonardo da Vinci drew machines that "flew."
4. Chuck Yeager, who broke the sound barrier, is a famous pilot.
5. His bravery, which I admire, continues to inspire pilots today.

EXERCISE B: Write each relative pronoun and, where possible, the noun to which it refers.

> **Example:** Harry Truman, who was President, was born in Missouri.
> **Answer:** who, Harry Truman

1. Truman once owned a store that specialized in men's clothing.
2. With whom did Truman own that store?
3. Truman married Bess Wallace, whose family was well known.
4. They had a daughter, whom they named Margaret.
5. Truman, who became a judge, was later elected vice-president.
6. He was selected by Franklin D. Roosevelt, whose presidency was strong.
7. When Roosevelt, who had polio, died, Truman was informed.
8. The news, which shocked him, also made him President.
9. Truman's strong opinions, which were many, were often controversial.
10. He made difficult decisions that changed history.

EXERCISE C: Use the relative pronoun in parentheses to combine each pair of sentences into one sentence with a main clause and a subordinate clause.

> **Example:** I was reading to my brother. My brother is four years old. (who)
> **Answer:** I was reading to my brother, <u>who</u> is four years old.

1. My brother loves books. My brother's name is Chuck. (whose)
2. I am reading him one story. He loves it. (that)
3. Chuck asks me many questions. Chuck listens carefully. (who)
4. The story is about a veterinarian. All the animals love him. (whom)
5. The story has a happy ending. It makes Chuck smile. (which)

Identifying and Using Demonstrative Pronouns

EXERCISE A: Write the demostrative pronoun in each sentence.

> **Example:** This should be an interesting class today.
> **Answer:** This

1. I think those are rather good examples.
2. Is there a better answer than that?
3. This is the first day of the rest of your life.
4. I think these are the books you misplaced.
5. We needed new curtains, but why those?

EXERCISE B: Write each demonstrative pronoun and its antecedent.

> **Example:** Those are beautiful flowers.
> **Answer:** Those, flowers

1. That appears to be an old stove.
2. Which of these are the best choices?
3. You know this is the way.
4. No, those are not new ideas.
5. This was her first visit.
6. What if these turn out to be valuable paintings?
7. Maybe those are the people we should invite.
8. I hope that isn't his only towel.
9. I suppose the oldest trees here are these.
10. That was the first hint we had.

EXERCISE C: Rewrite each sentence, completing it with the type of demonstrative pronoun indicated in parentheses.

> **Example:** (Singular) is the best pasta I've ever eaten!
> **Answer:** This is the best pasta I've ever eaten!

1. (Singular) is a famous Italian restaurant.
2. (Singular) is the waiter who will take your order.
3. May I have one of (plural), please?
4. (Plural) are all wonderful-sounding choices.
5. Look at (singular)—pasta in the shape of little bow ties!

Identifying and Using Indefinite Pronouns

EXERCISE A: Write the ten indefinite pronouns in the sentences.

> **Example:** Is anybody here?
> **Answer:** anybody

1. No one is here, but someone must have left on that light.
2. There's nothing unusual going on, I think.
3. Hey, did you hear something?
4. Much of the noise is in your mind!
5. Each is getting louder, and one is coming closer!
6. Here comes another! Run and hide, everyone!
7. Many will never come back here.

EXERCISE B: Write the indefinite pronoun in each sentence. Then label it as *singular* or *plural*.

> **Example:** Anyone is eligible to enter.
> **Answer:** anyone   singular

1. Everyone is excited about the contest, so none of the entries are wasted.
2. Many are entering more than once.
3. Some are filling out forms right now.
4. Much of the fun is thinking about the prizes.
5. Each is worth over one thousand dollars.
6. Can you actually win something for nothing?
7. Can you imagine anything like this one?

EXERCISE C: Rewrite each sentence, completeing it with an indefinite pronoun.

> **Example:** Will _____ help me, please?
> **Answer:** Will <u>someone</u> help me, please?

1. Has _____ left for the day?
2. There's _____ in the building.
3. Perhaps here is _____ who can help you.
4. I'd give _____ for an extra pair of hands!
5. _____ will be here in the morning.
6. Will you get _____ for me?
7. _____ are ever here this late.
8. I guess _____ have to get home for dinner.
9. If you need _____, just call me.
10. _____ of the work can wait until tomorrow.

Identifying and Using Intensive and Reflexive Pronouns

EXERCISE A: Write the intensive or reflexive pronoun in each sentence. Label each one as *intensive* or *reflexive*.

> **Example:** I baked that apple pie myself.
> **Answer:** myself (intensive)

1. Mom didn't think I could do it myself.
2. Help yourselves to some of this delicious pie.
3. The children cleaned the kitchen themselves.
4. We also baked some cookies ourselves.
5. Don't burn yourself on the hot stove!

EXERCISE B: Write the intensive or reflexive pronoun in each sentence. Label each one as *reflexive* or *intensive* and as *singular* or *plural*.

> **Example:** The artist signed that painting herself.
> **Answer:** herself (intensive, singular)

1. We made a wall mural ourselves.
2. I drew this part of the mural myself.
3. We watched ourselves near that wet paint.
4. The students themselves did all the work.
5. Our parents congratulated themselves on their artistic kids.

EXERCISE C: Write a reflexive or intensive pronoun on each blank line. Then label your choice as *intensive* or *reflexive* and as *singular* or *plural*.

> **Example:** The students _____ washed the cars.
> **Answer:** <u>themselves</u> (intensive, plural)

1. Band members earned _____ a chance to play in the Rose Bowl.
2. The band _____ doesn't have the money for the trip.
3. Arlene told _____ that a car wash would be a good idea.
4. We wanted to raise the money _____.
5. Mr. Sarowsky _____ donated his garage for the afternoon.
6. One car wash _____ won't raise all the money we need.
7. The students ask _____ what else they can do.
8. "Let's put on a play _____," suggests Nate.
9. I bought _____ a ticket to the play.
10. We threw _____ a party with the leftover funds!

Using Personal Pronouns Correctly

EXERCISE A: Write the personal pronoun that correctly completes each sentence. Label the pronoun as a *subject* or *object* pronoun.

    Example: Carol and (me, I) are working on a research paper.
    Answer: I (subject)

1. (We, us) and the librarian spent hours looking for books.
2. (She, Her) and (I, me) have a lot of work to do!
3. Those boys and (they, them) are almost finished.
4. Maybe another idea should be considered by (we, us).
5. (I, Me) think that (we, us) have a good plan.
6. (Her, She) and (me, I) take turns at the computer.
7. The teacher gave (us, we) an A on the paper!

EXERCISE B: Write an appropriate subject or object pronoun on each blank line. Then label your choice as a *subject* or *object* pronoun.

    Example: Chris and _____ went to the basketball game.
    Answer: he (subject)

1. A professional basketball game was a treat for _____.
2. Dad took _____ as a special surprise.
3. _____ and _____ saw the Orlando Magics play the New York Knicks.
4. The crowd cheered for _____.
5. The famous forward smiled at Dad and _____!
6. Watch _____ stuff the ball into the basket.
7. _____ jumped to our feet and cheered.
8. Dad and _____ asked _____ for an autograph after the game.

EXERCISE C: Use each pair of pronouns in an original sentence. Be sure to use subject and object pronouns correctly.

    Example: I, her
    Answer: <u>I</u> gave Adam and <u>her</u> some advice.

1. they, me
2. she, them
3. us, he
4. they, them
5 him, we

Using Interrogative and Relative Pronouns Correctly

EXERCISE A: Write the interrogative or relative pronoun that correctly completes each sentence. Label the pronoun as *interrogative* or *relative*.

> **Example:** To (who, whom) did Shakespeare dedicate his poems?
> **Answer:** whom (interrogative)

1. (Who, Whom) has never read a play by Shakespeare?
2. For (who, whom) was *Othello* written?
3. *Othello*, (who, whom) was a Moor, loved Desdemona.
4. Othello, (who, whose) jealousy was well known, suffered from this tragic flaw.
5. With (who, whom) did Shakespeare write his plays? No one!

EXERCISE B: Rewrite the paragraph, correcting any errors in the use of interrogative and relative pronouns.

> **Example:** With who did Richard Rodgers write *The Sound of Music?*
> **Answer:** With <u>whom</u> did Richard Rodgers write *The Sound of Music?*

The Sound of Music is about Maria, whom plans to become a nun. By who orders is she sent outside the convent to work? Maria becomes governess to seven children whom mother has died. Their father, whom is a naval officer and who they both respect and fear, is very strict. Maria, whose loves music, sings to the children. From who are they learning new songs? The Captain, who Maria secretly loves, begins to soften. Maria runs away but is sent back by the Mother Superior, to who she has gone for advice. The children, whom love her, rejoice.

EXERCISE C: Combine each pair of sentences by using a relative pronoun. Then write a question that the sentence could answer, using an interrogative pronoun.

> **Example:** We visited Paris. Paris is the capital of France.
> **Answers:** We visited Paris, <u>which</u> is the capital of France.
>
>   <u>Who</u> visited Paris?

1. We saw the Louvre Museum. The Louvre is one of the most famous museums in the world.
2. The Louvre's new entrance was designed by I. M. Pei. I. M. Pei is an American architect.
3. Another famous museum is the Musée d'Orsay. It had been a railroad station in Paris.
4. We found a museum tour guide. We admired her knowledge.

Using Indefinite and Reflexive Pronouns Correctly

EXERCISE A: Write the pronoun from the choice in parentheses that agrees with each underlined antecedent.

> **Example:** <u>Everyone</u> in the cafeteria stopped eating (his or her, their) lunch.
> **Answer:** his or her

1. <u>Many</u> of the students found (themselves, theirselves) staring.
2. Almost <u>no one</u> could keep (their, his or her) mouth from dropping.
3. <u>Neither</u> of the teachers could believe what (she, they) was seeing.
4. Why would the <u>movie star</u> let (hisself, himself) be seen—and at our school?
5. <u>All</u> my friends want his autograph for (his, their) collections.

EXERCISE B: Write the pronoun from the choice in parentheses that correctly completes each sentence.

> **Example:** As children, many future inventors disappointed (his, their) teachers.
> **Answer:** their

1. The children insist that they can handle the job (theirselves, themselves).
2. Why did neither of the rescued women recognize (her, their) family?
3. Somebody upstairs is playing (their, his or her) stereo too loudly.
4. I hope that you handled each of those fragile pieces by (their, its) edges!
5. Perry wants me to believe that he can make (himself, hisself) disappear.

EXERCISE C: Rewrite the sentences, correcting any errors in pronoun usage. If a sentence needs no changes, write *Correct*.

> **Example:** Band members must allow theirselves plenty of practice time.
> **Answer:** Band members must allow <u>themselves</u> plenty of practice time.

1. Any one of these stories will fascinate you with their plot.
2. Some of the better restaurants are listed with four stars by their names.
3. Rolanda and Marya quizzed theirselves on the material for the test.
4. Many of the homes had flowers or a tree near its front steps.
5. If everybody has memorized their script, the prompters will make theirselves available for rehearsal of the first two scenes.

Developing Your Style: Pronouns

EXERCISE A: Rewrite the sentences, replacing each underlined word or phrase with an appropriate pronoun.

Example: Mr. Lee and Karylle said that <u>Mr. Lee and Karylle</u> would plan the party.
Answer: Mr. Lee and Karylle said that <u>they</u> would plan the party.

1. Karylle made a list of <u>Karylle's</u> friends; she sent <u>Karylle's friends</u> invitations.
2. Karylle then asked Mr. Lee to tell <u>Karylle</u> the names of <u>Mr. Lee's</u> friends.
3. Mr. Lee's friends said that <u>Mr. Lee's friends</u> would be glad to come.
4. The party would be on Saturday, and <u>the party</u> would start at eight o'clock.
5. When Brenda and I promised that <u>Brenda and I</u> would provide the music, Karylle thanked <u>Brenda and me</u>.
6. Mr. Lee made sandwiches, and were <u>the sandwiches</u> ever delicious!
7. The guests played charades; each of <u>the guests</u> won a prize.

EXERCISE B: Rewrite each item in two ways. First, use a pronoun to replace the repeated noun. Then use a relative pronoun to combine the sentences.

Example: Vanessa and Ed are friends. Vanessa and Ed are always there for me.
Answer: Vanessa and Ed are friends. <u>They</u> are always there for me.

Vanessa and Ed are friends <u>who</u> are always there for me.

1. Ed sometimes tutors Vanessa and me. Ed is great at math.
2. Vanessa owns two dogs. The dogs' parents were both champions.
3. Vanessa is a special person. I can tell my secrets to Vanessa.
4. All people need friends. All people can trust friends.

EXERCISE C: Rewrite the paragraph. Replace repeated nouns with pronouns. Combine sentences with relative pronouns.

One of the first important summer movies was *Jaws*. *Jaws* was about a great white shark. It attacked swimmers in a resort town called Amity. In 1982, *E.T.*, another summer box-office smash, told the story of an alien. The alien is found and helped by a boy. More than ten years later, *Jurassic Park* appeared. *Jurassic Park* became the biggest money-making film of all time. *Jurassic Park* topped the list of spectacular summer movies.

Question Marks

Using Question Marks Correctly

EXERCISE A: If a sentence is punctuated correctly write *Correct*. If it is not, rewrite it correctly, adding or changing a period or a question mark.

> **Example:** Have you read *Kidnapped*.
> **Answer:** Have you read *Kidnapped?*

1. Did Robert Louis Stevenson write for children
2. I asked the librarian to recommend a book
3. He asked me what kinds of books I prefer.
4. "Do you like adventure stories" he inquired.
5. What do you think of when I say "treasure?"

EXERCISE B: Rewrite the items, adding any missing question marks or periods. (Some items contain two sentences.)

> **Example:** Two heads are better than one Don't you agree
> **Answer:** Two heads are better than one. Don't you agree?

1. The skating party last winter was great fun, wasn't it
2. We could plan another one Wouldn't that be great
3. Did I just hear you say, "no way"
4. You would rather not help Why not
5. Maria replied, "Why must we do all the work"
6. I wonder why parties are always our responsibility
7. Someone else should do the planning—but who
8. "Who would like to assist us," we asked the class

EXERCISE C: Rewrite the dialogue, adding any missing question marks or periods.

> **Example:** "What experience do you have" she asked.
> **Answer:** "What experience do you have?" she asked.

Mrs. Xing asked, "Have you done much baby-sitting"
"Certainly Hasn't everyone done some" I answered I can be a bit flip at times, can't I More politely, I continued, "Did you have time to read my references"
"They are good, aren't they" Mrs. Xing admitted "What exactly did Ms. Huang mean by 'usually excellent' Please explain that"

Quotation Marks

Using Quotation Marks Correctly

EXERCISE A: Rewrite each sentence, adding commas and quotations marks where needed.

    Example: It can't be Saturday already I moaned.
    Answer: "It can't be Saturday already," I moaned.

1. Mom laughed Come on, kids, get to work!
2. Must we clean the whole basement? sighed Peter.
3. That said Mom is the basic idea.
4. Wow! Mom later exclaimed. You kids did a great job!
5. I think groaned Peter that my back is broken.

EXERCISE B: Rewrite each sentence. Add commas, periods, question marks, and exclamation marks where needed.

    Example: "Wait" blared the announcer "Don't touch that dial"
    Answer: "Wait!" blared the announcer. "Don't touch that dial!"

1. "I suppose" sighed Gus "that we will never know the truth"
2. "I'll wait outside the store" said Carmen.
3. "These boxes are heavy" I gasped in dismay.
4. Did I hear you say "Give me a break"
5. "After lunch" I promised "I'll tell you everything"

EXERCISE C: Rewrite each sentence, adding any missing punctuation.

    Example: Mother, why did you do that she wailed.
    Answer: "Mother, why did you do that?" she wailed.

1. Our Scout leader said Be sure that the fire is out
2. I heard her remark I'm glad that job is done
3. Did he say There is no homework tonight
4. Don't play ball here shouted Mr. Grasso.
5. How Margo wondered can spiders walk on the ceiling
6. How can you just come out and say I refuse to help
7. She moaned My feet are absolutely killing me
8. I was furious when he announced This is a pop quiz
9. Who can say She sells seashells by the seashore
10. Would you please said Ms. King be kind enough to take a message

Other Uses of Quotation Marks

EXERCISE A: Rewrite each phrase, adding quotation marks where needed.

> **Example:** an article entitled America, the Polluted
> **Answer:** an article entitled "America, the Polluted"

1. the author, Josephine (Jo) McPherson
2. reads the poem Billboards
3. reference to the song America, the Beautiful
4. calls polluters a scourge on the land
5. oil executives' attitude, termed laid back

EXERCISE B: Write the word or phrase that should be in quotation marks and punctuate it correctly.

> **Example:** What is the origin of the song Yankee Doodle?
> **Answer:** "Yankee Doodle"

1. Why are Northerners referred to as Yankees?
2. Jonathan Yankee Jon Hastings was a farmer.
3. He used the word to mean what we might call cool.
4. I read that in a chapter entitled Colonial New England.
5. New York's Yankee Stadium is also known as the house that [Babe] Ruth built.

EXERCISE C: Rewrite each sentence, adding quotation marks where needed.

> **Example:** Please read Chapter 7, America at War.
> **Answer:** Please read Chapter 7, "America at War."

1. The audience sang Feelings with great feeling.
2. Crime on Mars, a story by Arthur C. Clarke, has a clever ending.
3. Ruth (Rutabaga) Remarque is a funny stand-up comic.
4. We played Swing Low, Sweet Chariot at the ball game.
5. Did Francisco really call our party swell?
6. The crime was committed by Leo The Leopard Lamas.
7. The May issue has an article entitled A Stitch in Time.
8. Poe's story The Pit and the Pendulum is unnerving.
9. I asked him to play, but he said he was just chilling.
10. Do you prefer Rudyard Kipling's poem If to Robert Frost's Birches?

Quotations

Distinguishing Between Direct and Indirect Quotations

EXERCISE A: Each item contains either an indirect quotation or a direct quotation that requires quotation marks. Write whether each item contains a *direct* or an *indirect* quotation.

> **Example:** The drama coach said that auditions would be held on Friday.
> **Answer:** indirect

1. Will you read for one of the leading roles, asked Simon.
2. Patricia asked herself if she dared try out for a part.
3. She asked Simon which role in *West Side Story* he was considering.
4. I'm hoping for the role of Tony, he said, and I think you'd be great as Maria.
5. Patricia gasped but promised that she'd think about it.

EXERCISE B: If an item contains a direct quotation, rewrite it as an indirect quotation. If it contains an indirect quotation, rewrite it as a direct quotation. Label each new item as containing a *direct* or an *indirect* quotation.

> **Example:** "I've read three books about Robert LaSalle," said Keiko.
> **Answer:** Keiko said that she'd read three books about Robert LaSalle. (indirect)

1. Mr. Jennings asked Keiko if she knew how our town got its name.
2. Keiko replied, "It was named for a famous French explorer."
3. "He explored the Mississippi River at length," she added, "learning much along the way."
4. Mr. Jennings admitted that he was impressed by Keiko's knowledge.

EXERCISE C: Use each sentence to create two sentences of your own. The first sentence should contain a direct quotation; the second should contain an indirect quotation. Add any other words that you think are needed. (The speaker is named in parentheses.)

> **Example:** Do you read the newspaper every day? (Mrs. Tolbert)
> **Answers:** "Do you read the newspaper every day?" Mrs. Tolbert asked Charisse.
>
> Mrs. Tolbert asked Charisse whether she read the newspaper every day.

1. Only the Sunday paper is delivered to my house. (Charisse)
2. Even then, I read just the sports section and the comics. (Charisse)
3. I rather enjoy the Sunday comics myself. (Mrs. Tolbert)
4. Do you know about the Metro, Arts, and Travel sections? (Mrs. Tolbert)
5. I guess there's more to a newspaper than one might think. (Charisse)

Using Quotations in Essays and Research Papers

EXERCISE A: Write whether each quotation supports statement *A* or statement *B*.

    A. The U.S. has the world's most varied weather.
    B. It's been a crazy winter.

    Example: "One day it would be fifty degrees, and the next day it would drop below
                 freezing!"
    Answer: B

1. "The traditional cool period—January and February—never arrived."
2. "The Midwest got hit with half a dozen killer snowstorms."
3. "The Gulf Stream stirs up storms along the East Coast."
4. "Pacific winds often lose their moisture over the coastal mountains, leaving much of the Far West too dry."
5. "Cold north winds hitting hot humid south winds on the Great Plains produce the world's strongest thunderstorms and tornadoes."
6. "Rains in the Pacific Northwest caused flooding throughout Washington and Oregon."
7. "Afternoon showers, which usually begin in June, started in March this year."
8. "Fog and clouds along the West Coast are created by cold ocean currents."
9. "Hurricanes from the Atlantic Ocean, the Gulf of Mexico, or the Caribbean Sea often damage southern coastal areas."
10. "We had snow this year! Imagine! Snow in Florida!"

EXERCISE B: Choose one of the following proverbs as a topic for a paragraph. Tell about an experience, real or imagined, that supports the proverb. Be sure to include the proverb in your paragraph as a quotation.

- "The early bird catches the worm."
- "Neither a borrower nor a lender be."
- "Variety is the spice of life."
- "You can't have your cake and eat it, too."
- "Never put off until tomorrow what you can do today."

EXERCISE C: Write a paragraph about these topics. Invent quotations as you write that support or expand your topic.

- An unusual vacation or field trip
- A class or family gathering
- A book, movie, or TV program that made a lasting impression
- A disagreement or debate about a current event

Writing Dialogue

EXERCISE A: Rewrite the dialogue, adding quotation marks and other necessary punctuation. Note that a new paragraph occurs whenever the speaker changes.

1. Are you ready to go yet, Kent? asked Ricardo.
2. Almost. I still have to let my mother know where I will be and how long I'll be gone, Kent replied.
3. Better hurry, urged Ricardo. You know they won't hold up the parade for us.
4. Do you suppose, asked Kent, that the 1904 Oldsmobile will be in the parade again this year?
5. I hope so, said Ricardo. That is my favorite. It has really been well taken care of.

EXERCISE B: Rewrite the dialogue, adding the needed punctuation and forming new paragraphs as needed.

(1) Terry, asked Ms. Rodriguez, have you completed your book report (2) I have finished the book, Ms. Rodriguez, but I haven't finished the written report yet, Terry answered. (3) What is the book you have chosen for your report? (4) I read *Big Red*. It's about an Irish setter. (5) I really liked it because Big Red reminded me of my dog. (6) I'm glad you liked it, Terry. Try to get that report in tomorrow.

EXERCISE C: Rewrite the dialogue, adding the necessary punctuation and forming new paragraphs as needed.

Have you ever been inside this cave I asked nervously. Sure, lots of times Tom answered confidently. Well, which way do we go, then I inquired. If we go left, we come to a wall. The other way leads deeper into the cave Tom explained. Let's go deeper he suggested. Okay, lead on I said. I came this way once and found an underground stream said Tom. Do you want to try to find it again he asked. Sure . . . Hey, what's this I exclaimed, pointing my flashlight at my feet It looks like a treasure chest Tom answered excitedly Let's take it outside where we can look at it more closely I said. Great idea! You grab that end said Tom, and we tried to carry the chest out of the cave.

Developing Your Style: Quotations

EXERCISE A: Create five sentences by matching each of the statements from #6-#10 with the quotation from #1-#5 that supports it. Change the wording of the statements as necessary for smoothness, but don't change any of the quotations.

> **Example:** Most claimed the membership drive was quite successful. "We enrolled 4,567 new members."
>
> **Answer:** "We enrolled 4,567 new members," claimed some teammates, most of whom claimed the membership drive a success.

1. "His work is some of the least creative I've ever seen."
2. "Hollinson seems to have lost his touch."
3. "Eating one of their pizzas is like chewing soggy cardboard!"
4. "They'll appreciate it more if they help build it."
5. "Everyone should write to this station for our book of safety tips."
6. Most students admitted that they didn't care for Paulo's Pizza Palace.
7. Coach Nickerson expressed regret at replacing the once-great forward.
8. Principal Sherry Adamson applauded the students' willingness to help construct pavilions for the fair.
9. Meteorologist Chen Li of WPXG said the seasonal lightning and thunderstorms accounted for many injuries.
10. A few art lovers, however, disagreed vehemently, siding instead with one patron who stood before a sculpture shaking her head.

EXERCISE B: Choose one of the pairs of topic sentences and quotations. Develop the item into a paragraph. As you write, create a second quotation to include.

1. "Move over! I can't see!" whispered Garth, shoving me onto the floor. "It's just hanging there, outside the window," he whispered, staring at the ball of light.
2. The sun blazed across the evening sky. "What a magnificent sunset!" Sandy sighed.
3. Jenny eyed the kitten with distaste. "Oh, it's cute, all right. But don't forget that kittens grow up to be cats!"
4. "This has been, without a doubt, the most boring afternoon of my entire life." Shawna's face was twisted with irritation.

EXERCISE C: Write a paragraph about one of these topics. Find a proverb or famous quotation to support the statements you make.

- Beauty
- Dogs
- Home
- Music

Semicolons

Using Semicolons Correctly

EXERCISE A: Rewrite each sentence, using semicolons where needed.

> **Example:** Beverly Cleary has lived in Yamhill, Oregon, Seattle, Washington, Oakland, California, and Berkeley, California.
>
> **Answer:** Beverly Cleary has lived in Yamhill, Oregon; Seattle, Washington; Oakland, California; and Berkeley, California.

1. Cleary had always wanted to be a writer she finally started when her husband bought her a new pencil sharpener.
2. Cleary's first book was *Henry Huggins* the main character was based on a boy from Cleary's childhood.
3. Characters in other stories include Ramona Quimby a mischievous girl, Beezus, her older sister, and twins Mitch and Amy.
4. Her earlier novels were mostly humorous however, some recent works have been concerned with realistic, serious problems.
5. Cleary's stories will remain popular because of their memorable characters, their funny, touching plots, and their subtle, inspirational encouragement.

EXERCISE B: If a sentence uses semicolons incorrectly, rewrite the sentence correctly. If a sentence needs a semicolon or other punctuation, rewrite it correctly.

> **Example:** This year was a very special birthday I turned thirteen.
>
> **Answer:** This year was a very special birthday; I turned thirteen.

1. My mother planned a big party for me she allowed me thirteen guests.
2. I invited Susan, my next-door neighbor, Juan, my best friend, and Lee, my cousin.
3. The food included pizza with thirteen toppings; salad with thirteen vegetables, and thirteen types of cookies.
4. Of course, my birthday is always special, it's on Halloween!
5. Among the costumed guests at my party were a green, hairy werewolf, a rock star with a guitar, and a purple and red dinosaur.

EXERCISE C: Add information to each group of words below to tell something about yourself. Use semicolons to separate clauses and to separate items in lists that contain commas.

> **Example:** I am a good cook
>
> **Answer:** I am a good cook; I especially enjoy making pasta.

1. My hobbies include
2. My best friend is so much fun
3. Among my heroes are
4. I always know when it's suppertime
5. My three favorite movies and their stars are

Sentences: Structure and Types

Identifying and Using Subjects and Predicates

EXERCISE A: Rewrite each sentence, drawing a line between the complete subject and the complete predicate. Underline the simple subject and the simple predicate.

> **Example:** The early bird gets the worm.
> **Answer:** The early <u>bird</u> /<u>gets</u> the worm.

1. Rain forms from moisture in the atmosphere.
2. The moisture in the air comes from evaporation.
3. Water is made of molecules.
4. Molecules of water escape into the air.
5. Warm air holds more water than cold air.
6. Droplets of water may form around tiny pieces of dust.
7. A cloud is a collection of these droplets.
8. A lower air temperature causes more droplets to form.
9. Air currents can hold them up no longer.
10. They fall to the earth as rain.

EXERCISE B: Write whether each group of words is a *complete subject* or a *complete predicate*. Then use the phrase in a sentence, adding the missing part.

> **Example:** were singing in a tree
> **Answer:** complete predicate   Two birds were singing in a tree.

1. the post office on the corner
2. is working in the basement
3. excellent cities for vacations
4. plenty of photographs
5. that piece of material
6. were arguing about the color
7. broccoli and cauliflower
8. become scarce at high altitudes
9. quiet strains of music
10. pulled her hat lower

EXERCISE C: In sentences #1-#2, write the complete subject; then add a new complete predicate. In sentences #3-#4, write the complete predicate; then add a new complete subject.

> **Example:** The basement was crowded with furniture and boxes.
> **Answers:** The basement <u>needed a good cleaning</u>.
>
> <u>The moving van</u> was crowded with furniture and boxes.

1. An overstuffed couch sagged beneath piles of books.
2. A delicate, old-fashioned birdcage tilted from the ceiling.
3. The birdcage would look wonderful decorated with flowers.
4. Most of the old toys could be fixed, cleaned, and repainted.

Identifying and Using Complements

EXERCISE A: Identify each complement in parentheses as a *direct object*, an *indirect object*, or an *object complement*.

> **Example:** What makes the (Hope Diamond) so (famous)?
> **Answer:** direct object / object complement

1. Diamond experts judge it (valuable) because of its color and clarity.
2. Its size and legend have made the (Hope Diamond) (famous).
3. Henry Philip Hope gave the (diamond) its name.
4. He paid a (diamond merchant) ($90,000) for the diamond in 1813.
5. Some people call the Hope Diamond (cursed).
6. It's said the diamond brought (Marie Antoinette) (death) by the guillotine.
7. A prince gave a French (actress) the stone and then shot her on stage.
8. According to legend, Jean Tavernier stole the (stone) from an idol.
9. Later, wild dogs tore (him) to pieces on the steppes of Russia.
10. True or not, the legends give the (diamond) (luster).

EXERCISE B: Write and identify the complements in the paragraph.

> **Example:** I consider the Grand Canyon the greatest national park.
> **Answer:** Grand Canyon (direct object)   national park (object complement)

The Colorado River carved the Grand Canyon. Congress made the Grand Cayon a national park in 1919. During our trip, Mom and I found the Grand Canyon beautiful. The setting sun made the canyon walls colorful. While there, Mom and I bought ourselves two large canteens, and sturdy hiking boots. We drank water as we hiked into the canyon. For two days, we made the bottom of the Grand Canyon our home. Our trip gave me a new passion.

EXERCISE C: Rewrite the paragraph, completing it with the complements designated in parentheses. Add articles or other words if necessary.

> **Example:** Leon's strange adventure gave (indirect object) (direct object).
> **Answer:** Leon's strange adventure gave <u>me</u> a <u>chill</u>.

Leon told (indirect object) a story about a tornado. His story made me (object complement). One day he had left (direct object) for school. It was 8:00 A.M. Leon said that the sky turned emerald green suddenly and that dogs began barking loudly. A high-pitched whine made him (object complement). He lost consciousness. The next he knew, he was sitting on his porch, and it was two hours later!

Identifying and Using Sentence Patterns

EXERCISE A: Complete each sentence with a word that fits the sentence pattern.

>**Example:** Mom and Dad gave (indirect object) two tickets to the concert.
>**Answer:** me

1. I (linking verb) very excited about it.
2. Immediately I called (direct object) with the news.
3. He (action verb) me for inviting him.
4. Of course, (subject) cheered and applauded for the band.
5. Never has a concert been so (predicate adjective)!

EXERCISE B: Write whether each sentence *matches* or *does not match* the sentence pattern in parentheses. If it does not match, rewrite it so that it matches. (Some sentences may need more changes than others.)

>**Example:** Yolanda showed a painting of herself.
>
>   (subject + action verb + indirect object + direct object)
>**Answer:**   does not match   Yolanda showed <u>me</u> a painting of herself.

1. She was eager to hear my opinion. (subject + action verb + direct object)
2. The little self-portrait was truly remarkable. (subject + linking verb + predicate adjective)
3. "You should do portraits of other people." (subject + action verb + indirect object + direct object)
4. Yolanda looked quite proud. (subject + action verb + linking verb + predicate adjective)
5. She was an artist, after all. (subject + linking verb + predicate noun)

EXERCISE C: Write five sentences about something that you like to do, using the sentence patterns below. (You may add other words, but do not change the pattern.) Unless an item directs otherwise, write declarative sentences.

>**Example:** (subject + action verb + direct object; question)
>**Answer:**   Can you see that skating rink?

1. (subject + linking verb + predicate nominative)
2. (subject + action verb + direct object)
3. (subject + linking verb + predicate adjective; exclamation)
4. (subject + action verb + indirect object + direct object; question)
5. (subject + action verb + direct object + action verb + action verb)

Identifying and Using Types of Sentences

EXERCISE A: Write whether each sentence is *declarative, interrogative, imperative,* or *exclamatory.* Then write the missing end mark.

Example: Do you rememeber the ranch we visited
Answer: interrogative ?

1. I've been going through our old photo album
2. What a great time we had there
3. There's that magnificent herd of buffalo we saw
4. Don't forget the wonderful barbecue
5. Don't you wish that we could go back there

EXERCISE B: Rewrite each sentence, changing it to the type of sentence named in parentheses.

Example: Does a dragonfly have four wings? (declarative)
Answer: A dragonfly has four wings.

1. Its wings appear fragile. (exclamatory)
2. Think about how those wings are strong enough to reach a speed of sixty miles per hour. (declarative)
3. The wings are shimmering like little rainbows. (interrogative)
4. You might notice how the insect's entire body shines. (imperative)
5. Does the dragonfly have remarkable eyes? (exclamatory)

EXERCISE C: Write a passage of dialogue about an upcoming school event. Use the types of sentences named in parentheses.

Example: MARCY: (exclamatory) (interrogative)
Answer: MARCY: What a great concert the band is planning! Are you going, David?

1. DAVID: (declarative)   (interrogative)
2. MARCY: (declarative)   (imperative)
3. DAVID: (interrogative) (declarative)
4. MARCY: (declarative)   (imperative)
5. DAVID: (exclamatory)   (declarative)

Identifying and Using Simple and Compound Sentences

EXERCISE A: Label each sentence as *simple* or *compound*. For sentences #1–#5, write the simple subject or subjects of each sentence. For sentences #6–#10, write the simple predicate or predicates of each sentence.

> **Example:** Several squirrels scolded me.
> **Answer:** simple   squirrels (subject) / scolded (predicate)

1. Each adult human has 206 bones in his or her body.
2. The skeleton is an amazing arrangement of bones.
3. A baby's skeleton has 350 bones, but many bones fuse.
4. The hands and arms have sixty bones.
5. Two or more bones meet at a joint.
6. Three kinds of joints allow bones to move.
7. Hinge joints swing, pivot joints rotate, and ball-and-socket joints do both.
8. Bones must have calcium, or they may not last a lifetime.
9. Many people get calcium from dairy products and leafy green vegetables.
10. Some people eat those foods, but they also take calcium tablets.

EXERCISE B: Label each sentence as *simple* or *compound*. If a sentence is compound, write the compound parts and underline the coordinating conjunction.

> **Example:** You wash the dishes, and I will dry them.
> **Answer:** compound   You wash the dishes, <u>and</u> I will dry them.

1. She sells real estate on weekends, but during the week she works at the hospital.
2. The marathon runners were completely exhausted.
3. Mindy lost her purse, and her whole family was upset.
4. Chip doesn't want to go to the party, nor does he want to meet us for lunch.
5. Ballet and gymnastics require strength and grace.

EXERCISE C: Rewrite the passage, combining several of its ten sentences. Your finished passage should contain four simple sentences and three compound sentences.

Apples are one of the oldest-known fruits eaten by humans. Remains of apples have been found in Stone Age villages! The Greeks were growing apples 2,200 years ago. The Romans carried them to Europe. Pilgrims and Puritans brought apple seeds and seedlings to America. The colonists dried apples. They used them to make cider and apple butter.

Pioneer Johnny Appleseed is credited with planting apple trees along the early American frontier. Many short stories and poems tell of Johnny's deeds. None of these folktales has ever been proven true.

Identifying and Using Complex and Compound-Complex Sentences

EXERCISE A: Write the number of main clauses and subordinate clauses in each sentence. Indicate whether the sentence is *complex* or *compound-complex*.

> **Example:** After the game was over, we went for pizza.
> **Answer:** One subordinate clause + one main clause = complex

1. It will be winter again before you know it.
2. Buildings fell when the earth shook, and terrified people filled the streets.
3. We left after the third quarter ended, for our team was losing.
4. A kitten dozed on the sill, where the sun shone warmly and brightly.
5. Skip acted as if he knew the secret, but he really was in the dark.

EXERCISE B: Label each sentence as *complex* or *compound-complex*. Then rewrite the sentence, changing the subordinate clause.

> **Example:** My sister, whose hobby is tennis, has entered a local tournament.
> **Answer:** complex   My sister, <u>who is one of our school's best tennis players,</u> has entered a local tournament.

1. Juan, who is in my Stamp Club, keeps buying stamps, although he has hundreds already.
2. Juan isn't the only person who collects something of worth.
3. Briana, who has a fantastic collection of marbles, has special display cases.
4. Roxana who has a collection bought special insurance to protect the items.
5. Art collectors whose paintings are valuable may install burglar alarms.

EXERCISE C: Add an independent clause to each group of words. Label the result as a *complex* or a *compound-complex* sentence.

> **Example:** since I moved away
> **Answer:** <u>Since I moved away,</u> I've made new friends, but I still miss you. (compound-complex)

1. whom I like very much
2. Bret interrupted Martha before she finished speaking
3. when lunch is over, Seth has gym
4. although Marty looked everywhere
5. Jack, who is his best friend, is not here
6. the garden that Mom planted bloomed beautifully
7. even though I paid close attention
8. when the school elections are held
9. since you pass the post office anyway
10. when she leaves, we will follow her

Spelling

Adding Prefixes and Suffixes

EXERCISE A: Study the words that are formed as shown. Write whether each word is *correct* or *incorrect* in its spelling. If it is incorrect, spell it correctly.

> **Example:** un + notice + ed = unoticed
> **Answer:** incorrect; unnoticed

1. il + legal + ly = ilegally
2. co + ordinate = cordinate
3. co + pilot + ed = copilotted
4. un + believe + able = unbelieveable
5. dis + qualify + ing = disqualifying
6. legislate + ive = legislateive
7. mis + shape + en = misshapen
8. in + fame + ous = infameous
9. anti + social = antisocial
10. re + arrange + ing = rearrangeing

EXERCISE B: Write the word in each pair that is spelled correctly.

> **Example:** preferrence / preference
> **Answer:** preference

1. useless / usless
2. irresponsable / irresponsible
3. untieing / untying
4. hopeful / hopfull
5. stubborness / stubbornness
6. arrival / arriveal
7. horriblely / horribly
8. peacefully / peacefuly
9. confussing / confusing
10. immobile / imobile

EXERCISE C: Add prefixes and/or suffixes to create words that will complete the sentences.

> **Example:** Kerry is (probable) the best gymnast in the school.
> **Answer:** probably

1. He can do (amaze) back flips and handstands.
2. He (grace) performs each part of his routine.
3. Kerry (organized) his routine again last week.
4. He put on a (beauty) demonstration in practice today.
5. Kerry says he is the (happy) when he works on gymnastics.

Choosing Correct Homophones

EXERCISE A: Write the homophone in parentheses that correctly completes each sentence.

> **Example:** The wind (blue, blew) through the crack in the window.
> **Answer:** blew

1. Matt needs to replace the hand (break, brake) on his bike.
2. The football team is (all ready, already) to leave for the game.
3. Trenton is the (capitol, capital) of New Jersey.
4. The jogger (passed, past) me five minutes ago.
5. Who is the (principal, principle) of your school?

EXERCISE B: Complete each sentence with an appropriate homophone from the list.

accept, except	desert, dessert	weigh, way
affect, effect	its, it's	shone, shown
coarse, course	plain, plane	their, there

1. My favorite _____ this year is language arts.
2. Barbara did _____ my invitation to the dance.
3. Do you think this dress is too _____ for the prom?
4. Trucks have to use that _____ station before they continue.
5. You should never _____ your teammates during a game.
6. Everyone is going to the event _____ Vince.
7. Has Julie _____ you her new dress?
8. The students left _____ books in homeroom.
9. What _____ does nicotine have on your body?
10. This old ring has lost _____ shine.

EXERCISE C: Rewrite the paragraph, correcting its ten homophone errors.

My family decided that its time for a vacation. To years had past since our last trip. We drove to Richmond, the capitol of Virginia. We hoped that the whether would be warm enough for swimming—but it was all together to cold for water sports! Since we had not packed warm clothes, we had to altar our plans. We traveled eastward threw the state toward Virginia Beach. We spent one weak basking in the sunlight of this coastal town. Before leaving for home, we made reservations for next year!

Applying Other Spelling Rules and Tips

EXERCISE A: Complete each word by adding *ie*, *ei*, *cede*, *ceed*, *ance*, or *ence*.

> **Example:** o c c u r r _ _ _ _
> **Answer:** o c c u r r<u>e n c e</u>

1. con _ _ _ _
2. a c c e p t _ _ _ _
3. p r o _ _ _ _
4. rec _ _ p t
5. _ _ g h t e e n
6. e x p e r i _ _ _ _
7. c a f f _ _ n e
8. v i o l _ _ _ _
9. s u c _ _ _ _ e d
10. d i s b e l _ _ f

EXERCISE B: Identify the misspelled word in each group. Then write it correctly.

> **Example:** light, releif, height
> **Answer:** relief

1. procede, recede, precede
2. weight, friend, conceipt
3. disappear, unatural, illegal
4. finally, occasionally, truthfuly
5. happiness, baronness, beautiful
6. species, either, wierd
7. noticeable, sieze, desirable
8. knowlege, heir, icicles
9. picnic, neccessary, nervous
10. supercede, succeed, recede

EXERCISE C: Rewrite the passage, correcting the misspelled words.

Usualy, the boys agrede on how to scedule thier day. One afternoon, however, they were argueing over how to spend some lesure time. Tim beleived that they shoud bicicyle to the lake and go fishing. Dan's choce of activity was hikeing thorough the woods with a picnick lunch. How should they procede? Finaly, after much discusion, they comprimised. They hiked to the lake and had a picinic lunch after fishing! As it turned out, it was a wonderfull experence!

Spelling Commonly Misspelled Words Correctly

EXERCISE A: Write the word in each pair that is spelled correctly.

> **Example:** absents / absence
> **Answer:** absence

1. desease / disease
2. cemetery / cematary
3. business / busness
4. labratory / laboratory
5. February / Febuary
6. eighth / eigth
7. occasion / ocasion
8. performance /performence
9. recommend / reccomend
10. truely / truly

11. embarass / embarrass
12. lisence / license
13. infanite / infinite
14. varity / variety
15. all right / alright
16. libary / library
17. jewelry / jewelery
18. harass / harrass
19. definite / defenite
20. mispell / misspell

EXERCISE B: Rewrite the sentences, correcting any misspellings. If a sentence needs no changes, write *Correct*.

> **Example:** I went to the library this week.
> **Answer:** Correct

1. They had a display on the enviarment.
2. The display is part of the permenent collection.
3. One book was all about the rythms of nature.
4. Another book presented facts about my neighberhood.
5. I picked up a pamphlit about building a bird feeder.

EXERCISE C: Correct the misspelled word or words in each pair. Then use the pair of words in an original sentence.

> **Example:** busness / restaurant
> **Answer:** The <u>restaurant</u> <u>business</u> requires hard work.

1. mischievious / neighbor
2. reccomend / technology
3. benifit / describe
4. genious / existence
5. foreign / goverment
6. pharmacy / sincerly
7. priviledge / jewelery
8. alright / embarras
9. fourty / libary
10. seperate / defenite

Underlining/Italics

Using Underlining/Italics Correctly

EXERCISE A: Rewrite each item, adding underlining or italics where needed.

  Example: boats like the Delta Queen
  Answer: *Delta Queen*

 1. books like Treasure Island
 2. magazines like Newsweek
 3. the Wall Street Journal or other newspapers
 4. z, the last letter of the alphabet
 5. Rodin's sculpture, The Thinker
 6. semper fidelis, the Marine motto
 7. the word serendipity
 8. three 7's in my phone number
 9. the warship, Merrimac
10. great films like Gone with the Wind

EXERCISE B: Rewrite the sentences, adding italics or underlining where needed.

  Example: Don't forget to write i before e (except after c, as in receipt).
  Answer: Don't forget to write *i* before *e* (except after *c*, as in *receipt*).

 1. Larry read both *The Yearling* and The Incredible Journey.
 2. He wrote his book report, however, on the Odyssey.
 3. Larry's hometown paper The Boston Globe, reviews only current books, however.
 4. This classic by Homer gave James Joyce the idea to title his novel, Ulysses.
 5. In Greek mythology, some characters have a flaw called hubris.
 6. This Greek word is nearly a synonym for the word pride.
 7. I wonder if some athletes featured in Sports Illustrated have too much pride.
 8. Another Homer created the painting called Snap the Whip.
 9. In another myth, Jason and the Argonauts sailed on the ship Argo.
10. Larry remembered to dot his i's and cross his t's in his report.

EXERCISE C: Write original sentences that include this information. Be sure to use underlining or italics correctly.

   • names of two magazines
   • name of a newspaper
   • names of one novel and one movie
   • names of one work of art and one long musical work or play
   • one word and one letter needing special attention

Verbals

Identifying and Using Participles and Participial Phrases

EXERCISE A: Each sentence contains one participle or participial phrase. Write the participle or participial phrase.

> **Example:** Established in 1973, a dog-sled race is one of the world's greatest challenges.
> **Answer:** Established in 1973

1. The Iditarod Sled Dog Race is a thrilling event.
2. Dog-sled drivers, referred to as "mushers," must be in excellent physical condition.
3. Mushers stand on runners behind the sled, pumping with one foot.
4. Susan Butcher, completing the race in slightly more than eleven days, won the Iditarod in 1990.
5. Sharing the winner's podium with her dogs, she accepted the prize money graciously.

EXERCISE B: Write the participial phrase in each sentence and underline the participle. Then write the word that the phrase modifies.

> **Example:** Singing softly to herself, Rosana continued on her way.
> **Answer:** <u>Singing</u> softly to herself, (Rosana)

1. The facts, known to only a few people, were a shock to the rest.
2. Miguel, swallowing hard, looked at us with embarrassment.
3. He brought us two articles cut from yesterday's newspaper.
4. Trying to be helpful, the children only got in the way.

EXERCISE C: Use the participial phrases to write ten sentences about an imaginary trip to the zoo. Underline the participle in each sentence. After each sentence, write the noun or pronoun that the phrase modifies.

> **Example:** Walking through the gate
> **Answer:** <u>Walking</u> through the gate, I immediately saw the elephants. (I)

1. scattered on the ground
2. chewing on bananas
3. hidden from view
4. disguised in their spots
5. slithering across a rock
6. perched on a limb
7. stretching his neck
8. screeching in the distance
9. spreading his tail feathers
10. caked with mud

Identifying and Using Gerunds and Gerund Phrases

EXERCISE A: Write the gerund or gerund phrase in each sentence.

> **Example:** Making quilts was a necessity as well as an art form for early settlers.
> **Answer:**   Making quilts

1. Quilting began with fabric cut into special shapes.
2. "Piecing" the quilt into a large rectangle could take many hours.
3. The easiest step was sewing a large single piece of fabric onto the back of the patchwork top.
4. Quilters enjoyed naming their quilts with titles drawn from everyday life.
5. Joining long strips of fabric into squares formed a "Log Cabin" pattern.

EXERCISE B: Write the gerund phrase in each sentence and underline the gerund. Then write how the gerund is used—as a *subject*, a *direct object*, or an *object of the preposition*.

> **Example:** Working hard was part of Tomás Rivera's childhood.
> **Answer:**   <u>Working</u> hard (subject)

1. Tomás Rivera remembers picking fruits and vegetables for half the year.
2. Frequent moves made attending school regularly a problem.
3. Getting an education, therefore, became very important to him.
4. He later wrote stories about growing up as a worker in the field.
5. Writing the book *y no se lo trago la tierra* (*Earth Did Not Swallow*) earned him a much-deserved book award.

EXERCISE C: Use the gerund phrases to write ten sentences about a visit to the mall or to a favorite store. After each sentence, underline the gerund phrase and tell how it is used—as a *subject*, a *direct object*, a *predicate nominative*, or an *object of the preposition*.

> **Example:** Going to the mall
> **Answer:**   <u>Going to the mall</u> is our favorite pastime. (subject)

1. smelling the food
2. devouring a pizza
3. spending much money
4. looking at new styles
5. listening to new music
6. watching other shoppers
7. meeting friends
8. playing video games
9. studying the window displays
10. browsing in the bookstore

Identifying and Using Infinitives and Infinitive Phrases

EXERCISE A: Each of these sentences contains one infinitive phrase. Write the infinitive phrase.

> **Example:** Do you like to read African folktales?
> **Answer:** to read African folktales

1. A chief of the Ashanti was trying to find a husband for his daughter.
2. Three brothers in another land all hoped to wed her.
3. One day the first brother was surprised to see her in his mirror.
4. He and his brothers decided to fly to her in a magic hammock.
5. Which brother will the daughter want to marry?

EXERCISE B: Each sentence contains one infinitive phrase. Write the infinitive phrase and underline the infinitive. Then write whether the infinitive phrase functions as a *noun*, an *adjective*, or an *adverb*.

> **Example:** Almost everyone has a dream to pursue.
> **Answer:** <u>to pursue</u> (adjective)

1. Goals can be difficult to achieve.
2. Julie told us about her plans to become an engineer.
3. Her goal, to understand everything about computers, is ambitious.
4. Herb's dream is to sail around the world in his own boat.
5. Will Juan follow my suggestion to choose a teaching career?

EXERCISE C: Use the infinitives to write ten sentences about attending a sports event. Write whether each infinitive phrase functions as a *noun*, an *adjective*, or an *adverb*.

> **Example:** to go
> **Answer:** On Friday night I decided <u>to go</u> to the football game. (noun)

1. to kick
2. to catch
3. to tackle
4. to avoid
5. to huddle
6. to make
7. to cheer
8. to fumble
9. to score
10. to win

Using Verbals Correctly

EXERCISE A: Write whether each sentence contains a *misplaced modifier*, a *dangling participle*, or a *split infinitive*. Then write the incorrectly used verbal.

Example: The painter climbed the ladder holding the paint bucket.
Answer: misplaced modifier   holding the paint bucket

1. The painter reached the top rung breathing a sigh of relief.
2. Painting the ceiling, the paint splattered the man's face.
3. He tried to quickly shield his eyes with his hand.
4. Dropping his brush, the floor was sticky with paint.
5. The painter started to slowly and carefully climb down the ladder.

EXERCISE B: Rewrite each sentence that contains an incorrect use of a verbal. If a sentence needs no changes, write *Correct*.

Example: Arriving at her workshop, the new invention was on the table.
Answer: Arriving at her workshop, <u>she saw the new invention on the table.</u>

1. Mrs. Canton planned to slowly work today.
2. The inventor inspected it carefully holding the machine in her hands.
3. Placing it back on the table, the machine was out of batteries.
4. Putting in fresh batteries, she tried out her latest invention.
5. The machine started to break apart whirring loudly.

EXERCISE C: Rewrite the paragraph, correcting any errors in the use of verbals.

Example: Buying a new pair of shoes, they were on sale.
Answer: Buying a new pair of shoes, <u>Darnell noticed they were on sale.</u>

   The salesclerk tried to slyly hide the sale sign. Darnell asked to see the manager realizing what had happened. The manager tore up the sign apologizing for the mistake. Paying half price for the shoes, the manager smiled weakly. The clerk handed Darnell the package hanging his head in shame.

Developing Your Style: Verbals

EXERCISE A: Rewrite the sentences. Use participial phrases, gerunds, and infinitives to make the sentences clearer and more interesting. Combine sentences where appropriate.

> **Example:** Coach Eliot led the team to the finals. He stopped at the press box for questions.
> **Answer:** <u>Leading the team to the finals</u>, Coach Eliot stopped at the press box to answer questions.

1. The coach guided the team. He wasn't scheming for an award as the best coach of the year.
2. The honor of a win isn't half as satisfying to Coach Eliot as to know that his players tried their best.
3. He arrived first at the victory party. Coach Eliot remembers his congratulations to each member of the team.
4. Coach Eliot started as the players' drill instructor. He became their lifelong friend.

EXERCISE B: Rewrite the sentences, using verbals to improve their clarity and style.

> **Example:** Elaine worked hard for her good grades. It paid off for her.
> **Answer:** <u>Working hard to earn good grades</u> paid off for Elaine.

1. Elaine addressed her fellow graduates. She quoted a line from a poem for their inspiration.
2. She remembers her use of gestures for emphasis of her main points.
3. Elaine praised her audience for their accomplishment of many things in junior high school.
4. She urged them for continuation of their good work in high school.
5. The audience applauded loudly. They gave her a standing ovation.

EXERCISE C: Rewrite the following paragraph, using verbals to improve the style of writing.

> **Example:** The President held a press conference. He appeared confident.
> **Answer:** <u>Holding a press conference</u>, the President appeared confident.

The President spent a grueling week for promotion of his economic policies. He talked to lawmakers on Capitol Hill. He labored for the gain of support of members of Congress. Of course, the President didn't expect their approval automatically. That's why he decided for an appearance on television. The President recognized the importance of the public's support. He took to the airwaves for his message.

Verbs

Identifying and Using Action Verbs and Linking Verbs

EXERCISE A: Label each underlined verb as *action* or *linking*.

Example: Your brother seems happy at school.
Answer: linking

1. Five hundred students <u>attend</u> Walnut Street School.
2. The students <u>are</u> in grades one through eight.
3. Mrs. Scott <u>has been</u> the principal for four years.
4. Mrs. Scott <u>seems</u> happy in her job.
5. She <u>encourages</u> the students to do their best.

EXERCISE B: Label each underlined verb as *action* or *linking*. If it is an action verb, tell whether the action is *physical* or *mental*. If it is a linking verb, write the words that it links.

Example: Mrs. Mann is my bus driver.
Answer: linking   Mrs. Mann/driver

1. Jonah <u>rides</u> a bus to school each day.
2. He always <u>sits</u> in the same uncomfortable seat.
3. The ride <u>is</u> long and boring.
4. His classmates <u>sound</u> too noisy.
5. They <u>yell</u> across the aisle to one another.
6. Jonah often <u>feels</u> sorry for the driver.
7. He <u>wonders</u> how she can concentrate on the road.
8. Jonah <u>envies</u> his friend Ricardo.
9. Ricardo <u>looks</u> handsome in his new jacket.
10. He <u>walks</u> home every day.

EXERCISE C: Rewrite the paragraph, completing it with verbs. Label each new verb as *action* or *linking*.

　　Walnut Street School _____ a canned-food drive. Everyone _____ excited about the activity. Their school spirit _____ contagious! Even the faculty _____ in the drive. The principal alone _____ 127 cans. The drive _____ three weeks and _____ 842 cans. Local charities _____ the boxes and _____ them to needy families. Everyone _____ pleased with the success of the drive.

Identifying and Using Transitive Verbs and Intransitive Verbs

EXERCISE A: Write the ten verbs in the paragraph. Label each verb as *transitive* or *intransitive*.

    Example: The town carnival started today.
    Answer: started—transitive

    Our town holds a carnival each year in June. Adults and children enjoy this annual event. Children like the Ferris wheel; it stretches into the clouds like a skyscraper! Adults often play the games of chance. The prizes for these games are donated by local businesses. Last year, one winner received a trip to Disney World! A new car is first prize this year. Members of the community prepare the refreshments. The mayor's chocolate cake tastes delicious!

EXERCISE B: Write the verb in each sentence and label it as *transitive* or *intransitive*. If it is transitive, name the word to which the action carries.

    Example: Hank washed his family's car.
    Answer: washed—transitive / car

1. Many students are members of sports teams.
2. Twenty-six students have joined the track team.
3. Some students run relay races.
4. Other students enjoy the hurdles.
5. Jackie just loves the high jump.
6. Myra seems excellent at short-distance sprints.
7. The relay team had a practice race.
8. Their combined time was five minutes.
9. All the athletes have worked hard this week.
10. Their next meet looks very promising.

EXERCISE C: Use each verb to write two sentences. In the first sentence, use the verb as a transitive verb; in the second, use it as an intransitive verb.

    Example: study
    Answer: Tonight we <u>will study</u> Chapter 4 of our science book. (transitive)
                We <u>studied</u> right after dinner. (intransitive)

1. believe
2. cook
3. sing
4. answer
5. look

Identifying and Using Main Verbs and Helping Verbs

EXERCISE A: Write the verb phrase in each sentence and underline each main verb. Do not include any words that separate parts of a verb phrase.

> **Example:** Did anyone see the accident?
> **Answer:** Did <u>see</u>

1. Ryan and Dwayne were waiting in the park.
2. The boys had not been there very long.
3. They were expecting Ryan's brother Stewart.
4. They were watching the workers across the street.
5. The workers had been repainting the corner building.
6. Should the boys have been watching the traffic?
7. A bicycle rider was speeding around the corner.
8. The cyclist could have been more careful, too!
9. Ryan might have been seriously injured.
10. Luckily, he did not break any bones.

EXERCISE B: Write each sentence, adding the number of helping verbs shown in the parentheses.

> **Example:** By noon the rain (2) falling hard.
> **Answer:** By noon the rain <u>will be</u> falling hard.

1. Someone (2) closed the window.
2. Your friend (1) feeling better this morning.
3. Amanda (2) looking for you all day.
4. A report about the accident (2) written.
5. Your guinea pigs (1) escaped from their cage again.

EXERCISE C: Complete each sentence with a main verb (MV) and one or more helping verbs (HV).

> **Example:** Mrs. Hwang's students (HV) (HV) (MV) the Far East.
> **Answer:** Mrs. Hwang's students <u>have been studying</u> the Far East.

1. Penny (HV) (MV) a report about Japan.
2. Her uncle, Jared, (HV) (MV) the island nation.
3. (HV) Stella (MV) Thailand for her report?
4. She (HV) (MV) Thai food in a restaurant.
5. The students (HV) (HV) (MV) their reports all next week.

Identifying and Using Verb Forms, Number, and Person

EXERCISE A: Write the two verbs in each sentence. Then write the person and number of their subjects.

    Example: Jonathan swims on Mondays and jogs on Wednesdays.
    Answer: swims, third person singular jogs, third person singular

1. "Jeff, did you know that I have joined a health club?"
2. Leslie knows the importance of exercise but rarely finds the time.
3. We walk three miles every day after we eat breakfast.
4. I began a jogging program, but it hurt my knees too much.
5. My doctor says that a brisk walk is the best exercise for me.

EXERCISE B: Rewrite the sentences, correcting any verbs that do not agree with their subjects. If a sentence needs no changes, write *Correct*. After each sentence, write the person and number of each agreeing subject and verb.

    Example: Tennis have always been one of Jim's favorite activities.
    Answer: Tennis <u>has been</u> one of Jim's favorite activities. third person singular

1. "Do you and Marie take tennis lessons at the Caswell Center?"
2. He have improved his serve and his forehand.
3. Richard's level of skill surpass mine.
4. Anh's love of tennis inspire and challenge me.
5. Both tennis and golf requires much hand-eye coordination.
6. I am taking lessons on Tuesdays and Thursdays.
7. Are you and Gerri registering for lessons?
8. We will sign up and plays doubles.

EXERCISE C: Complete the dialogue. Each sentence should show the person and number in parentheses. Also make sure that verbs agree with subjects.

    Example: second person singular
    Answer: GRACE: Are you going to the band picnic?

OLIVIA: first person singular
GRACE: second person singular
OLIVIA: first person singular; third person plural
GRACE: third person plural

Identifying and Using Simple Tenses

EXERCISE A: Write the present, past, and future tense of each verb. For present tense, show two forms.

    Example: walk
    Answer: walk/walks, walked, will walk

  1. miss
  2. watch
  3. scamper
  4. select
  5. play
  6. plan
  7. prepare
  8. copy
  9. think
10. go

EXERCISE B: Complete each sentence, using the verb and tense in parentheses.

    Example: Walter (love-present) Virginia Hamilton's books.
    Answer: Walter <u>loves</u> Virginia Hamilton's books.

  1. Virgina Hamilton (be-past) the youngest of five children.
  2. Hamilton's childhood experiences (influence-past) her writing.
  3. Her grandfather (escape-past) from slavery to Ohio.
  4. Historians (remember-future) Hamilton's hometown in Ohio as an important stop on the Underground Railroad.
  5. Her novel *Arilla Sun Down* (focus-present) on stories about her grandmother.
  6. *M.C. Higgins, the Great* (win-past) the National Book Award and the Newbery Award in the same year.
  7. Many of Hamilton's books (concern-present) themselves with the past.
  8. She also (write-present) stories about today's problems.
  9. Today she and her husband (live-present) in Yellow Springs, Ohio.
10. Virginia Hamilton (continue-future) to write novels for young adults on contemporary issues and historical events.

EXERCISE C: Use each verb to write three sentences—one in the present tense, one in the past tense, and one in the future tense.

  1. jump
  2. carry
  3. display
  4. drop
  5. write

Identifying and Using Perfect Tenses

EXERCISE A: Write each underlined verb and label its tense as *present perfect, past perfect,* or *future perfect.*

> **Example:** Johnny <u>had performed</u> in three school plays.
> **Answer:** past perfect

1. Some children <u>have gone</u> horseback riding during their free time.
2. Others <u>will have played</u> computer games for hours.
3. Leroy <u>has built</u> many model airplanes and cars.
4. Elena once <u>had collected</u> seashells as a hobby.
5. Our neighbors <u>will have collected</u> coins and paper money from each country on their tour.

EXERCISE B: Complete each sentence, using the verb and tense in parentheses.

> **Example:** The photographer (take-past perfect) pictures at the circus.
> **Answer:** The photographer <u>had taken</u> pictures at the circus.

1. We (move-present perfect) the furniture in the den.
2. After dinner Ron (grumble-past perfect) about doing the dishes.
3. Each contestant (spell-future perfect) difficult words.
4. Vi (build-past perfect) the new computer by herself.
5. Who (use-present perfect) all the adhesive tape?

EXERCISE C: Write five sentences, using perfect tenses as directed below.

1. Write a simple declarative sentence that contains two present perfect verbs.
2. Write a question that contains a past perfect verb.
3. Write a compound declarative sentence that contains one present perfect and one past perfect verb.
4. Write a question that contains a future perfect verb.
5. Write an exclamatory sentence that contains one present perfect verb.

Identifying and Using Progressive Forms of Verb Tenses

EXERCISE A: Write the progressive form for each verb and tense listed. Use the form of the verb that would agree with a subject that is third person singular.

> **Example:** run (present perfect)
> **Answer:** has been running

1. climb (present)
2. read (future)
3. visit (present perfect)
4. explain (past)
5. study (future perfect)
6. practice (future)
7. act (past perfect)
8. travel (past)
9. lie (present perfect)
10. see (past perfect)

EXERCISE B: Write the tense and form of the five verbs that show a continuing action.

> **Example:** We are entering our gardening projects in the county fair.
> **Answer:** are entering (present progressive)

1. My friends and I are taking good care of our gardens.
2. By next week, we will have been working on them for four months.
3. My friend Scott will be competing against me.
4. I had not been thinking much about gardening until this year; however, I have been thinking about it quite a bit lately.

EXERCISE C: Rewrite each sentence, using the verb tense and form in parentheses. Then use a different verb, keeping the same tense and form, in a sentence of your own.

> **Example:** We (learn-present progressive) about ancient Rome.
> **Answer:** We <u>are learning</u> about ancient Rome.

1. Last week, we (discuss-past progressive) ancient Greece.
2. This week, we (see-present perfect progressive) similarities between the two cultures.
3. Right now, we (view-present progressive) a video about some of the services that the Roman government (provide-past progressive) for its people on a daily basis.
4. Our teacher says that she (quiz-future progressive) us on this material soon!

Identifying and Using Irregular Verbs

EXERCISE A: Complete each item so that it shows the present, the past, and the past-participle form of the verb.

> **Example:** _____, chose, _____
> **Answer:** <u>choose</u>, chose, <u>chosen</u>

1. sing, _____, _____
2. _____, drew, _____
3. _____, _____, gone
4. see, _____, _____
5. _____, drank, _____
6. _____, _____, spoken
7. _____, thought, _____
8. write, _____, _____
9. _____, _____, rung
10. _____, grew, _____

EXERCISE B: Write the form of the verb in parentheses that correctly completes each sentence. Then label it as *past* or *past participle* in form.

> **Example:** We have (hear) a tape about underwater life.
> **Answer:** heard   past participle

1. The scientist had (speak) about sea creatures.
2. I (think) that it was a fascinating presentation.
3. The tape has (leave) me with new ideas.
4. I have (begun) to consider a career in marine biology.
5. In fact, I (swim) ten laps today—to get in shape!

EXERCISE C: Write sentences to complete this dialogue. Use the past or past participle of the underlined word. Label the form.

> **Example:** RHONDA: Where did she <u>say</u> that she saw that sweater?
> **Answer:** DONNA: She <u>said</u> that she saw it at Flynn's. (past)

1. RHONDA: In which department did she <u>find</u> it?
2. DONNA:
3. RHONDA: How did she <u>get</u> the money for it?
4. DONNA:
5. RHONDA: Did she <u>wear</u> it to school yet?
6. DONNA:
7. RHONDA: Did Aimee really <u>buy</u> the same sweater?
8. DONNA:
9. RHONDA: Do you think that she'll <u>take</u> it back?
10. DONNA:

Identifying and Using Active and Passive Voice

EXERCISE A: Write the ten verbs in the paragraph. Label each one as *active voice* or *passive voice*.

  Example: Ice cream has been enjoyed by people for a long time.
  Answer: has been enjoyed   passive voice

   Ice cream is eaten by people around the world. However, no one knows the origin of this dessert. The recipe for water ices was brought to Europe by Marco Polo in the thirteenth century. Years later, Europeans made a type of ice cream. When they added ice and snow to cream and fruit, a frozen dessert was created. Recipes for this treat were carried to North America by colonists. For many years, ice cream was made at home. In the nineteenth century, the first ice-cream manufacturing plant was established. Today, most ice cream is produced in such plants.

EXERCISE B: Write whether each sentence contains a verb in the *active voice* or the *passive voice*. Then rewrite the sentences, changing the active voice to the passive voice and the passive voice to the active voice.

  Example: The meal was eaten by Joel.
  Answer: passive   Joel <u>ate</u> the meal.

   1. A restaurant has been visited by my family.
   2. Favorite desserts were eaten by all of us.
   3. My sister favored custard pie.
   4. Dad paid the bill.
   5. Now some exercise will be needed by my family!

EXERCISE C: Write ten sentences. Use the verbs listed below.

  Example: visit: passive, past
  Answer: The patient <u>was visited</u> by her family.

   1. buy: passive, present perfect
   2. buy: active, past
   3. read: active, past
   4. read: passive, future
   5. read: passive, future perfect

Using Easily Confused Verbs Correctly

EXERCISE A: Write the verb from the choice in parentheses that correctly completes each sentence.

   Example: Aunt Polly (laid, lay) her knitting in her lap.
   Answer: laid

   1. Everyone was (sitting, setting) in the room when Old Tom entered.
   2. Old Tom soon (lay, laid) sleeping on the floor.
   3. We (leave, let) that old hound sleep anywhere he likes.
   4. Uncle Dave (lain, laid) Old Tom's food dish in the corner.
   5. Now he has (set, sit) Old Tom's water dish beside it.

EXERCISE B: Write the correct form of *set/sit*, *leave/let*, or *lie/lay* on the blank line. (For some sentences, more than one answer is possible).

   Example: _____ me pick up a bus schedule.
   Answer: Let

   1. A passenger _____ down at the front of the bus.
   2. He _____ his package on the seat next to him.
   3. After a time, he _____ the package on his lap.
   4. He looked tired, as if he wanted to _____ down.
   5. "_____ me alone," his expression seemed to say.

EXERCISE C: Rewrite each sentence, correcting any confused verb. If a sentence needs no changes, write *Correct*.

   Example: Have you ever set in the park on a spring day?
   Answer: Have you ever <u>sat</u> in the park on a spring day?

   1. The workers have just lain new tiles around the fountain.
   2. They've set up a special fountain for kids, too.
   3. They'll leave anybody play in the fountain.
   4. Yesterday, I set in the rose garden.
   5. Some rose petals laid on the flower bed.

Using Principal Parts of Verbs Correctly

EXERCISE A: Choose the verb form in parentheses that correctly completes each sentence.

> **Example:** Cindy (lended, lent) me her new hat.
> **Answer:** lent

1. I had (taken, took) it with me to the lake.
2. We (rode, ridden) across the lake in a speedboat.
3. I (worn, wore) it while I was in the boat.
4. I should've (knowed, known) to hold onto the hat!
5. The wind (blew, blown) the hat across the lake.

EXERCISE B: Rewrite the sentences, correcting any misused verb forms. If a sentence needs no changes, write *Correct*.

> **Example:** Native Americans have growed corn for ten thousand years.
> **Answer:** Native Americans have <u>grown</u> corn for ten thousand years.

1. Native Americans teached the Pilgrims to plant corn.
2. They had given the Pilgrims seeds to grow corn.
3. Every day the corn risen higher and higher.
4. They leaved it to dry in the sun.
5. Some of the Pilgrims' first crop was took back to Europe.

EXERCISE C: Complete each sentence with the correct form of the verb in parentheses.

> **Example:** Joey (give) us some peppers from his garden.
> **Answer:** Joey <u>gave</u> us some peppers from his garden.

1. I (bite) into one without thinking.
2. I probably should have (choose) a sweet pepper.
3. How that spicy pepper (sting) my tongue!
4. I could have (drink) a gallon of water.
5. I never (know) that anything could be so hot!

Using Tense Sequence Correctly

EXERCISE A: Choose the verb in parentheses that correctly completes each sentence.

> **Example:** Once we have finished, we (packed, will pack) our belongings.
> **Answer:** will pack

1. I felt ashamed that I (mistreated, had mistreated) her.
2. When she had worked here, she (was, had been) kind.
3. As we worked together, she (changed, had changed).
4. I now fear that I (misjudged, have misjudged) her.

EXERCISE B: If the sentence is correct, write *Correct*. If it is not, change the second verb to correct the tense sequence. Rewrite the sentence.

> **Example:** We were ashamed that we witnessed the event.
> **Answer:** We were ashamed that we <u>had witnessed</u> the event.

1. Janice felt sorry that she disturbed our sleep.
2. We were nervous until we flew a few times.
3. I began to sense that I had miscalculated.
4. Don't you wish that you answered him first?
5. Were you surprised when Luke told you the news?
6. I feel better now that I filled out my application.
7. After you have completed the task, call me.
8. Gerald polished the silver although he did it earlier.
9. When Sis has written, I always answered.
10. Having watched the show, I quietly went to bed.

EXERCISE C: Write the form of the verb in parentheses that correctly completes each sentence.

> **Example:** We are concerned now that you (explain) the problem.
> **Answer:** have explained

1. In the past, when duty has called, we (respond).
2. I was instantly alarmed that he (speak) so boldly.
3. It was clear that Tia (catch) the largest fish.
4. Doesn't she wish that she (write) to her aunt?
5. If Marsh was your pilot, you now (fly) with the best.

Developing Your Style: Using Vivid, Precise Verbs

EXERCISE A: Rewrite the sentences, replacing each underlined verb with a more vivid, precise verb.

Example: The museum <u>shows</u> the best collection of modern art in the country.
Answer: The museum displays the best collecttion of modern art in the country.

1. The visitors <u>walk</u> through the gallery and <u>see</u> the paintings.
2. Some artists <u>write</u> their names on their artwork in clear, bold letters while others <u>write</u> theirs carelessly.
3. "You see, the glass frames <u>save</u> the paintings," the guide <u>says</u>.
4. Although many people <u>like</u> the paintings, they <u>enjoy</u> the sculpture garden more.

EXERCISE B: Rewrite the sentences, completing them with vivid, precise verbs. Write each sentence.

Example: The host _____ famous people onto his show.
Answer: The host <u>invited</u> famous people onto his show.

1. One guest _____ politics with the host; another guest _____ about Hollywood stars.
2. The singer _____ into the spotlight and _____.
3. The people _____ and _____ for their favorite rock star.
4. When the comedienne _____ on the polished floor, she _____.
5. Because she _____ her knee, she _____ off the stage.

EXERCISE C: Rewrite the paragraph, replacing ten vague verbs or verb phrases with more vivid, precise verbs.

The ill-mannered passenger went aboard the train and walked down the aisle. First, the passenger sat in his chair and then looked quickly through the newspaper. Later, he drank some water and breathed loudly when he fell asleep. As the train moved into the station, the conductor said, "Last stop!" Suddenly, the startled passenger arose from his seat and stepped from the train onto the platform.

Developing Your Style: Choosing the Active Voice

EXERCISE A: In each pair of sentences, write the letter of the sentence that uses the active voice.

Example: a. The play was performed by members of the Drama Club.

b. Members of the Drama Club performed the play.

Answer: b

1. a. Ms. Hall directed the students.
   b. The students were directed by Ms. Hall.
2. a. The part of the robot was played by Rolando.
   b. Rolando played the part of the robot.
3. a. Did Duncan print the programs?
   b. Were the programs printed by Duncan?
4. a. The sets had to be painted in a hurry.
   b. They had to paint the sets in a hurry.

EXERCISE B: Rewrite each sentence, changing the verb from passive voice to active voice and making other necessary changes.

Example: The school variety show was broadcast by the cable station.
Answer: The cable station broadcast the school variety show.

1. All the windows in the house were washed by the cleaning crew.
2. The whole family was fascinated by the birth of the kittens.
3. The financial records are being maintained by the treasurer.
4. Will all our changes be recommended by the school board?
5. Your position has been defended well.
6. The battle had been fought and won by poor farmers.
7. How wonderfully the piano is being played by Lenore!
8. This year the team will be coached by Mr. Hirsch.
9. Had one question been asked by a girl in the back row?
10. The championship has been won by our girls' basketball team!

EXERCISE C: Write ten sentences about important events in your life. Use active-voice verbs in all ten sentences.

Example: Detroit <u>is</u> my birthplace.

Answer Key

Grammar, Usage, and Mechanics

Abbreviations

Writing Abbreviations Correctly, EXERCISE A
1. New Hampshire—NH
2. United Nations—UN
3. meter—m
4. Thursday—Thurs.; in the afternoon—P.M.
5. Professor—Prof.; Doctor—Dr.

Writing Abbreviations Correctly, EXERCISE B
1. Maj.
2. Mt.
3. Wed.
4. g
5. in.
6. MO
7. km
8. Feb.
9. CIA
10. TN

Writing Abbreviations Correctly, EXERCISE C

Order:
1. 1 4-<u>lb.</u> box of oranges
   2 4-<u>oz.</u> coffee cakes

2. 1 6-<u>kg</u> country ham
   NOTE: MUST ARRIVE BY
   <u>WED., OCT.</u> 12

Ship To:
<u>Dr.</u> Rachel <u>L.</u> Adams
12 <u>N.</u> Water <u>Dr., Apt.</u> 3-C
Weston, <u>VT</u> 05161
<u>Atty.</u> Carlos Rivera, <u>Jr.</u>
273 Basin <u>Blvd. E.</u>
Houston, <u>TX</u> 77215

Addresses

Writing Addresses Correctly, EXERCISE A
1. 81 <u>55th Ave.</u>/Apartment <u>12</u>-A
2. <u>100</u> Irving <u>St.</u>/Akron, OH 44313
3. They live in Gresham Township, Baltimore County.
4. Deliver the materials to me at 86 Pinto <u>Street</u>, Unity, <u>Maine</u> 04285.

Writing Addresses Correctly, EXERCISE B
1. <u>14</u> Day St./Fayette, AL 35555; <u>14</u> Day <u>Street</u>, Fayette, <u>Alabama</u> 35555
2. Forest Hills/Queens County, NY; Forest Hills, Queens County, <u>New York</u>
3. <u>45</u> James Ave./Ogden, UT 84401; <u>45</u> James <u>Avenue</u>, Ogden, <u>Utah</u> 84401
4. 12 Elm St., Apartment <u>6</u>/Hickory, NC 28601; 12 Elm <u>Street</u>, Apartment <u>6</u>, Hickory, North Carolina 28601

Writing Addresses Correctly, EXERCISE C

269 65th Avenue
Ames, IA 50010
May 29, 1995

Hartford Minerals
31 Lloyd Street
Suite 22-B
Hartford, CT 06101

Dear Hartford Minerals:

   Please note our change of shipping address to 10 Cypress Street , Indianapolis, Indiana 46222. Thank you.

Sincerely,

Ed Haines

Adjectives

Identifying Adjectives and Their Functions, EXERCISE A
1. many—resources, natural—resources
2. the—source, largest—source
3. fir—trees, tall—trees, majestic—trees
4. Sixty—kinds, state—treasures
5. Large—sections, this—state, few—people
6. Many—farms, small—farms
7. many—harbors, fine—harbors, natural—harbors
8. That—park, well-known—park, rainy—forests

Identifying Adjectives and Their Functions, EXERCISE B
1. Most—snakes (how many), a—stare (which one/how many), glassy—stare (what kind)
2. Few—kinds (how many), harmful—kinds (what kind)
3. The—family (which one), colubrid—family (what kind/which one), tropical—forests (what kind)
4. some—features (how many), lizardlike—features (what kind)
5. Coral—snakes (what kind), multicolored—rings (what kind)
6. The—tails (which one), young—rattlesnakes (what kind), one—button (how many), round—button (what kind), shiny—button (what kind)
7. This—sidewinder (which one), little-known—sidewinder (what kind), unusual—tracks (what kind)

Identifying Adjectives and Their Functions, EXERCISE C
Answers will vary; possible answers are given.
1. I felt sleepy and reluctant to get up.
2. The morning sky was clear and sunny.
3. The history teacher explained a complicated system of grading.
4. The menu included greasy hamburgers and delicious potatoes.
5. Jane rattled on about the rock concert at the new stadium.

Identifying and Using Proper Adjectives, EXERCISE A
1. English
2. Asian
3. Buddhist
4. Mexican
5. Japanese

Identifying and Using Proper Adjectives, EXERCISE B
1. Kentuckian—stables
2. American—scholar
3. British—company
4. German—students, Canadian—film
5. Midwestern—winter

Identifying and Using Proper Adjectives, EXERCISE C
Answers will vary; possible answers are given.
1. The <u>American</u> flag flew at half-mast.
2. I am proud of my <u>Native American</u> heritage.
3. That <u>Bostonian</u> monument is a real piece of history.
4. Please pass me some <u>Japanese</u> sushi.
5. The <u>Spanish</u> dictionary proved to be an invaluable aid.

Identifying and Using Demonstrative and Indefinite Adjectives, EXERCISE A
1. some (indefinite) students
2. that (demonstative) table
3. These (demonstrative) plants, several (indefinite) nutrients
4. This (demonstrative) chart, certain (indefinite) types
5. no (indefinite) fair
6. Every (indefinite) visitor, those (demonstrative) experiments
7. much (indefinite) fuss

Identifying and Using Demonstrative and Indefinite Adjectives, EXERCISE B
Answers will vary; possible answers are given.
1. <u>Several</u> letters from Union and Confederate soldiers are quite moving. (indefinite)
2. <u>This</u> book ought to contain a <u>few</u> little-known facts. (demonstrative; indefinite)
3. You'll find good information in <u>these</u> articles about the Battle of Shiloh. (demonstrative)
4. You'll get <u>little</u> help from the magazine, however. (indefinite)
5. You might watch <u>some</u> video documentaries and take notes on them. (indefinite)
6. I wonder if <u>many</u> people today realize how tragic <u>those</u> years were. (indefinite; demonstrative)
7. <u>All</u> fighters of <u>that</u> war have passed away, but their stories remain. (indefinite; demonstrative)

Identifying and Using Demonstrative and Indefinite Adjectives, EXERCISE C
Answers will vary; possible answers are given.
1. I'll tie up <u>this</u> pile of newspapers.
2. Get <u>another</u> bucket of water, Katy; the water is too dirty to use.
3. If you don't use <u>those</u> roller skates, Cathy, why do you keep them?
4. How glad I am that we don't have to clean the garage <u>every</u> week!
5. Wow! Look at the size of <u>that</u> cobweb!
6. Way to go, Cathy—show the dirt <u>no</u> mercy!
7. We should sort through <u>these</u> old clothes; maybe we can give <u>some</u> items away.
8. <u>Most</u> garages aren't this clean after only a <u>few</u> hours' work.

Comparing with Adjectives, EXERCISE A
1. tall, <u>taller</u>, <u>tallest</u>
2. <u>tiny</u>, <u>tinier</u>, tiniest
3. <u>colorful</u>, more colorful, <u>most colorful</u>
4. smooth, <u>smoother</u>, <u>smoothest</u>
5. <u>good</u>, <u>better</u>, best
6. <u>bold</u>, bolder, <u>boldest</u>
7. <u>bad</u>, worse, <u>worst</u>
8. <u>frantic</u>, <u>more frantic</u>, most frantic
9. little, <u>less</u>, <u>least</u>
10. far-fetched, <u>more (less) far-fetched</u>, <u>most (least) far-fetched</u>

Comparing with Adjectives, EXERCISE B
1. Last week, Pete hit the (most spectacular; superlative) home run of the year.
2. Kathleen is (more [less] worried; comparative) than I am about our upcoming camping trip.
3. That's the (most refreshing; superlative) breeze I've felt all day!
4. Are you (jealous; positive) that I got (more; comparative) attention than you did?
5. Of all the cheerleaders, Loni comes up with the (most creative; superlative) routines.
6. I feel (calm; positive) right now, but I'll feel even (better; comparative) when this is over!
7. After the intermission, the band played (livelier; comparative) tunes than they had offered before, and the audience responded with (more enthusiastic; comparative) applause, than at the beginning of the performance.

Comparing with Adjectives, EXERCISE C
Answers will vary; possible answers are given.
1. The county has some old farmhouses, but the Yoder place was <u>older</u> than any of the others.
   Some people say that it's the <u>oldest</u> farmhouse in this part of the state.
2. The sounds were <u>more mysterious</u> than the mere howling of dogs.
   They were the <u>most mysterious</u> noises that Travis had ever heard.
3. In fact, I had <u>less</u> attention for his stories than usual.
   I had the <u>least</u> amount of patience when Ben started talking about haunted houses.
4. My confidence now was <u>less sure</u> than it had been a few minutes earlier.
   I felt <u>least sure</u> when Travis challenged me to explore the place with him.

Using Adjectives Correctly, EXERCISE A
1. incorrect
2. correct
3. incorrect
4. incorrect
5. correct

Using Adjectives Correctly, EXERCISE B

1. That's the <u>saddest</u> story you've ever told.
2. This wallpaper design is <u>more interesting</u> than that one.
3. The fever was <u>worse</u> in the morning than at night.
4. You are the <u>most agreeable</u> friend I have.
5. After studying the two maps, she picked the <u>more detailed</u> one.
6. Correct
7. The friends grew <u>closer</u> every day.
8. Would the relish tray or the fruit salad be <u>easier</u> for you to bring?
9. Correct
10. Of the two sisters, Carla is the <u>more</u> sharp-tongued.

Using Adjectives Correctly, EXERCISE C

AUDRA: John Ford may have been the <u>most successful</u> filmmaker in the world.

ELIZA: I know. His Westerns were the <u>most popular</u> movies of all time. His stars had the <u>broadest</u> appeal across age groups of any filmmaker.

AUDRA: John Ford may have been <u>more successful</u> than Alfred Hitchcock.

ELIZA: Of all Hitchcock's movies, I think *North by Northwest* is the <u>most respected</u>.

Developing Your Style: Using Precise Adjectives, EXERCISE A

1. a <u>cloudless</u> sky
2. a <u>glistening</u> dewdrop
3. the <u>deafening</u> waterfall
4. a <u>putrid</u> skunk odor
5. a <u>footsore</u> hiker
6. a <u>vibrant</u> red
7. the <u>haunted</u> house
8. a <u>mellow</u> voice
9. a <u>spectacular</u> view
10. an <u>endless</u> wait

Developing Your Style: Using Precise Adjectives, EXERCISE B

Answers will vary; possible answers are given.

1. Some tools had <u>twisted</u> shapes.
2. The wood handles were wet and <u>musty</u>.
3. A <u>winding</u> trail of dirt led to the door.
4. Outside, the color of the shed looked <u>rusted</u>.
5. We could hear <u>chattering</u> starlings nearby.

Developing Your Style: Using Precise Adjectives, EXERCISE C

Answers will vary; possible answers are given.

At the <u>bustling</u> terminal, the weary commuters hustled to board their <u>teeming</u> buses. Joan spotted a <u>gleaming</u> bus at the end of the long platform. Holding a ticket in her <u>clenched</u> fist, she walked with a <u>cautious</u> step toward the bus. With the lights off, it appeared <u>gloomy</u> inside. Suddenly, a <u>helpful</u> bus driver asked Joan if she were lost. She showed him her <u>crumpled</u> ticket. "Oh, that's your bus over there," he said in a <u>cheerful</u> voice. He was pointing to the bus with the <u>glaring</u> headlights and <u>sputtering</u> engine.

Developing Your Style: Avoiding Overuse of Adjectives, EXERCISE A

1. b
2. a
3. b
4. a

Developing Your Style: Avoiding Overuse of Adjectives, EXERCISE B
1. A computer's <u>memory</u> is enhanced by microchips.
2. Computers <u>process</u> the information.
3. They also <u>solve</u> complicated problems.
4. Mom and Dad recently <u>purchased</u> a home computer.
5. We <u>celebrated</u> the purchase.

Developing Your Style: Avoiding Overuse of Adjectives, EXERCISE C
Answers will vary; possible answers are given.
1. Do coyotes live up to their <u>reputation</u>?
2. The coyote can be found on the <u>prairies</u> of western North America.
3. It <u>howls</u> at night.
4. The coyote can <u>deceive</u> its enemies.
5. Does the coyote's <u>cleverness</u> match the fox's slyness?

Adverbs

Identifying Adverbs That Modify Verbs, EXERCISE A
1. First, dye
2. carefully, pull
3. often, uses
4. everywhere, sell
5. forever, lasts

Identifying Adverbs That Modify Verbs, EXERCISE B
1. almost, To what extent?
2. Now, When?
3. outside, Where?
4. Then, When?; thoughtfully, In what manner?
5. rather, To what extent?
6. here, Where?
7. today, When?; beautifully, In what manner?
8. since, When?

Identifying Adverbs That Modify Verbs, EXERCISE C
Answers will vary; possible answers are given.
1. speedily; The waiter walked <u>quickly</u> to the table.
2. Then, clumsily; <u>Next</u> he <u>awkwardly</u> handed the menu to the diner.
3. nearly, quickly; The glass of water <u>almost</u> fell, but the diner caught it <u>deftly</u>.
4. late, briskly; When dinner arrived <u>tardily</u>, the diner rose <u>abruptly</u>.
5. Soon, nervously; <u>Suddenly</u> the manager appeared and <u>emotionally</u> appologized to the diner.
6. quickly; A new plate of food appeared <u>rapidly</u>.

Identifying Adverbs That Modify Adjectives and Other Adverbs, EXERCISE A
1. every, four (adjective)
2. rather, simply (adverb)
3. much, more competitive (adjective)
4. extremely, well (adverb)
5. truly, amazing (adjective)

Identifying Adverbs That Modify Adjectives and Other Adverbs, EXERCISE B
1. slightly spoiled, absolutely adorable
2. relatively slowly, almost hourly
3. always fresh, uncommonly clean
4. rather large, amusingly puzzled

Identifying Adverbs That Modify Adjectives and Other Adverbs, EXERCISE C
Answers will vary; possible answers are given.
1. extremely; The student scored <u>very</u> high marks on his reports.
2. most; He approached his work <u>quite</u> vigorously.
3. especially; Other students did not work <u>so</u> hard.
4. usually; Their reports were <u>typically</u> inaccurate.
5. highly; The teacher was <u>rather</u> outraged.
6. sorely; The <u>extremely</u> inadequate facts were unacceptable.
7. somewhat; She concluded, <u>relatively</u> angrily, that changes were necessary.
8. singularly; She asked the <u>exceptionally</u> clever student to display his work.
9. rather; She ordered the others to do their research <u>fairly</u> thoroughly.
10. slightly; Are the students <u>somewhat</u> nervous about their new assignment?

Distinguishing Adverbs from Adjectives and Prepositions, EXERCISE A
1. adverb
2. adverb
3. adjective
4. preposition
5. adjective
6. adverb
7. adverb
8. adjective
9. adverb
10. preposition

Distinguishing Adverbs from Adjectives and Prepositions, EXERCISE B
1. since; preposition, adverb
2. through; preposition, adverb
3. early; adverb, adjective
4. up; adverb, preposition

Distinguishing Adverbs from Adjectives and Prepositions, EXERCISE C
Answers will vary; possible answers are given.
1. There's an <u>outside</u> chance that they will win.
2. He wore his shirt <u>outside</u> his jeans.
3. Put the kettle <u>on</u> the stove.
4. Turn the light <u>on</u>.
5. The girls lined up on the <u>right</u> side of the gym.
6. He was told to go <u>right</u> home.
7. They waited <u>under</u> the overpass.
8. Either climb over the fence or crawl <u>under</u>.
9. While Kyla climbed the ladder, I waited <u>below</u>.
10. In playing cards, the jack is ranked <u>below</u> the queen.

Comparing with Adverbs, EXERCISE A

1. more softly, most softly
2. higher, highest
3. more nearly, most nearly
4. worse, worst
5. more casually, most casually
6. sooner, soonest
7. more habitually, most habitually
8. farther, farthest (or further, furthest)
9. better, best
10. less, least

Comparing with Adverbs, EXERCISE B

1. comparative
2. superlative
3. superlative
4. comparative
5. comparative
6. comparative
7. superlative
8. comparative
9. superlative
10. comparative

Comparing with Adverbs, EXERCISE C

1. hardest (superlative)
2. more cautiously (comparative)
3. earlier (comparative)
4. most safely (superlative)
5. best (superlative)

Using Adverbs Correctly, EXERCISE A

1. incorrect
2. incorrect
3. correct
4. incorrect
5. incorrect
6. incorrect
7. incorrect
8. correct
9. incorrect
10. incorrect

Using Adverbs Correctly, EXERCISE B

1. Probably no one you know has had an adventure <u>anything</u> like his.
2. Stevens was <u>all ready</u> to take a trip around the world on his bicycle, so he left San Franciso in 1884.
3. Unpaved roads and mountainous terrain made Stevens's trip <u>very</u> uncomfortable at times.
4. Hardly <u>anyone</u> who read the newspaper failed to follow his journey around the globe or applaud him for a job done so <u>well</u>.

Using Adverbs Correctly, EXERCISE C

Answers will vary; possible answers are given.

CARA: Nothing <u>will</u> keep me out of the talent show this year. I'm going to sing <u>well</u> enough to win in the vocal category! In fact, I've <u>already</u> started rehearsing! Can you play a musical instrument?

RAVI: I can play the clarinet, but not too <u>well</u>. I'm not <u>bad</u> on the guitar, though.

Developing Your Style: Adverbs, EXERCISE A

Answers will vary; possible answers are given.

1. unexpectedly, suddenly
2. nervously, anxiously
3. swiftly, quickly
4. securely, tightly
5. hurriedly, hastily

Developing Your Style: Adverbs, EXERCISE B

Answers will vary; possible answers are given.

1. Andy <u>carefully</u> baited his hook.
2. <u>Then</u> he confidently cast the line halfway across the lake.
3. A large fish nibbled <u>hungrily</u> on the bait.
4. Andy <u>gradually but confidently</u> gave the fish some line.
5. The fish swam <u>very slowly</u> toward the dock.
6. The fish <u>suddenly</u> jerked the cork under the water.
7. Andy <u>excitedly</u> reeled in the line.
8. <u>Next</u>, he <u>expertly</u> removed the hook from the bass's mouth.
9. The landed bass was <u>impressively</u> large.
10. It <u>immediately</u> flopped off the pier and into the water.

Developing Your Style: Adverbs, EXERCISE C

Answers will vary; possible answers are given.

1. I sun myself <u>lazily</u> on the beach.
2. I <u>eagerly</u> read library books.
3. I sleep <u>unusually</u> late every day.
4. I <u>frequently</u> ride my bike by the ocean.
5. I quite <u>contentedly</u> eat ice-cream cones.

Apostrophes

Using Apostrophes in Possessives and Contractions, EXERCISE A

1. Benjamin<u>'s</u> novel
2. a poet<u>'s</u> rhyme
3. everybody<u>'s</u> favorite singer
4. two months<u>'</u> work
5. three writers<u>'</u> poetry
6. you<u>'d</u>
7. don<u>'t</u>
8. Correct
9. they<u>'re</u>
10. Sam<u>'ll</u>

Using Apostrophes in Possessives and Contractions, EXERCISE B
1. panel's
2. hasn't
3. hers
4. She'll
5. won't
6. movie's, his
7. teachers'
8. wouldn't, supporters'

Using Apostrophes in Possessives and Contractions, EXERCISE C
Julia thought that <u>she'd</u> like to make a surprise party, but Nancy wasn't going along with the idea. She believes that <u>nobody's</u> ever happy about being surprised. Still, <u>Nancy's</u> sister thought that Jennifer would enjoy all the fuss. The <u>friends'</u> problem <u>wasn't</u> resolved until the next <u>day's</u> meeting. Jennifer had guessed her <u>pals'</u> plan and <u>didn't</u> hesitate to talk to them about it. She said, "I <u>don't</u> mind a surprise party, so long as there <u>aren't</u> too many people there."

Other Uses of Apostrophes, EXERCISE A
1. dot your *i*<u>'s</u> and cross your *t*<u>'s</u>
2. Count by *10*<u>'s</u>
3. *7*<u>'s</u> that look like *z*<u>'s</u>
4. a glut of *!*<u>'s</u>
5. so many *very*<u>'s</u> in that poem
6. "Blowin<u>'</u> in the Wind"
7. three *5*'s in her telephone number
8. use *&* <u>'s</u>, not *+*<u>'s</u>
9. the speaker drops all initial *h*<u>'s</u>
10. "Lend me an <u>'</u>elping <u>'and</u>," he'll say.

Other Uses of Apostrophes, EXERCISE B
1. The storyteller presented "Dancin<u>'</u> and Prancin<u>'</u> with the Lady of the Moon."
2. He said that he'd heard enough *once upon a time*<u>'s</u> and *happily ever after*<u>'s</u> to last a lifetime.
3. He asked his audience, "Have you been mindin<u>'</u> your *p*<u>'s</u> and *q*<u>'s</u>?"
4. The moral of his tale was "If *if*<u>'s</u> and *and*<u>'s</u> were pots and pans, there'd be no need for tinkers."
5. You'd better get <u>'em</u> to come here quickly.

Other Uses of Apostrophes, EXERCISE C
1. Hal always makes *A*<u>'s</u> and *B*<u>'s</u>; getting *C*<u>'s</u> would crush him.
2. When do you change the *y*<u>'s</u> to *i*<u>'s</u>?
3. The room resounded with *no*<u>'s</u> when she asked if we wanted a test.
4. "I was <u>zoomin'</u> down the road, <u>feelin'</u> the wind <u>'round</u> my helmet."
5. There are two *n*<u>'s</u> and two *s*<u>'s</u> in *unnecessary*.
6. Correct
7. Using too many *!*<u>'s</u> can actually reduce the impact of your writing.
8. Correct
9. Jimmy asked, "Can you <u>'ear</u> me when I say <u>'ello</u>?"
10. Correct

Appositives

Identifying and Punctuating Appositives, EXERCISE A
1. an African-American hero, Harriet Tubman
2. Yvonne, my best friend
3. the great baseball player, Henry Aaron
4. her favorite author, Jean Fritz
5. Robert E. Lee, the American general

Identifying and Punctuating Appositives, EXERCISE B
Answers will vary; possible answers are given.
1. Mr. Grant, my English teacher, wants to see me this afternoon.
2. Would you take these books to Mrs. Willis, the principal's secretary?
3. My mother, a registered nurse, should take a look at that cut.
4. We took the bus to Baseline Road, the stop nearest the school.
5. The poet Emily Dickinson is one of my favorite writers.

Identifying and Punctuating Appositives, EXERCISE C
Answers may vary slightly; possible answers are given.
1. The Corning Glass Works, a company that makes glass, has developed more than 100,000 kinds of glass.
2. Safety glass, a substance used for car windshields, is made of layers of glass and plastic.
3. The first glass objects, creations of unknown artisans, were made thousands of years ago.
4. Venice, a city in Italy, was a center for manufacturing glass.
5. American designer Louis Tiffany created many beautiful objects from glass.

Developing Your Style: Appositives, EXERCISE A
1. Correct
2. Sherlock Holmes, a brilliant detective, can solve any mystery.
3. Dr. Watson, a good friend, assists Holmes in solving his cases.
4. The character of Holmes was based on a real person, Dr. Joseph Bell.
5. Holmes's trademark, a curved pipe, is familiar to most people.

Developing Your Style: Appositives, EXERCISE B
Answers may vary slightly; possible answers are given.
1. Gary Paulsen wrote *Dogsong, a book about the Iditarod Sled Dog Race,* in 1984.
2. The Iditarod, a thousand-mile race, is run from Anchorage to Nome, Alaska.
3. *Dogsong* won an important award, the Newbery Honor Book, from the American Library Association.
4. Another book, *The Voyage of the Frog,* reveals Paulsen's love of water sports.
5. *The Voyage of the Frog,* the story of a boy lost at sea, is based on an event in Paulsen's own life.

Developing Your Style: Appositives, EXERCISE C
Answers will vary; possible answers are given.
1. The victim, Penelope Peacock, had been murdered.
2. A bottle of poison, cyanide, lay near the body.
3. I noticed the first clue, a muddy footprint, in the hall.
4. The second clue, a smudged fingerprint, gave me an idea.
5. My prime suspect, the cook, had bought a bottle of rat poison.

Capitalization

Capitalizing Names and Titles of People, EXERCISE A

1. <u>D</u>r. <u>W</u>atson
2. <u>S</u>ir <u>A</u>rthur
3. <u>F</u>rankenstein's monster
4. <u>E</u>mily <u>D</u>ickinson's poems
5. <u>Y</u>esterday I read a sonnet by <u>S</u>hakespeare.
6. <u>L</u>angston <u>H</u>ughes
7. <u>J</u>ames <u>T</u>hurber's <u>W</u>alter <u>M</u>itty
8. <u>T</u>.<u>S</u>. <u>E</u>liot
9. <u>M</u>s. <u>D</u>orothy <u>P</u>arker
10. <u>Y</u>ou're right, <u>L</u>ord <u>W</u>embley!

Capitalizing Names and Titles of People, EXERCISE B

1. <u>I</u> told <u>M</u>rs. <u>W</u>hittaker what <u>I</u>'d heard.
2. Hey, <u>D</u>ad, have your heard the joke yet?
3. After <u>D</u>r. <u>R</u>uiz read the joke, she told it to <u>S</u>ally and <u>C</u>helsea.
4. <u>S</u>ally and <u>C</u>helsea sent the joke to <u>M</u>r. <u>T</u>.<u>J</u>. <u>G</u>oodman, who publishes *Ha-Ha* magazine.
5. <u>M</u>r. <u>G</u>oodman asked <u>M</u>s. <u>E</u>llen <u>P</u>arnell to illustrate the joke.

Capitalizing Names and Titles of People, EXERCISE C

1. *Little Women* is a novel by <u>L</u>ouisa <u>M</u>ay <u>A</u>lcott.
2. It tells about the <u>M</u>arch <u>f</u>amily.
3. There are four sisters: <u>M</u>eg, <u>J</u>o, <u>B</u>eth, and <u>A</u>my.
4. <u>M</u>rs. <u>M</u>arch's first name is <u>M</u>armee.
5. They live next to <u>M</u>r. <u>L</u>awrence and his son, <u>T</u>heodore.
6. <u>T</u>heodore's nickname is <u>L</u>aurie.
7. A tutor is in love with <u>J</u>o.
8. Correct
9. Who is your favorite character, <u>M</u>om?
10. Mother likes <u>M</u>eg, but I think that <u>A</u>unt <u>M</u>arch and <u>J</u>ohn <u>B</u>rooke are also very interesting characters.

Capitalizing Name of Places, EXERCISE A

1. the <u>O</u>hio <u>R</u>iver
2. <u>P</u>ark <u>A</u>venue
3. <u>S</u>an <u>J</u>oaquin <u>V</u>alley
4. <u>A</u>lbuquerque, <u>N</u>ew <u>M</u>exico
5. the <u>S</u>ahara <u>D</u>esert
6. <u>P</u>rince <u>E</u>dward <u>I</u>sland
7. <u>Y</u>ellowstone <u>N</u>ational <u>P</u>ark
8. <u>M</u>editerranean <u>S</u>ea
9. <u>P</u>eople's <u>R</u>epublic of <u>C</u>hina
10. a <u>E</u>uropean country

Capitalizing Name of Places, EXERCISE B
1. The continent of <u>N</u>orth <u>A</u>merica includes the countries of <u>C</u>anada, the <u>U</u>nited <u>S</u>tates, and <u>M</u>exico.
2. The region called the <u>G</u>reat <u>P</u>lains extends from the <u>C</u>anadian provinces of <u>A</u>lberta, <u>S</u>askatchewan, and <u>M</u>onitoba through the central <u>U</u>nited <u>S</u>tates into northern <u>T</u>exas.
3. The <u>M</u>iddle <u>W</u>est includes the states of <u>I</u>llinois, Indiana, <u>I</u>owa, <u>K</u>ansas, <u>M</u>ichigan, <u>M</u>innesota, <u>M</u>issouri, <u>N</u>ebraska, <u>O</u>hio, and <u>W</u>isconsin.
4. The <u>M</u>ississippi <u>R</u>iver flows from <u>M</u>innesota to <u>L</u>ouisiana, where it empties into the <u>G</u>ulf of <u>M</u>exico.

Capitalizing Name of Places, EXERCISE C
Greetings from <u>G</u>reat <u>B</u>ritain! Our trip has been wonderful. We arrived at <u>G</u>atwick <u>A</u>irport last Sunday. We took a train to <u>V</u>ictoria <u>S</u>tation and then the underground to our hotel in <u>E</u>arl's <u>C</u>ourt <u>R</u>oad. The sites in <u>L</u>ondon were marvelous, especially <u>K</u>ensington <u>G</u>ardens and the <u>T</u>hames <u>R</u>iver. We traveled north to <u>Y</u>ork, which is on the <u>N</u>orth <u>S</u>ea. Tomorrow we will reach <u>E</u>dinburgh, <u>S</u>cotland.

Capitalizing Other Names, EXERCISE A
1. before <u>W</u>orld <u>W</u>ar I
2. Buckingham <u>P</u>alace
3. *The <u>S</u>ound of <u>M</u>usic*
4. speaking in <u>I</u>talian
5. "The <u>P</u>it and the <u>P</u>endulum"
6. African-<u>A</u>merican art
7. the <u>B</u>ible
8. the <u>N</u>ew <u>Y</u>ork <u>S</u>tock <u>E</u>xchange
9. after the <u>G</u>reat <u>D</u>epression
10. drive a <u>P</u>ontiac *Bonneville*

Capitalizing Other Names, EXERCISE B
1. Can you imagine driving in a *Model T* <u>F</u>ord?
2. How tall is the <u>C</u>hrysler <u>B</u>uilding, Ginny?
3. Can you speak <u>P</u>ortuguese?
4. Will you take <u>A</u>merican <u>H</u>istory 101 next year?
5. Have you ever visited <u>M</u>ount <u>R</u>ushmore?
6. When did the battle between the *<u>M</u>onitor and the <u>M</u>errimac* take place?
7. Was the <u>B</u>attle of <u>Y</u>orktown part of the <u>R</u>evolutionary <u>W</u>ar?
8. In which countries do many people practice <u>B</u>uddhism?
9. Have you ever seen *The <u>H</u>unchback of <u>N</u>otre <u>D</u>ame?*
10. Can you remember the lyrics to "The <u>S</u>tar-<u>S</u>pangled <u>B</u>anner"?

Capitalizing Other Names, EXERCISE C
Answers will vary; possible answers are given.
1. My favorite movie is *<u>Singing in the Rain</u>*.
2. One song that really gets on my nerves is "<u>Beautiful Dreamer</u>."
3. I think that the landmark that best represents the United States is <u>the Statue of Liberty</u>.
4. I would like to join <u>the Peace Corps</u> someday.
5. If I could travel backward in time, I would like to see <u>the Boston Tea Party</u>.

Using Capitals to Mark Beginnings of Sentences and Direct Quotations, EXERCISE A
1. Swimming is my favorite sport, but I do not like diving.
2. Marie said to Lena, "You and I could go to the pool this afternoon."
3. Lena said, "What a good idea! We can practice our synchronized swimming routine."
4. The lifeguard called them over. The two partners left the pool.
5. Will we find deck chairs in the sun?

Using Capitals to Mark Beginnings of Sentences and Direct Quotations, EXERCISE B
1. Julio said, "Many houses in Mexico are built of adobe."
2. "Yes," agreed his mother. "Our family grew up in an adobe house."
3. Correct
4. "Well," said Uncle Raimundo, "this climate is not appropriate for adobe. When they get damp, adobe bricks will crumble."
5. "Oh, well," said Julio, "if I can't live in an adobe house, I'm glad I got to see one in person."

Using Capitals to Mark Beginnings of Sentences and Direct Quotations, EXERCISE C
1. Humorous author Mark Twain wrote *The Prince and the Pauper* in 1882. It is an entertaining tale of reversed identities. The prince of England, Edward, and a London street beggar named Tom Canty exchange places. Their adventures take them into parts of the world that they had never before encountered.
2. "My favorite book is *The Prince and the Pauper*," said Christa. "It is everything a novel should be. It's funny, exciting, and perceptive. If you enjoy reading this book, you will also like *A Connecticut Yankee in King Arthur's Court*."

Using Capitals to Mark Other Beginnings, EXERCISE A
1. The next line is "Thou art more lovely and more temperate."
2. The final couplet is "So long as men can breathe, or eyes can see/So long lives this, and this gives life to thee."
3. Delia wrote "Dear Mom and Dad" at the top of the card.
4. The first entry in Ike's outline was "I. The South Pole."
5. Beneath that came "A. The southern end of Earth's axis."

Using Capitals to Mark Other Beginnings, EXERCISE B
1. "Here a star, and there a star,/Some lose their way!" (Emily Dickinson)
2. Dear Sir or Madam:
3. Dear Editor of the *Cleveland Plain Dealer*,
4. Dearest Melanie,
5. I.   The attack on Pearl Harbor
    A. Took place on Dec. 7, 1941
    B. Naval base attacked by Japanese
    C. War declared the next day

Using Capitals to Mark Other Beginnings, EXERCISE C
1. "Dark brown is the river,/Golden is the sand, . . ." (Robert Louis Stevenson)
2. Dearest Senator:
3. Correct
4. II. Discovery of buoyancy
    A. Bathtub experiment
    B. Volume can be measured by displacement of water

Clauses

Identifying and Using Main and Subordinate Clauses, EXERCISE A
1. main clause
2. phrase
3. subordinate clause
4. main clause
5. subordinate clause

Identifying and Using Main and Subordinate Clauses, EXERCISE B
Rewritten sentences will vary; possible answers are given.
1. main clause; <u>Since we have extra time</u>, I want to go over some things.
2. subordinate clause
3. main clause; <u>If you want to get a drink of water</u>, do it now.
4. main clause; Place your papers on my desk <u>before you leave the room</u>.
5. subordinate clause

Identifying and Using Main and Subordinate Clauses, EXERCISE C
Rewritten sentences will vary; possible answers are given.
1. When we visited the marine museum, <u>we saw many strange sights</u>.
2. Since one shark has been there for years, <u>it has become a favorite attraction</u>.
3. Although horseshoe crabs are not really crabs, <u>they are also known as king crabs</u>.
4. Wherever we went, <u>our guide pointed out interesting facts</u>.
5. <u>We also watched a film about marine life</u> before we left.

Identifying and Using Adjective Clauses, EXERCISE A
1. that scared everyone
2. who interrupts all the time
3. which many people once rode
4. who won many awards
5. whose essay took first prize

Identifying and Using Adjective Clauses, EXERCISE B
1. that have similar meanings, words
2. who wrote "Jabberwocky," poet
3. that is well behaved, dog
4. which is sixty miles from here, Chicago
5. that has become very popular, sport
6. whom everyone likes, coach
7. that help the blind, Dogs
8. whose mother has just arrived, children
9. who wrote under the name of George Sand, Aurore Dupin
10. that is coming from downstairs, music

Identifying and Using Adjective Clauses, EXERCISE C
Answers will vary; possible answers are given.
1. A person <u>who is always smiling</u> cheers up a room.
2. The passengers <u>whose flight was delayed</u> waited impatiently.
3. The sketch <u>that Su Lin and Martin admired</u> cost six-hundred dollars!
4. Do you want honey, <u>which many people like</u>, in your tea?
5. Peter, <u>whom the police had suspected</u>, was found to be completely innocent.

Distinguishing Between Restrictive and Nonrestrictive Clauses, EXERCISE A
1. nonrestrictive
2. restrictive
3. nonrestrictive
4. restrictive
5. nonrestrictive

Distinguishing Between Restrictive and Nonrestrictive Clauses, EXERCISE B
1. who seems quite shy, nonrestrictive
2. which can surprise you, nonrestrictive
3. that bewilder strangers, restrictive
4. who understand him, restrictive
5. whom he most amazes, restrictive
6. whom I adore, nonrestrictive
7. whose looks are so ordinary, restrictive
8. that folks expect him to be dull, restrictive
9. that leave me howling, restrictive
10. whose patience is limited, nonrestrictive

Distinguishing Between Restrictive and Nonrestrictive Clauses, EXERCISE C
1. Danielle comes from Marseilles, which is in southern France.
2. Correct
3. My city, which has a port as well, may seem similar.
4. Correct
5. My cousin Emily, who works there, will give us a behind-the-scenes tour.

Identifying and Using Adverb Clauses, EXERCISE A
1. Before
2. so that
3. wherever
4. When

Identifying and Using Adverb Clauses, EXERCISE B
1. so that they would be comfortable, why
2. when they rode along the highway, when
3. Before spring comes, when
4. Because her family speaks Russian at home, why
5. if you would speak up, under what condition
6. while you slice the tomatoes, when
7. as if we had never met, how
8. After the games were over, when
9. because I admire her, why
10. Until you finish eating, when

Identifying and Using Adverb Clauses, EXERCISE C
Answers will vary; possible answers are given.
1. Jason chuckled under his breath <u>as soon as he heard</u>.
2. <u>If he wished to do so</u>, Jason would stand on his head.
3. Jason paced in a circle <u>while he waited</u>.
4. Jason tapped his toes <u>because he was happy</u>.

Using Clauses Correctly, EXERCISE A

1. faulty subordination; John chose the terrier
2. Correct
3. faulty subordination; his doubts were now gone
4. faulty subordination; John took his new pet home
5. Correct

Using Clauses Correctly, EXERCISE B

1. Correct
2. She will be late for her appointment unless the package is delivered on time.
3. She will accept it if the new refrigerator is not damaged.
4. Correct
5. She can call her mother at work if there is a problem.

Using Clauses Correctly, EXERCISE C

1. Although you don't have homework, you should study.
2. Unless you are a speed reader, it will take you hours.
3. If you could read a book each week, you would be quite literate.
4. Because the book is nonfiction, it may take you more time.
5. When you write your own book, you can make it any length.

Developing Your Style: Clauses, EXERCISE A

Some answers may vary slightly; possible answers are given.

1. Supervisors train new editors, who may be inexperienced.
2. The new edition is longer because it has more words.
3. When new words were added, some old words were dropped.
4. You'll find the meaning if you look it up in a dictionary.
5. Before they added foreign foods, they called restaurant owners.

Developing Your Style: Clauses, EXERCISE B

Answers will vary; possible answers are given.

1. If you send in your answers, we'll print your responses.
2. Unless you print your name and address, we won't know who you are.
3. Although you may send us a fax, we'd prefer a mailed entry.
4. Since the deadline is next week, you have no time to lose.
5. While there are no guarantees, you can be a winner!

Developing Your Style: Clauses, EXERCISE C

Answers will vary; possible answers are given.

1. <u>I like the wintertime</u> although I have no favorite season.
2. <u>Although we had a harsh winter</u>, we never missed a day of school.
3. <u>We had to borrow a sled</u> because we didn't have one of our own.
4. <u>Since I can't ski</u>, I need to take lessons.
5. <u>Indoor sports are fun, too</u>, when you can't play outside.
6. <u>Springtime is best</u> because the flowers are in bloom.
7. <u>If I could choose any sport</u>, I would pick basketball.
8. <u>Since we moved here</u>, I've met two new friends.
9. We'll stay at the beach <u>unless the weather gets too hot</u>.
10. <u>This storm broke all records</u> because it was quite fierce.

Colons

Using Colons Correctly, EXERCISE A

1. 1:30 P.M.
2. Dear Mr. Morrison:
3. Caution : Open Door Slowly
4. 11:00 A.M.
5. To Whom It May Concern:

Using Colons Correctly, EXERCISE B

1. Sift together the following: the cornmeal, the flour, and the salt.
2. The train leaves at 3:15 P.M. and arrives at 4:02 P.M.
3. The sign read, "Caution: Wet Floor."
4. Use these methods to prepare the fish: broiling, baking, or grilling.
5. In Florida we saw several kinds of citrus trees: lemon, orange, lime, and grapefruit.

Using Colons Correctly, EXERCISE C

Dear Student:

Welcome to Pleasant Valley Middle School! During your first visit, plan to do the following: locate your classrooms, meet your new teachers, and look at your new textbooks. Your daily schedule will be as follows: classes from 8:30 A.M. to 11:30 A.M.; lunch from 11:45 to 12:15; and classes from 12:30 P.M. to 3:00 P.M. Remember that at Pleasant Valley, we have one simple rule: treat others as you would like to be treated.

Commas

Using Commas with Coordinating Conjunctions, EXERCISE A

1. Carmen is my best friend, and she knows it.
2. Everyone likes going to parties, yet no one likes to plan them.
3. Receiving presents is wonderful, but giving them is even better.
4. Can you come, or will you be busy that night?
5. Roger didn't show up, nor did he offer me a good explanation.

Using Commas with Coordinating Conjunctions, EXERCISE B

Answers will vary; possible answers are given.
1. The tapes belong to Li and Sun, but the CD player is mine.
2. The littler children began to cry, for they were lost.
3. The storyteller talked on and on, yet no one grew tired of listening.
4. Shall we order Chinese food, or would the twins rather eat pizza?
5. Maritza would not look at anyone, nor would she answer our questions.
6. Dad made a pasta salad, and Uncle Greg prepared the fish.
7. Many birds had flown south, but the sparrows remained.
8. I had set the alarm, yet it did not go off.
9. Darrell was fond of his sister, and he often bought her presents.
10. Shall we read a story, or shall we watch television?

Using Commas with Coordinating Conjunctions, EXERCISE C

Answers may vary slightly; possible answers are given.
1. Dogs make good pets, but I prefer cats.
2. Do you want to go out tonight, or would you rather stay home?
3. I like the new girl, and I'll tell her so.
4. French is a beautiful language, yet I think I'd rather learn Spanish.
5. I have not broken the club rules, nor will I.

Using Commas with Adjectives, EXERCISE A
1. massive, thick
2. cold, murky
3. fierce, huge, diabolical
4. numerous vicious (no comma)
5. bold, fearless

Using Commas with Adjectives, EXERCISE B
1. majestic, proud
2. cooling, refreshing
3. Correct
4. Correct
5. sleek, swift
6. rough, wiry
7. dark, dusty, drab
8. sobbing, shaking; soft, sweet
9. intelligent, outgoing, level-headed

Using Commas with Adjectives, EXERCISE C
Answers will vary; possible answers are given.
1. A heavy, cold lump was forming in her throat.
2. With a smart, snappy salute, the lieutenant greeted the colonel.
3. Wearing your seat belt is a simple, important habit to learn.
4. They heard weird, spine-chilling, terrifying laughter from the top of the stairs.
5. A menacing, beastly shadow appeared on the wall.

Using Commas with Subordinating Conjunctions, EXERCISE A
1. While you're up, would you bring me something from the kitchen?
2. If you had a choice, would you rather have a cookie or an apple?
3. Although I like junk food, I'd rather have a home-cooked meal.
4. Whatever we have for dinner, my brother always wants something else.
5. Until you've tried my recipe, you don't know how good okra can be.

Using Commas with Subordinating Conjunctions, EXERCISE B
1. Before you answer the question, be sure you know the facts.
2. After all we've been through together, how can you treat me this way?
3. Correct
4. Correct
5. While you're in town, I hope you'll pay us a visit.

Using Commas with Subordinating Conjunctions, EXERCISE C
Answers will vary; possible answers are given.
1. Until I started junior high school, I never had so much homework.
2. Whether you like Mr. Decker or not, you have to appreciate his talent.
3. Because I want to do well, I'll study hard for this exam.
4. After school today, do you want to study at my house?
5. Whenever we have midterms, I always worry that I'm not going to pass.
6. As I told you before, I can't define the word *conjunction*.
7. Unless I'm mistaken, I did very well on that test.
8. When I think about it, I really respect that teacher.
9. Since I took that exam, I've chosen English as my favorite subject.
10. My parents are getting me a tutor if I don't do well in this class. (no comma)

Using Commas with Introductory Words and Phrases, EXERCISE A

1. As the fifteenth child of former slaves, Bethune
2. During that time in South Carolina, most
3. At the invitation of a teacher, Mary
4. Excelling as a student, she
5. With the help of wealthy businesspeople, Bethune

Using Commas with Introductory Words and Phrases, EXERCISE B

Answers may vary slightly; possible answers are given.

1. Annoyed by our antics, the teacher frowned at us.
2. On the other hand, how do we know she can be trusted?
3. Puzzled by its contents, we decided to open the box.
4. According to the news on the radio, the information is correct.
5. Under its mop of hair, the dog had tiny black eyes.

Using Commas with Introductory Words and Phrases, EXERCISE C

Answers will vary; possible answers are given.

1. Cramming my books into my backpack, I hurried out.
2. Waiting for the bus, I waved to a friend.
3. Near the front of the bus, I found a seat.
4. Starving for a snack, I ate some popcorn.
5. On the way to a friend's house, I wrecked my bike.
6. Working on our homework, we made good progress.
7. Satisfied with our progress, we played basketball for a while.
8. By the end of the afternoon, we had finished our math.
9. After helping with the dishes, I watched television.
10. Tired from my studies, I went to bed.

Using Commas with Interrupters, EXERCISE A

1. Brooks, winner of a Pulitzer prize, grew up in Chicago.
2. She has served, moreover, as a consultant to the Library of Congress.
3. Her poetry, which draws from African-American experiences, can be harsh and yet moving.
4. A number of poets, I believe, had their roots in Chicago.
5. Carl Sandburg, who wrote the poem "Chicago," is one of the most famous.

Using Commas with Interrupters, EXERCISE B

1. The meal, in general, was quite delicious.
2. The bread, an old family recipe, contains two packages of yeast.
3. It rose, as you can imagine, over the edges of the pan.
4. We were, meanwhile, chopping vegetables for the goulash.
5. You wonder, I suppose, about the seasoning in the goulash.
6. Correct
7. Those black specks, which look like pepper, may be something else.
8. The bread, on the other hand, seems perfect.
9. Its crust, for example, is a golden brown.
10. We bought the dessert, an apple cobbler, at the bakery.

Using Commas with Interrupters, EXERCISE C

Answers will vary slightly; possible answers are given.

1. The meal, to tell the truth, was pretty simple.
2. My specialty, hamburgers, begins with a good quality of meat.
3. Sometimes, if I have the time, I will add chopped onions to the meat.
4. The salad, torn lettuce and raw vegetables, doesn't take long to make.
5. Be sure, of course, to clean up afterward!

Using Commas in Series, EXERCISE A
1. An architect designs buildings, selects materials, and supervises construction.
2. The architect should consider where the structure will be built, what the purpose of the building will be, and how much the construction will cost.
3. Wright's designs combine rough stone, stained glass, and natural wood.
4. Admirers find his designs exciting, bold, and original.
5. Tourists see his work at the Guggenheim Museum, Taliesin West, and Fallingwater.

Using Commas in Series, EXERCISE B
1. Tired, dirty, and hungry, the hikers arrived at their campsite.
2. The Spanish test covered grammar, poetry, and vocabulary.
3. We walked over the bridge, through the field, and around the hill.
4. The breakfast specials were fried eggs, oatmeal, and griddle cakes.
5. When it is your turn, Jan, throw the dice, move your piece on the board, read the instructions on the card, and do as the card says.

Using Commas in Series, EXERCISE C
Answers will vary; possible answers are given.
1. He, she, and I counted all our money.
2. We had looked through Jim's pockets, under my mattress, and in Kelly's purse.
3. We didn't know which movie was showing, how we were going, or who was going with us.
4. We were all tired, hungry, and bored.
5. We ate rapidly, caught the bus, and ran to the theater.

Using Commas with Direct Quotations, EXERCISE A
1. Marnie asked, "Do you think we'll see the monster?"
2. "It first appeared in the sixth century," the guide claimed.
3. "According to legend," he continued, "St. Columba was the first to see it."
4. "Well," Marnie commented, "scientists haven't been able to find the creature."
5. Marnie suddenly shouted, "Something is stirring up the water!"

Using Commas with Direct Quotations, EXERCISE B
1. "Many years ago," she began, "there was no daylight in the land."
2. "Where can we get light?" the Inuit asked.
3. The Crow said that daylight could be found in the far north.
4. "Please fly there and bring us some daylight," the chief pleaded.
5. Correct
6. "I can become a piece of dust," he thought, "and hide in a baby's ear."
7. "Ask for some daylight to play with," Crow whispered to the baby.
8. "Father," the baby asked, "may I have a ball of daylight to play with?"
9. "Of course," replied his father.
10. Crow decided, "I'll resume my bird shape now, snatch the ball with my beak, and carry it home!"

Using Commas with Direct Quotations, EXERCISE C
Answers may vary slightly; possible answers are given.
1. Mom asks, "How far is it to Gatlinburg?"
2. My sister Jane wonders, "When are we going to eat?"
3. Dad comments, "The highest point in the park is Clingman's Dome."
4. Suddenly Dad exclaims, "The car needs gas!"
5. Jane glumly remarks, "There are no service stations in the park."

Other Uses of Commas, EXERCISE A

1. September 20, 1953
2. Los Angeles, CA 90038
3. Very truly yours,
4. 3,356 kilometers
5. $71,590.60
6. 14,583 employees
7. Dear Mr. and Mrs. Tranh,
8. 56,650 acres
9. 1,515,263 miles
10. 1,920,000 square feet

Other Uses of Commas, EXERCISE B

1. Dear Ramona,
2. On June 11, 1994, I visited the Empire State Building.
3. It is 1,250 feet tall, 100 feet shorter than the World Trade Center.
4. The building weighs 365,000 tons.
5. Write me at 57 Bank Street, New York, New York 10014.

Other Uses of Commas, EXERCISE C

Dear Rosa,

We got back from Disney World yesterday! Did you know that it covers more than 27,400 acres? When Walt Disney died on December 15, 1966, he had just begun building his "Magic Kingdom" in Orlando. Our vacation cost $1,236.15 this year.

Luisa wrote me last week. Her mom loves her new job. The company she works for has 17,500 employees. Luisa's new address is 392 First Avenue, Glencoe, IL 60022. Luisa's sixteenth birthday is on July 1, 1994. Don't forget!

Your friend,
Graciela

Using Comma Sense, EXERCISE A

1. The car is in the driveway.
2. The funny sound is near the curb.
3. The car is near the curb.
4. Pedro finishes the drink with a gulp.

Using Comma Sense, EXERCISE B

1. When Peter disappeared for an hour, no one noticed.
2. When Peter disappeared, for an hour no one noticed.
3. After we searched under the truck in the barn, we finally found him.
4. After we searched under the truck, in the barn we finally found him.

Using Comma Sense, EXERCISE C

Because of the bad weather everywhere in the North, many people are taking vacations. When Jasmine called us from Pennsylvania, there was a cry of surprise. Throwing some clothes into a suitcase, with the dog she jumped into her car. Before we even thought, she was heading south!

Commonly Confused or Misused Words

Commonly Confused or Misused Words I, EXERCISE A
1. already
2. lend
3. complement
4. advice
5. effect

Commonly Confused or Misused Words I, EXERCISE B
1. incorrect, Except
2. incorrect, Besides
3. incorrect, a lot
4. correct
5. incorrect, all right

Commonly Confused or Misused Words I, EXERCISE C
1. Correct
2. I wanted to go very <u>badly</u>.
3. <u>Fewer</u> kids were going than originally had signed up for the trip.
4. Our teacher <u>accepted</u> an invitation to eat lunch with the museum director.
5. He said that it was quite a <u>compliment</u> to our class.

Commonly Confused or Misused Words II, EXERCISE A
1. hear
2. piece
3. as if
4. principal
5. past

Commonly Confused or Misused Words II, EXERCISE B
1. <u>It's</u> time to sign up for a dog-training class.
2. My puppy is not doing <u>well</u> at home.
3. Correct
4. I managed to teach him to <u>lie</u> down on command.
5. However, I cannot allow him to run <u>loose</u> outside.

Commonly Confused or Misused Words II, EXERCISE C
Answers will vary; possible answers are given.
1. I found a <u>loose</u> sock in the dryer./I always <u>lose</u> socks in the dryer.
2. I feel <u>good</u> about my chances./I did <u>well</u> on the exam.
3. Did you <u>hear</u> about the accident?/<u>Here</u> is the newspaper account.
4. Help me <u>lay</u> the cloth on the table./I will <u>lie</u> down before dinner.
5. Time <u>passed</u> slowly./She lived in the <u>past</u>.
6. Mr. Baines is our school <u>principal</u>./He comes up with a new rule or <u>principle</u> each day.
7. I hope for <u>peace</u> in the world./Give me a <u>piece</u> of paper.
8. The horse bowed <u>its</u> neck./<u>It's</u> quite a docile animal.
9. You can <u>learn</u> Spanish./I could <u>teach</u> you in a month.
10. You are dressed <u>as if</u> it were still summer./You are dressed <u>like</u> a Floridian.

Commonly Confused or Misused Words III, EXERCISE A

1. stationery
2. whose
3. whether
4. sit
5. really

Commonly Confused or Misused Words III, EXERCISE B

1. A <u>stationary</u> front is resting directly overhead.
2. Correct
3. <u>You're</u> bound to hear people ask, "Hot enough for you?"
4. Is there any question more annoying <u>than</u> that?
5. Ignore them, <u>regardless</u> of their persistence.

Commonly Confused or Misused Words III, EXERCISE C

Answers will vary; possible answers are given.

1. Is that a <u>real</u> diamond?/Are you <u>really</u> going to get married?
2. We <u>set</u> the table./The family will <u>sit</u> down.
3. When I am <u>stationary</u> all day, I get stiff./Working in a <u>stationery</u> store gives little time for exercise.
4. I love cold <u>weather</u>./I don't care <u>whether</u> we have snow or sunshine.
5. The shoes were <u>too</u> expensive./We bought <u>two</u> pairs.
6. He likes chocolate better <u>than</u> vanilla./<u>Then</u> he will order chocolate mousse.
7. Did you hear <u>their</u> commercial?/<u>There</u> it is again.
8. Do gentlemen still <u>raise</u> their hats?/Do they <u>rise</u> from their chairs?
9. I have been calling <u>your</u> house for hours./<u>You're</u> always on the phone.
10. <u>Who</u> ordered the pizza?/To <u>whom</u> shall I give the bill?

Conjunctions

Identifying and Using Coordinating Conjunctions, EXERCISE A

1. and
2. or
3. or
4. and
5. yet

Identifying and Using Coordinating Conjunctions, EXERCISE B

Some answers may vary slightly; possible answers are given.

1. Are those birds crows <u>or</u> wrens?
2. Artie <u>and</u> Fran finished the race, tired <u>but</u> proud.
3. I must leave soon, <u>so</u> you'll have to take over.
4. We pushed <u>and</u> prodded the cow, <u>yet</u> it would not move.
5. Derek jumped <u>and</u> shuddered, <u>for</u> the lightning had startled him.

Identifying and Using Coordinating Conjunctions, EXERCISE C
Answers will vary; possible answers are given.
1. We could eat <u>and</u> watch the sunset on the beach <u>or</u> from our hotel.
2. The sand along one beach is black <u>yet</u> soft, <u>so</u> let's go there.
3. Surfing <u>and</u> diving would be a challenge, <u>for</u> I have never done either.
4. Coconuts <u>or</u> pineapples sound tasty—<u>but</u> I don't know about poi!
5. Unfortunately, I don't have enough money, <u>nor</u> would my parents let me go on such a vacation without them.

Identifying and Using Correlative Conjunction, EXERCISE A
1. Both . . . and
2. either . . . or
3. neither . . . nor
4. not only . . . but also
5. both . . . and

Identifying and Using Correlative Conjunctions, EXERCISE B
Some answers may vary slightly; possible answers are given.
1. The crocodile is <u>neither</u> as heavy <u>nor</u> as slow as the alligator.
2. Both reptiles are well suited <u>not only</u> for walking <u>but also</u> for swimming.
3. However, <u>neither</u> the alligator <u>nor</u> the crocodile walks as much as it swims.
4. Since <u>both</u> their eyes <u>and</u> their nostrils are higher than the rest of their heads, both beasts can watch for prey while floating in the water.
5. Would you dare to get close to <u>either</u> an alligator <u>or</u> a crocodile?

Identifying and Using Correlative Conjunctions, EXERCISE C
Answers will vary; possible answers are given.
1. We will <u>either</u> fly <u>or</u> drive to California.
2. <u>Neither</u> Marianne <u>nor</u> Juliette came to visit me.
3. I <u>not only</u> played my radio <u>but also</u> did my homework.
4. Good writing will be <u>both</u> concise <u>and</u> clear.
5. We told <u>either</u> Phil <u>or</u> Holly about the movie.
6. <u>Both</u> nails <u>and</u> a hammer are in the toolbox.
7. Did the children <u>not only</u> sing <u>but also</u> dance?
8. <u>Either</u> a new car <u>or</u> a new home can be expensive.
9. The music was <u>neither</u> very sweet <u>nor</u> very well played.
10. <u>Both</u> archaeology <u>and</u> physics really interest me.

Identifying and Using Subordinating Conjunctions, EXERCISE A
1. because
2. Since
3. although
4. Wherever
5. If

Identifying and Using Subordinating Conjunctions, EXERCISE B

Answers may vary slightly; possible answers are given.

1. <u>Once</u> I got used to the routine, I began to enjoy the work.
2. <u>Although</u> my schedule varies, I try to walk at least three dogs a day.
3. We make quite a picture <u>as</u> we walk along.
4. Usually, the dogs take me <u>where</u> they want to walk.
5. The dogs are nice <u>when</u> they behave themselves.
6. <u>Since</u> I started this job, I've made about thirty dollars.
7. <u>If</u> all goes well, I'll reach my goal in another five or six weeks.
8. I'll be able to go shopping <u>because</u> I've earned the cash.
9. <u>After</u> I finish the job, but <u>before</u> I spend my money, I'll consider my options.
10. <u>When</u> I earn money, I try to save part of it.

Identifying and Using Subordinating Conjunctions, EXERCISE C

Answers may vary slightly; possible answers are given. Subordinating conjunctions are underlined.

1. d <u>When</u> I had a problem last week, I couldn't think of a solution.
2. a <u>Although</u> I was shy about asking, I finally went to my sister.
3. b She's easy to talk to <u>because</u> she's a good listener.
4. e <u>As</u> I talked to her, she asked me some questions.
5. c The issues became clear <u>after</u> we spoke about them.

Identifying and Using Conjunctive Adverbs, EXERCISE A

1. however
2. furthermore
3. therefore
4. also
5. nevertheless

Identifying and Using Conjunctive Adverbs, EXERCISE B

Answers may vary; possible answers are given.

1. Australia has beautiful beaches; <u>however,</u> it also has scorching deserts.
2. Ayers Rock is in the middle of one desert; <u>thus,</u> tourists must brave the heat to visit it.
3. Western Australia is mostly desert; <u>nevertheless,</u> sheep graze there.
4. Kangaroos are a delight to tourists; koalas <u>also</u> are popular.
5. Despite its cuddly image, the koala has sharp, curved claws; <u>consequently,</u> tourists should be careful around these Australian "teddy bears."

Identifying and Using Conjunctive Adverbs, EXERCISE C

Answers may vary; possible answers are given

1. She needed to write faster; <u>therefore,</u> Sue decided to learn word processing.
2. She had used a computer; <u>accordingly,</u> she read the manual.
3. The instructions seemed clear; <u>nevertheless,</u> she couldn't get the machine to double-space.
4. Sue hit the *I* key by itself; she <u>also</u> pressed it and *Control* at the same time.
5. The combination opened the *Help* function; <u>consequently,</u> Sue found the instructions she needed.

Using Conjunctions Correctly, EXERCISE A

1. or (correct)
2. because (incorrect)
3. But (incorrect)
4. or (correct)
5. like (incorrect)

Using Conjunctions Correctly, EXERCISE B

Answers will vary; possible answers are given

1. Sometimes, <u>however</u>, a definition may be difficult to understand.
2. The dictionary may use the word in a sentence. (Delete <u>So</u>)
3. <u>Using a word</u> in a sentence often makes its meaning clearer.
4. You might consider a thesaurus, <u>as</u> many students do.
5. It's <u>also</u> fun just to skim the pages of a dictionary or a thesaurus.

Using Conjunctions Correctly, EXERCISE C

Answers will vary; possible answers are given.

   Daisy had to take her cats to the veterinarian. Bibs and Thomas needed vaccinations, <u>and</u> Hartley needed vitamins. Daisy called the three, but they seemed to know Daisy's purpose. (Delete <u>So</u>) The two males hid under the bed, <u>but</u> Bibs couldn't find a hiding place. She raced around the house <u>as if</u> she were a miniature tornado. Daisy finally caught her <u>because</u> Bibs ran into a corner. Then Daisy went after the other two. She could wear herself out getting under the bed, <u>or</u> she could outwit them. Daisy coaxed Thomas out with a cat treat. Hartley, <u>however,</u> stayed where he was, <u>as if</u> he knew that Daisy was trying to trick him. (Delete <u>So</u>) As she walked to the front door, Daisy talked about the good time that the others would have. (Delete <u>And</u>) Hartley, fooled by the sound of her voice, was at the front door before Daisy got there.

Developing Your Style: Conjunctions, EXERCISE A

Some answers may vary; possible answers are given.

1. also; addition
2. consequently; cause/effect
3. when; time
4. furthermore; addition
5. therefore; cause/effect
6. because; cause/effect
7. while; time
8. however; contradiction
9. after; time
10. but; contradiction

Developing Your Style: Conjunctions, EXERCISE B

1. <u>As it got darker, the girls</u> turned back toward camp.
2. They walked <u>faster; consequently, they</u> sighted camp as darkness fell.
3. <u>Because the fire had been out for many hours,</u> the girls built a new one.
4. <u>Once the fire crackled merrily, the girls</u> enjoyed its light and warmth.
5. The firelight was soon <u>gone; however, the dark night</u> seemed friendly.

Developing Your Style: Conjunctions, EXERCISE C

Some answers may vary slightly; possible answers are given.

1. The lawn is <u>brown because there has been</u> a water shortage.
2. It hasn't <u>rained; consequently, the level</u> at the reservoir is down.
3. People can't fill their swimming <u>pools, either, but nobody</u> has complained.
4. Water has been <u>rationed; nevertheless,</u> many continue to waste water.
5. <u>As I watch water running down the street, the waste</u> upsets me.

Contractions

Identifying and Forming Contractions, EXERCISE A

1. is not
2. we will/ we shall
3. we had/ we would
4. they have
5. does not
6. I am
7. will not
8. that is
9. you are
10. Mary is/ Mary has

Identifying and Forming Contractions EXERCISE B

1. hasn't
2. could've, wasn't
3. Where's
4. didn't, they're
5. They'll

Identifying and Forming Contractions, EXERCISE C

1. isn't
2. can't
3. they'll
4. I'm, don't
5. We're
6. I'll
7. Where's
8. hasn't
9. It's
10. should've

Distinguishing Between Possessive Pronouns and Contractions, EXERCISE A

1. c
2. e
3. d
4. a
5. b

Distinguishing Between Possessive Pronouns and Contractions, EXERCISE B

1. Your
2. Theirs
3. They're, their
4. who's
5. It's

Distinguishing Between Possessive Pronouns and Contractions, EXERCISE C

1. <u>Whose</u> dog is this?
2. Is this <u>your</u> dog?
3. Correct
4. I can tell because I recognize <u>its</u> markings.
5. <u>Their</u> house is three blocks away.
6. You're certain to get a reward for finding <u>their</u> dog.
7. Look, <u>there's</u> Mrs. Gordon!
8. She says that the dog isn't <u>theirs</u>!
9. Correct
10. If you can't find the owners, maybe it's <u>your</u> dog now!

Dashes

Using Dashes Correctly, EXERCISE A

1. Wells wrote numerous books—nearly one hundred, in fact.
2. Many of his books—for example, *The Time Machine*—became science-fiction classics.
3. Wells's future world has two social classes—the Morlocks and the Eloi.
4. The Morlocks—they live underground—do all the work.
5. The Eloi—they live on the earth's surface—simply enjoy life.

Using Dashes Correctly, EXERCISE B

1. Texarkana, Texas—its name comes from the letters of three adjoining states—was the hometown of Scott Joplin.
2. Correct
3. Ragtime music—its name comes from the expression "ragged time"—had its origins in the complex rhythms of African music.
4. In 1976 Joplin's ragtime opera won an award—the Pulitzer Prize!
5. Had he been alive, he might have started to say, "Well, it's about ti—."

Using Dashes Correctly, EXERCISE C

Answers will vary; possible answers are given.

1. Duke Ellington and Scott Joplin played the same type of instrument—the piano.
2. Jazz—no one is sure where the actual name came from—developed from the music of enslaved Africans.

Dates

Writing Dates Correctly, EXERCISE A

1. <u>Tuesday</u>, March 16
2. September 11<u>,</u> 1550
3. Correct
4. the 1920<u>'</u>s
5. Correct
6. Correct
7. <u>Labor Day</u>
8. Correct
9. the <u>F</u>ourth of July
10. <u>Friday</u><u>,</u> <u>May</u> 27<u>,</u> 1994

Writing Dates Correctly, EXERCISE B

1. My little brother was born the day after <u>Christmas</u>.
2. That made <u>December 26, 1986,</u> a very important day in our house.
3. Last year, Dad's birthday came on a <u>Saturday</u>; Grandpa's birthday fell on the <u>Friday</u> before.
4. The two of them had a big party with music from the 1940's—a great way to start the <u>winter</u>!
5. I think <u>Monday</u> is the best day for a holiday!

Writing Dates Correctly, EXERCISE C

Answers will vary; possible answers are given.

1. My best friend's birthday is <u>September 21, 1982</u>.
2. When <u>summer</u> comes, we can go to the beach!
3. My favorite holiday is <u>New Year's Eve</u>; this year, it falls on a <u>Tuesday</u>.
4. The music that I like best comes from the <u>1960's</u>.
5. On <u>July 4, 1776</u>, the Declaration of Independence was signed.

Double Negatives

Avoiding Double Negatives, EXERCISE A

1. Carlene <u>didn't get any straws</u> for us. OR Carlene <u>got no straws</u> for us.
2. I <u>have never seen</u> a mountain range, have you? OR I <u>haven't ever seen</u> a mountain range, have you?
3. Judy <u>never wrote us anything</u> about her engagement. OR Judy <u>wrote us nothing</u> about her engagement.
4. The President <u>hadn't answered any</u> of the questions. OR The President <u>had answered none</u> of the questions.
5. I <u>never told anybody</u> about the hiding place. OR I <u>told nobody</u> about the hiding place.

Avoiding Double Negatives, EXERCISE B

1. These railroad tracks <u>have had no use</u> in years. OR These railroad tracks <u>haven't had any use</u> in years.
2. Correct
3. Correct
4. His shoulder pads <u>didn't help</u> on that tackle. OR His shoulder pads <u>hardly helped</u> on that tackle.
5. My favorite red shoes <u>haven't got any marks</u> on them. OR My favorite red shoes <u>have got no marks</u> on them.

Avoiding Double Negatives, EXERCISE C

Answers will vary; possible answers are given.

1. By May 20, scarcely <u>any</u> plants or shrubs had bloomed.
2. We <u>didn't</u> see green leaves on the trees anywhere.
3. <u>Nothing</u> about this springtime weather seemed normal.
4. Farmers couldn't plant <u>any</u> crops until the beginning of June.
5. They had <u>barely</u> enough time to plant before summer arrived.

Ellipses

Using Ellipsis Points Correctly, EXERCISE A
1. omission within a sentence
2. pause
3. omission between sentences
4. omission within a sentence

Using Ellipsis Points Correctly, EXERCISE B
1. "The more we love . . . the less we flatter," Molière once wrote.
2. I am honored . . . thrilled to be here.
3. Correct
4. As my friend said, "I am humble. . . .This is great."

Using Ellipsis Points Correctly, EXERCISE C
1. The period . . . is a single dot.
2. A colon is a pair of dots. . . . It is used in front of lists.
3. The ellipsis . . . what can I say about it?
4. It . . . well . . . it is rarely used.

Exclamation Points

Using Exclamation Points Correctly, EXERCISE A
1. What an amazing plot it had!
2. I couldn't believe it when the house caught on fire!
3. Whew! What a relief that Cara survived!
4. Wow! What an ending!
5. "Fire! Fire!" they exclaimed hurriedly.

Using Exclamation Points Correctly, EXERCISE B
1. We're trying to decide what to do. I've got it!
2. We'll build a snow-dinosaur. What a blast!
3. Whew! This is hard work.
4. How great it will look when it's finished!
5. It's finished at last. Hooray!

Using Exclamation Points Correctly, EXERCISE C
Some answers may vary; possible answers are given.

DAD:	The smoke alarm? Get out of the house—now!
MANNY:	You, too, Dad! I can smell the smoke!
DAD:	Ready, Son? Let's run for it!
MANNY:	Whew! We made it!
DAD:	I'm so glad we're both out! Let's get to our neighbor's phone.

Gender

Using Gender References Correctly, EXERCISE A
1. she
2. it
3. its
4. his
5. his or her

Using Gender References Correctly, EXERCISE B
1. masculine and feminine, he or she
2. neuter, it
3. neuter, it
4. masculine, he
5. masculine, his
6. neuter, it
7. masculine, him
8. masculine, He
9. masculine and feminine, he or she
10. masculine and feminine, him or her

Using Gender References Correctly, EXERCISE C
    You probably think that Mother Goose was not real, but many scholars believe that <u>she</u> actually lived. However, each has <u>his or her</u> own opinion of exactly who <u>he or she</u> thinks Mother Goose really was. Some claim that she was the Queen of Sheba; others that she was Queen Bertha, the wife of the famous medieval king Charlemagne. Some scholars argue that they know she was Elizabeth Goose of colonial Boston. No one can prove <u>his or her</u> theory, but everyone likes to think that <u>his or her</u> opinion is right.

Hyphens

Using Hyphens Correctly, EXERCISE A
1. the ex-President
2. a well-known singer
3. pro-British forces
4. Correct
5. Ask the hotel mana-
   ger to come inside.
6. two-thirds vote
7. self-defense
8. Correct
9. my sister-in-law
10. Correct

Using Hyphens Correctly, EXERCISE B
1. His report seemed long-winded to us./re-port
2. The mayor-elect was seated in the audience./seat-ed
3. A well-liked comedian introduced the acts./intro-duced
4. The theme was a re-creation of our town's founding./found-ing
5. Forty-five children performed in the show./chil-dren
6. One high-spirited child read a poem./high-spirited
7. People in pre-Civil War dress pranced around./Peo-ple
8. Did you grumble that the show seemed un-American?/grum-ble
9. Our great-aunt should see this depiction!/great-aunt
10. To call this unpatriotic is a half-baked notion./no-tion

Using Hyphens Correctly, EXERCISE C
Hyphenated words at the ends of lines may vary; possible hyphenations are given.

　　Grandma claims to be all-knowing when it comes to diet and nutrition. She has a post-Depression mentality about the need to eat one-quarter cup of carrots a day. If it were up to her, we'd eat ninety-two cups of carrots each year! I don't mean it as a put-down, but I honestly think that Grandma behaves as though she's my mother-in-law.

Nouns

Identifying and Using Common and Proper Nouns, EXERCISE A
1. proper
2. common
3. proper
4. proper
5. common
6. proper
7. common
8. proper
9. common
10. proper

Identifying and Using Common and Proper Nouns, EXERCISE B
Answers will vary; possible answers are given.
1. C, Rio Grande
2. P, car
3. C, Liberty Street
4. P, city
5. C, James Madison
6. P, continent
7. C, Jackie Robinson
8. C, "Happy Birthday"
9. P, holiday
10. P, country

Identifying and Using Common and Proper Nouns, EXERCISE C

Answers will vary; possible answers are given.

1. Alaska, P; state, C; <u>Swtizerland</u> is a beautiful <u>country</u>.
2. Ned, P; sweaters, C; socks, C; cashier, C; <u>Archie</u> took two <u>shirts</u> and some <u>belts</u> to the <u>clerk</u>.
3. Labor Day, P; family, C; Indian Island Park, P; On <u>Memorial Day</u>, the <u>troop</u> camped at <u>Highland Acres</u>.
4. announcement, C; Wednesday, P; excitement, C; The <u>alert</u> on <u>Tuesday</u> was met with great <u>panic</u>.
5. United Nations, P; role, C; fight, C; hunger, C; The <u>World Health Organization</u> plays an active <u>part</u> in the <u>struggle</u> against <u>disease</u>.
6. Annette, P; cousin, C; "Yankee Doodle Dandy," P; Independence Day, P; <u>Wayne</u>, my <u>brother</u> sings "<u>Jingle Bells</u>" every <u>Christmas Eve</u>.

Identifying and Using Collective Nouns, EXERCISE A

1. herd
2. faculty
3. collection
4. mob
5. congress
6. club
7. audience
8. pack
9. squadron
10. group

Identifying and Using Collective Nouns, EXERCISE B

1. faculty
2. committee
3. crowd
4. community
5. squad
6. team
7. throng
8. band
9. audience
10. flock

Identifying and Using Collective Nouns, EXERCISE C

Answers will vary; possible answers are given.

1. The campers were startled by a <u>flock</u> of Canadian geese.
2. The <u>quartet</u> presented a medley of Civil War songs.
3. The <u>audience</u> has been applauding for five minutes!
4. What a large <u>herd</u> of cows is grazing on the hillside!
5. In the United States, <u>Congress</u> has the power to enact laws.
6. Does the <u>squad</u> have practice today?
7. The police ordered the angry <u>mob</u> to disperse.
8. The <u>Drama Club</u> is rehearsing its spring play.
9. The leader of our <u>troop</u> collected money from the annual cookie sale.
10. My aunt plays flute in the <u>Boston Philharmonic</u>.

Identifying and Using Concrete and Abstract Nouns, EXERCISE A

1. abstract
2. concrete
3. concrete
4. abstract
5. abstract
6. concrete
7. abstract
8. concrete
9. abstract
10. concrete

11. abstract
12. concrete
13. concrete
14. abstract
15. abstract
16. abstract
17. concrete
18. abstract
19. concrete
20. abstract

Identifying and Using Concrete and Abstract Nouns, EXERCISE B

1. senator
2. smile
3. bed
4. mother
5. tombstone
6. rags
7. medicine
8. snapshot
9. toys
10. book

Identifying and Using Concrete and Abstract Nouns, EXERCISE C

Sentences will vary; possible sentences are given

1. intelligence, abstract; book, concrete; Do you really think that reading that <u>book</u> will increase your <u>intelligence</u>?
2. circus, concrete; happiness, abstract; <u>Happiness</u> gets top billing when the <u>circus</u> comes to town.
3. sorrow, abstract; tree, concrete: According to local legend, a scene of great <u>sorrow</u> occurred beneath that <u>tree</u>.
4. generosity, abstract; toys, concrete: A sackful of <u>toys</u> was evidence of Mrs. Blaine's <u>generosity</u>.
5. patriotism, abstract; flag, concrete; I think that <u>patriotism</u> is a lot more than just standing when the <u>flag</u> passes by.
6. lilacs, concrete; delight, abstract; The Thompsons' porch, decorated with <u>lilacs</u>, was a <u>delight</u> to behold.
7. fear, abstract; monster, concrete; You need have no <u>fear</u> of Coach Buckner, for he's not really the <u>monster</u> he appears.
8. democracy, abstract; president, concrete; Nancy's election as club <u>president</u> was an example of <u>democracy</u> in action.
9. cat, concrete; sleepiness, abstract; Because of her <u>sleepiness</u> my usually alert <u>cat</u> missed that mouse.
10. cousin, concrete; Islam, abstract; Before he got married, my <u>cousin</u> converted to <u>Islam</u>.

Spelling Plural Nouns Correctly, EXERCISE A

1. houses	11. wives
2. mice	12. sisters-in-law
3. foxes	13. tomatoes
4. babies	14. series
5. children	15. crises
6. landladies	16. women
7. bushes	17. knives
8. monkeys	18. beliefs
9. classes	19. duties
10. echoes	20. bacteria

Spelling Plural Nouns Correctly, EXERCISE B

1. oxen
2. boxes
3. brothers-in-law
4. men
5. speeches
6. thieves
7. donkeys
8. sheep
9. teeth
10. pianos

Spelling Plural Nouns Correctly, EXERCISE C

Sentences may vary slightly; possible sentences are given.

1. Please return the library <u>books</u> to the proper <u>shelves</u>.
2. It was hard to tell the <u>heroes</u> from the <u>villains</u>.
3. The <u>cats</u> landed on their <u>feet</u>.
4. <u>Flocks</u> of <u>geese</u> flew overhead.
5. We bought new <u>fish</u> for our <u>aquariums</u>.
6. I'm afraid that the <u>dishes</u> broke when they fell.
7. Please pass the mashed <u>potatoes</u> and the <u>broccoli</u>.
8. Have the <u>leaves</u> turned color yet?
9. They visited large <u>cities</u> on their <u>trips</u>.
10. We studied the <u>journeys</u> of the European <u>explorers</u>.

Developing Your Style: Choosing Specific, Concrete Nouns, EXERCISE A

Related nouns will vary; possible answers are given.

1. ocean, Indian Ocean
2. game, checkers
3. animal, chimpanzee
4. worker, physical therapist
5. politician, Lyndon B. Johnson
6. country, Zaire
7. clothing, jeans
8. vehicle, motorcycle
9. color, turquoise
10. emotion, anger

Developing Your Style: Choosing Specific, Concrete Nouns, EXERCISE B

Answers will vary; possible answers are given.

1. We saw a wonderful <u>violinist</u> at the <u>street fair</u>.
2. Last <u>Christmas</u>, I got a <u>bicycle</u>.
3. The story was about people from <u>Venus</u> who visit Earth in a <u>starship</u>.
4. Is that <u>Uncle Timothy</u> eating <u>spaghetti</u>?
5. The technician fixed our <u>washing machine</u> with a <u>wrench</u>.

Developing Your Style: Choosing Specific, Concrete Nouns, EXERCISE C

Answers will vary; possible answers are given.

My <u>cousins</u> live on a farm, and I can hardly wait to visit each year. <u>Brad</u> and I climb into the back seat of our <u>minivan</u> as my <u>mother</u> sits impatiently behind the wheel. Then we're off, zooming past <u>mountain peaks</u> and <u>maple trees</u> as we travel across the <u>country</u>. Sometimes we play "<u>Twenty Questions</u>," as we travel. We know we've arrived when we hear the <u>squawking</u> of <u>chickens</u> from the barn, which is painted <u>red</u>. We unload our <u>suitcases</u> and take them inside. In the evening, <u>Aunt Flora</u> gives us lots of <u>chicken</u> and <u>corn</u> to eat and <u>lemonade</u> to drink. Then we listen to <u>Uncle Roy</u> play "<u>Red River Valley</u>" on the <u>harmonica</u>, and my heart is filled with <u>delight</u>.

Numerals

Ways of Writing Cardinals and Ordinals, EXERCISE A

1. At that time, school began at <u>eight</u> o'clock.
2. The children attended school <u>six</u> days a week.
3. On the <u>seventh</u> day, they often worked in the fields.
4. <u>Forty-five</u> children learned in a single room.
5. When they reached <u>ninth</u> grade, they graduated.

Ways of Writing Cardinals and Ordinals, EXERCISE B

1. eight hundred sixty, cardinal
2. 27, cardinal
3. forty-third, ordinal
4. two hundred twelve, cardinal
5. seven hundred tenth, ordinal
6. thirty-eight, cardinal
7. ninety-second, ordinal
8. one thousand five hundred, cardinal
9. 51st, ordinal
10. three thousand four hundred nine, cardinal

Ways of Writing Cardinals and Ordinals, EXERCISE C

1. My aunt showed me <u>five</u> old photographs.
2. <u>Three</u> of them showed my parents.
3. In the <u>third</u> photograph, I was a baby.
4. Correct
5. We went into the attic around <u>seven</u> o'clock.
6. Correct
7. She told me stories of <u>three hundred</u> different relatives.
8. Correct
9. <u>Eighteen</u> of my relatives lived on a farm.
10. The <u>nineteenth</u> member of that family worked on Wall Street.

Using Numerals Correctly, EXERCISE A

1. <u>1:30</u> A.M.
2. <u>1611</u>
3. A. The Land of Oz
    <u>1.</u> South
    <u>2.</u> North
4. <u>1200</u> Main Street
5. I sold <u>5</u> bow ties, <u>29</u> neckties, and <u>45</u> hair ribbons.

Using Numerals Correctly, EXERCISE B

Report of March 12, 1994

I.   Missing animals
A. Collie from <u>14</u> Jazz Street
B. Beagles from <u>900</u> Creole Lane
  <u>1.</u> Called in at <u>10</u> A.M.
  <u>2.</u> Called in at <u>3</u> P.M.
II.   Found animals
A. Report on <u>2</u> terriers and 120 cats
B. Collie from Jazz Street found at <u>12</u> Pine Place

Using Numerals Correctly, EXERCISE C

<u>18</u> Stewart Avenue
Apartment <u>10</u>-B
June 26, <u>1995</u>

Dear Jack,

I hope you can attend our Independence Day Party on Saturday from <u>3:00</u> P.M. till evening. We had a great time in 1993, and I'm sure this party will be <u>five</u> times better. We plan to (1) eat barbecued chicken, (2) play softball, and <u>(3)</u> dance to the music of a seven-piece band. Of course we will also have a display of <u>85</u> zillion fireworks! I've invited <u>5</u> relatives, <u>16</u> of my closest friends, and around 250 neighbors!

Your friend,

Diana

Parentheses

Using Parentheses Correctly, EXERCISE A

1. There are two things I like about school: (1) vocational training and (2) playing basketball in gym class.
2. Most of the kids I know feel the same way about school as I do. (I'm obviously not talking about "Brains" Applegate, the class genius.)
3. Our gym teacher (a man who obviously doesn't understand kids) says that I have to improve my skills.
4. Still, when we moved to this town (only a month ago, come to think of it), I couldn't really play basketball, and I didn't know anything about woodworking.

Using Parentheses Correctly, EXERCISE B
1. The Greek god Apollo (the son of Zeus and Leto) is often depicted driving a chariot across the sky.
2. Poseidon (the god of the sea) is usually shown wearing a crown, carrying a trident, and riding in a chariot drawn by dolphins.
3. Aphrodite (known to the Romans as Venus) was said to have risen from the sea.
4. Some people think (although I can't understand why) that studying mythology is boring.

Using Parentheses Correctly, EXERCISE C
1. Watching and feeding birds (something I've enjoyed doing for years) is a wonderful hobby.
2. Many birds (pigeons and sparrows, for example) are commonly found in urban areas.
3. In about 1850, the house sparrow was first introduced to North America. (It was in Brooklyn, New York, to be exact.)
4. If you decide to feed the birds (and it really is a lot of fun), you should continue feeding them throughout the winter and into the early spring.

Periods

Using Periods at the Ends of Sentences and Direct Quotations, EXERCISE A
1. Kyle said, "Maybe you should think about a performance poem."
2. As the name suggests, a performance poet is also an actor."
3. Some performance poets use live jazz, strobe lights, or even alarm clocks as they present their work.
4. "I'll do it," Raynell agreed. "Later, though, I want you to help me rehearse."
5. "First, I must read to my little sister," Kyle noted.

Using Periods at the Ends of Sentences and Direct Quotations, EXERCISE B
1. One of Emerson's best-known poems is "Concord Hymn."
2. It was written for the dedication of a memorial in Concord, Massachusetts.
3. Poems for special occasions are called, naturally, "occasional poetry."
4. On April 19, 1775, colonial farmers at Concord battled British soldiers.
5. Their clash signaled the "official" beginning of the Revolutionary War.
6. Emerson called it "the shot heard 'round the world."
7. In 1837, a monument was erected at the site; it was dedicated on July Fourth.
8. "Concord Hymn" was sung to a hymn tune known as "Old Hundredth."
9. "That tune is still used in churches today."
10. "It is not uncommon for one hymn tune to be used for several hymns," she added.

Using Periods at the Ends of Sentences and Direct Quotations, EXERCISE C
1. In music class, Mr. Charles explained that all drums are beaten. "Well, he noted, "there is one exception—the friction drum." He showed us a picture of a drum with a hole through its skin. Then he said, "By pulling a string or stick through the hole, the musician produces the desired sound." Mr. Charles also told us that the "talking drums" of Africa help people communicate.

2. Mr. Charles then said, "Let's take a closer look at drums in orchestras." He explained that every orchestra includes a set of kettledrums. "Of course," he explained, "you may know kettledrums by their Italian name—timpani." Mr. Charles added, "Some 'orchestras' in Asia consist entirely of different kinds of drums. The drums, which are lacquered, are beautiful to see as well as hear."

Other Uses of Periods, EXERCISE A
1. Dr. Dolores E. Hernandez
2. B. G. Singh, Ph.D.
3. Prof. J. R. R. Tolkien
4. the Rev. Mary T. Jefferson
5. $4.70
6. 16.5
7. 1.65
8. $20.22
9. $222.00
10. 38.083

Other Uses of Periods, EXERCISE B
1. Half of seven dollars is $3.50, isn't it?
2. In 1867, William H. Seward arranged the purchase of Alaska.
3. The memorial service was arranged by Capt. Ron Hayes and M. R. Bryant.
4. At a height of 1.40 meters, the bookcase was just right for Hassan's room.
5. *The War of the Worlds* was written by H. G. Wells, not Robert A. Heinlein.

Other Uses of Periods, EXERCISE C
1. *The Way to Rainy Mountain*, by N. Scott Momaday, mixes history and legend.
2. If we split our twelve-dollar debt three ways, we'll each owe $4.00.
3. A 19.8-kilometer race is just a little shorter than twenty kilometers.
4. With those dark glasses, Terri, you look like a CIA spy!
5. I need ten dollars, but I'm a little short; could you lend me $1.15?

Phrases

Identifying and Using Types of Phrases, EXERCISE A
1. prepositional phrase
2. appositive phrase
3. prepositional phrase
4. gerund phrase
5. participial phrase, infinitive phrase
6. appositive phrase, prepositional phrase
7. participial phrase, appositive phrase

Identifying and Using Types of Phrases, EXERCISE B
1. infinitive, adjective; prepositional, adverb
2. participial, adjective
3. gerund, noun; infinitive, noun
4. appositive, noun; prepositional, adverb
5. prepositional, adverb
6. participial, adjective; gerund, noun

Identifying and Using Types of Phrases, EXERCISE C
Sentences will vary; possible sentences are given.
1. infinitive, prepositional; My parents like <u>to go bowling</u> <u>in the evening</u>.
2. gerund; <u>Preparing dinner</u> takes them about half an hour.
3. prepositional; I go to school <u>at eight o'clock</u> every morning.
4. appositive, gerund; My math teacher, <u>Miss Johnson</u>, enjoys <u>playing softball</u>.
5. participial; <u>Having exited the interstate</u>, Mom reaches her job downtown.
6. gerund; Her job involves accounting and <u>interviewing job applicants</u>.
7. appositive, infinitive; My sister, <u>the oldest of three children</u>, is hoping <u>to get better grades this year</u>.

Using Commas with Phrases, EXERCISE A
1. Having handed in our permission slips, we went outside to wait for the bus.
2. Correct
3. At the head of the line, our teacher decided to do a quick head count.
4. After counting several times, she realized that somebody was missing.
5. Correct

Using Commas with Phrases, EXERCISE B
1. Feeling <u>ill is</u> never a pleasant experience.
2. My mother, a very sympathetic person, offered to borrow books for me.
3. Leaving work early, she went straight to the library.
4. The <u>librarian working that afternoon was</u> glad to be of assistance.
5. In the fiction section in the "New Titles" rack, she choose some novels for me.

Using Commas with Phrases, EXERCISE C
   Being an early riser, Samantha decided to read a chapter of her book before breakfast. Turning the pages quietly, she tried not to wake either of her sisters. In her bed across the room, her older sister slept soundly. Miriam, a sophomore in high school, often spent hours on her homework. Their sister Emily also shared the room. Emily, clutching a teddy bear to her chest, was in the third grade. Her teacher, Ms. Douglas, also had been Samantha and Miriam's teacher. The girl holding the book glanced at the clock. Noticing it was late, she carefully marked her place. Just then, Miriam's alarm clock went off, startling the two sleeping sisters.

Using Phrases Correctly, EXERCISE A
Answers will vary; possible answers are given.
1. <u>Eating my dinner last night, I</u> heard a knock at the door.
2. not a sentence
3. The <u>farmer, in her new overalls, milked</u> the cow.
4. not a sentence
5. <u>The monkeys are my favorite attraction when I visit the zoo</u>.

Using Phrases Correctly, EXERCISE B
Answers will vary; possible answers are given.
1. <u>The glass slipped out of his hand while he was drinking lemonade</u>.
2. Standing silently in the doorway, <u>he waited</u>.
3. Divers <u>with strong arms</u> carried the treasure from the sunken ship.
4. To win the game, <u>they strategized</u>.
5. Sitting by the window, <u>she knitted</u>.

Using Phrases Correctly, EXERCISE C
Answers will vary; possible answers are given.

    To be a good photographer <u>requires patience</u>. Books can be very helpful <u>to a person learning the art of photography</u>. Browsing in the photography section in bookstores and libraries <u>is always fun and informative</u>. <u>With their</u> sharp angles and interesting shadows, <u>buildings and other urban structures are subjects that appeal to some photographers</u>. Heading outdoors with my camera, <u>I find that nature</u> is my favorite subject. Bursting with enthusiasm, <u>I notice that</u> flowers and wildlife seem to demand my attention. <u>I am delighted to</u> breathe the fresh, clean air. <u>I once saw a gray squirrel hanging from a tree limb</u>. Unfortunately, while <u>I was</u> focusing my camera, the squirrel ran away. I could have taken a better picture of the squirrel <u>if I had used a tripod</u>.

Developing Your Style: Phrases, EXERCISE A
Answers will vary; possible answers are given.
1. Felicia, <u>my neighbor</u>, wrote a story.
2. The story is about a girl <u>baking cookies</u>.
3. <u>To sell her cookies</u>, the girl goes <u>into the village</u>.
4. <u>Talking to the town baker</u>, she decides <u>to go to school to study baking</u>.
5. <u>While she is in baking school</u>, the girl learns that <u>making delicious cookies</u> is the love of her life.

Developing Your Style: Phrases, EXERCISE B
Answers will vary; possible answers are given.
1. <u>In the beginning</u>, the club met <u>in Caroline's basement</u>.
2. The original members <u>of the club</u> made plans <u>to help the homeless</u>.
3. <u>After a while</u>, new members joined the club.
4. Club members took a trip <u>to the city</u> <u>to see the homeless shelter</u>.
5. <u>During their visit</u>, they learned something <u>about the problem</u>.
6. <u>Volunteering at the shelter</u> was the club's greatest accomplishment.
7. <u>Raising money</u> was another achievement.
8. Some of the members <u>of the club</u> decided <u>to prepare goals</u>.
9. Barry, <u>the club president</u>, and Kenny, <u>the treasurer</u>, thought of a way <u>to raise money</u> for the animal shelter.
10. <u>Helping their children</u>, some parents came up with the idea <u>to have a carnival</u> in the neighborhood.

Developing Your Style: Phrases, EXERCISE C
Answers will vary; possible answers are given.

    <u>Proceeding cautiously</u>, the cat was surprised <u>to see so many people</u>. <u>Before long</u>, she saw a boy <u>wearing a blue jacket</u>. The boy stopped <u>to pet the cat</u>. <u>Sensing her hunger</u>, he took the cat home <u>to give her some food</u>. The cat, <u>uncertain of her new surroundings</u>, explored the house <u>from top to bottom</u>. <u>Stepping outside</u>, she heard a noise <u>from across the street</u>. A large dog, <u>a German shepherd</u>, was barking <u>in the yard</u>. <u>Fearing the dog</u>, the cat ran away. <u>Looking around</u>, she knew she was lost <u>in the big city</u>. <u>After a while</u>, the cat <u>with the white paws</u> found her way home, but she never forgot the boy <u>in the blue jacket</u>.

Possessive Forms

Identifying and Forming Possessive Nouns and Pronouns, EXERCISE A
1. Our, Jack's
2. His, their, friends'
3. My, family's
4. our, my, grandmother's

Identifying and Forming Possessive Nouns and Pronouns, EXERCISE B

1. their
2. guests'
3. ours
4. potato's
5. girl's, mine
6. yours, Michelle's
7. hers, its

Identifying and Forming Possessive Nouns and Pronouns, EXERCISE C

1. The day was <u>ours</u> to spend any way we chose.
2. Correct
3. My two older <u>sisters'</u> boyfriends are twin brothers!
4. The old maple shed <u>its</u> leaves as the weather turned chilly.
5. The children's game ended when <u>their</u> mother called them.

Using Possessive Forms Correctly, EXERCISE A

1. hers
2. whose
3. Sam and Laura's
4. their, they're

Using Possessive Forms Correctly, EXERCISE B

1. incorrect, theirs
2. incorrect, Yours
3. incorrect, There's
4. correct
5. incorrect, Hers
6. correct
7. incorrect, Robert's and Jana's
8. incorrect, their
9. incorrect, its
10. incorrect, ours

Using Possessive Forms Correctly, EXERCISE C

1. I was looking for my coat, but I think I took <u>yours</u> by mistake.
2. Do you know <u>whose</u> turn it is?
3. I'd like to help you, but <u>there's</u> nothing I can do.
4. Correct
5. We gave them a set of <u>his and her</u> towels for their anniversary.
6. That cat looks like <u>ours</u>, but <u>it's</u> really theirs.

Developing Your Style: Streamlining Sentences with Possessive Forms, EXERCISE A

1. Jack London was one of <u>America's most popular writers</u>.
2. <u>Jack London's first home</u> was in Oakland, California.
3. London grew up along <u>that city's rough-and-tumble waterfront</u>.
4. It's no wonder that <u>his first jobs</u> were connected with the sea.
5. He worked as a <u>ship's seaman</u> and in other jobs around the waterfront.

Developing Your Style: Streamlining Sentences with Possessive Forms, EXERCISE B

Answers may vary slightly; possible answers are given.

1. Brian and Ana went to <u>their school's library</u>.
2. <u>Brian and Ana's research project</u> was the history of libraries.
3. About 5,500 years ago, ancient scholars learned to record <u>people's ideas</u>.
4. One of <u>the Egyptians' great discoveries</u> was papyrus, a kind of paper.
5. <u>Today's libaries</u> are simply more advanced storage systems.

Developing Your Style: Streamlining Sentences with Possessive Forms, EXERCISE C
Answers may vary; possible answers are given.

New Guinea's people tell a story to explain the cuckoo's strange behavior. In the story, the forest god's son had died. The god was sad and asked the animals to sing for him. The animals sang until they became tired and stopped. Finally, the only animal who could still be heard was the cuckoo. She sang her song until the god told her to stop. He was so happy with the singing that he told her she would never have to build a nest or care for her eggs again; other birds would do that for her. So to this day, the cuckoo lays eggs in other birds' nests.

Prepositions

Identifying and Using Prepositions and Prepositional Phrases, EXERCISE A
1. of America's most popular novels
2. Through this story; with Jo March
3. like the Alcott family; in many ways
4. on November 29, 1832
5. under a financial burden; for money
6. After *Little Women*; along with *Little Men*

Identifying and Using Prepositions and Prepositional Phrases, EXERCISE B
Answers will vary; possible answers are given.
1. outside; Rachel left her bicycle by the garage.
2. beneath; The rock sank under the waves.
3. Because of; With his bad cold, Emilio can't sing tonight.
4. in front of; Deanna waited quietly near the supermarket.
5. until; Do you mean that the work won't be finished before next week?

Identifying and Using Prepositions and Prepositional Phrases, EXERCISE C
Answers will vary; possible answers are given.
1. The wall behind the bookcase had not been painted. (adjective)
2. If you want a job like mine, you could deliver groceries to Mr. and Mrs. Ramirez. (adjective; adverb)
3. During the snowstorm, we stayed inside, drank cocoa, and played games. (adverb)
4. At 10:00 P.M., a shout suddenly broke the silence. (adverb)
5. The park near Duane's house is a wonderful place to play soccer. (adjective)
6. In spite of our plans, the dinner was ruined when a frying pan on top of the stove caught fire. (adverb; adjective)
7. I'm looking for the driver with the checkered shirt; have you seen him? (adjective)
8. The pails against the back door are the ones we should use. (adjective)

Using Prepositions Correctly, EXERCISE A
1. correct
2. incorrect
3. incorrect
4. incorrect
5. incorrect

Using Prepositions Correctly, EXERCISE B
Answers will vary; possible answers are given.
1. My brother's opinions about what to see first were <u>different from</u> mine.
2. We got separated, and I wasn't sure <u>where he had gone</u>.
3. I finally found him and asked him <u>where he'd been</u>.
4. He showed me an exhibit with fish that were very <u>different from</u> those that you see around here.

Using Prepositions Correctly, EXERCISE C
Answers will vary; possible answers are given.
　　First, we go to the rides. We walk around to choose the best rides. I'm looking for the roller coaster. It's different from any other roller coaster that I've ever ridden. We'll get a map so that we won't get lost.

Developing Your Style: Using Prepositional Phrases in Transitions, EXERCISE A
Some answers may vary; possible answers are given.
1. c
2. d
3. e
4. a
5. b

Developing Your Style: Using Prepositional Phrases in Transitions, EXERCISE B
Answers will vary; possible answers are given.
1. <u>Above the clouds</u>, the jet soared toward Europe.
2. <u>Down the street</u> lives my cousin Valentina.
3. <u>Like a rocket</u>, the rabbit scampered for home.
4. <u>Toward the road</u> the loose ball rolled.
5. I must watch these children <u>until midnight</u>.
6. <u>Together with his sister</u>, Ben apologized to Mrs. Wade.
7. <u>Without hesitation</u>, the fire fighters rushed into the burning building.
8. <u>During the discussion</u>, the opponents accused the mayor of wrongdoing.
9. I have resided in the same town <u>for many years</u>.
10. <u>After the rain</u>, the sun rose high in the sky.

Developing Your Style: Using Prepositional Phrases in Transitions, EXERCISE C
Answers will vary; possible answers are underlined.
　　<u>In the championship soccer game</u>, the Hawks took on the Force. The Hawks scored three goals in the first quarter. <u>At this quick score</u>, the Force became rattled. <u>Across the field</u>, their offensive players moved slowly. <u>Near the goal</u>, the defensive players stood. <u>During a time-out</u>, the coach told his players to forget the score. <u>After the time-out</u>, the team came alive and regained their confidence. <u>For the remainder of the game</u>, the players kept their position. <u>Before halftime</u>, the Force answered with two goals. <u>Throughout the second half</u>, their momentum continued. <u>With only five minutes left</u>, the Force tied the game. <u>At the one-minute mark</u>, they scored the winning goal.

Developing Your Style: Avoiding Prepositional Phrases in Strings, EXERCISE A
1. b
2. a
3. b
4. a

Developing Your Style: Avoiding Prepositional Phrases in Strings, EXERCISE B
Answers will vary; possible answers are given.
1. The van is equipped with a television above the passenger's window.
2. During the high-school dance, the lights in the cafeteria suddenly went out.
3. You will find the cat underneath the bed in the upstairs room.
4. Dan exercised continuously for twenty minutes.

Developing Your Style: Avoiding Prepositional Phrases in Strings, EXERCISE C
Answers will vary; possible answers are given.

ADAM: Yes! I went last night with some high-school friends from the band. We played games in the carnival's midway.

ROBIN: I will go tonight, but I intend to enjoy rides with my friends all evening.

ADAM: The only ride I enjoy is the Ferris wheel. I love looking at the city from it. It makes me feel like a bird flying among the clouds!

ROBIN: My favorite ride is the roller coaster. I love zooming around curves like a racer in a luge competition.

Pronouns

Identifying and Using Personal Pronouns, EXERCISE A
1. My, first person; It, third person
2. I, first person
3. his, third person
4. It, third person; it, third person
5. her, third person
6. he, third person; you, second person; his, third person

Identifying and Using Personal Pronouns, EXERCISE B
1. them, third person plural
2. our, first person plural
3. she, third person singular
4. I, first person singular; you, second person singular or plural

Identifying and Using Personal Pronouns, EXERCISE C
1. I
2. you
3. It
4. them

Identifying and Using Interrogative Pronouns, EXERCISE A
1. Which
2. whom
3. What
4. Who
5. Whose

Identifying and Using Interrogative Pronouns, EXERCISE B
1. whom
2. Which, paintings
3. Whose
4. what
5. Who, person

Identifying and Using Interrogative Pronouns, EXERCISE C
Answers will vary; possible answers are given.
1. <u>Who</u> was the star of *The Jazz Singer?*
2. <u>Which</u> was the first movie to win an Academy Award?
3. <u>Who</u> starred in *Wings?*
4. <u>Who</u> directed many terrifying movies?
5. <u>Whose</u> was the vision that became *Star Wars?*
6. Of the three *Star Wars* films, <u>which</u> is the one that you like most?
7. <u>What</u> is the title character in the *Beethoven* movies?
8. To <u>whom</u> was Disney's *Beauty and the Beast* dedicated?
9. <u>Which</u> was the film named Best Picture of 1939?
10. <u>Who</u> was the first African American to win an Academy Award?

Identifying and Using Relative Pronouns, EXERCISE A
1. whose
2. whom
3. that
4. who
5. which

Identifying and Using Relative Pronouns, EXERCISE B
1. that, store
2. whom
3. whose, Bess Wallace
4. whom, daughter
5. who, Truman
6. whose, Franklin D. Roosevelt
7. who, Roosevelt
8. which, news
9. which, opinions
10. that, decisions

Identifying and Using Relative Pronouns, EXERCISE C
Answers will vary; possible answers are given.
1. My brother, <u>whose</u> name is Chuck, loves books.
2. I am reading him one story <u>that</u> he loves.
3. Chuck, <u>who</u> listens carefully, asks me many questions.
4. The story is about a veterinarian <u>whom</u> all the animals love.
5. The story, <u>which</u> makes Chuck smile, has a happy ending.

Identifying and Using Demonstrative Pronouns, EXERCISE A
1. those
2. that
3. This
4. these
5. those

Identifying and Using Demonstrative Pronouns, EXERCISE B
1. That, stove
2. these, choices
3. this, way
4. those, ideas
5. This, visit
6. these, paintings
7. those, people
8. that, towel
9. these, trees
10. That, hint

Identifying and Using Demonstrative Pronouns, EXERCISE C
Answers may vary; suggested answers are given.
1. <u>This</u> is a famous Italian restaurant.
2. <u>That</u> is the waiter who will take your order.
3. May I have one of <u>these</u>, please?
4. <u>Those</u> are all wonderful-sounding choices.
5. Look at <u>that</u>—pasta in the shape of little bow ties!

Identifying and Using Indefinite Pronouns, EXERCISE A
1. No one, someone
2. nothing
3. something
4. Much
5. Each, one
6. another, everyone
7. Many

Identifying and Using Indefinite Pronouns, EXERCISE B
1. Everyone, singular; none, plural
2. Many, plural
3. Some, plural
4. Much, singular
5. Each, singular
6. something, singular; nothing, singular
7. anything, singular; one, singular

Identifying and Using Indefinite Pronouns, EXERCISE C

Answers will vary; possible answers are given.

1. Has <u>everyone</u> left for the day?
2. There's <u>no one</u> in the builing.
3. Perhaps here is <u>someone</u> who can help you.
4. I'd give <u>anything</u> for an extra pair of hands!
5. <u>Some</u> will be here in the morning.
6. Will you get <u>something</u> for me?
7. <u>Few</u> are ever here this late.
8. I guess <u>most</u> have to get home for dinner.
9. If you need <u>anything,</u> just call me.
10. <u>Most</u> of the work can wait until tomorrow.

Identifying and Using Intensive and Reflexive Pronouns, EXERCISE A

1. myself (intensive)
2. yourselves (reflexive)
3. themselves (intensive
4. ourselves (intensive)
5. yourself (reflexive)

Identifying and Using Intensive and Reflexive Pronouns, EXERCISE B

1. ourselves (intensive, plural)
2. myself (intensive, singular)
3. ourselves (reflexive, plural)
4. themselves (intensive, plural)
5. themselves (reflexive, plural)

Identifying and Using Intensive and Reflexive Pronouns, EXERCISE C

1. themselves (reflexive, plural)
2. itself (intensive, singular)
3. herself (reflexive, singular)
4. ourselves (intensive, plural)
5. himself (intensive, singular)
6. itself (intensive, singular)
7. themselves (reflexive, plural)
8. ourselves (intensive, plural)
9. myself (reflexive, singular)
10. ourselves (reflexive, plural)

Using Personal Pronouns Correctly, EXERCISE A

1. We (subject)
2. She (subject), I (subject)
3. they (subject)
4. us (object)
5. I (subject), we (subject)
6. She (subject), I (subject)
7. us (object)

Using Personal Pronouns Correctly, EXERCISE B
Some answers may vary; possible answers are given.
1. me (object)
2. me (object)
3. He (subject), I (subject)
4. them (object)
5. me (object)
6. him (object)
7. We (subject)
8. I (subject), him (object)

Using Personal Pronouns Correctly, EXERCISE C
Answers will vary; possible answers are given.
1. <u>They</u> came to my sister and <u>me</u> with a question.
2. Adam and <u>she</u> wondered if we could help <u>them</u>.
3. Adam looked at Gloria; "Tell <u>us</u> what to do," <u>he</u> asked.
4. Did <u>they</u> know that we would give <u>them</u> only our opinions?
5. Our advice must have disappointed Ruth and <u>him</u>, but <u>we</u> had to say what we thought.

Using Interrogative and Relative Pronouns Correctly, EXERCISE A
1. Who (interrogative)
2. whom (interrogative)
3. who (relative)
4. whose (relative)
5. whom (interrogative)

Using Interrogative and Relative Pronouns Correctly, EXERCISE B
   The Sound of Music is about Maria, <u>who</u> plans to become a nun. By <u>whose</u> orders is she sent outside the convent to work? Maria becomes governess to seven children <u>whose</u> mother has died. Their father, <u>who</u> is a naval officer and <u>whom</u> they both respect and fear, is very strict. Maria, <u>who</u> loves music, sings to the children. From <u>whom</u> are they learning new songs? The Captain, <u>whom</u> Maria secretly loves, begins to soften. Maria runs away but is sent back by the Mother Superior, to <u>whom</u> she has gone for advice. The children, <u>who</u> love her, rejoice.

Using Interrogative and Relative Pronouns Correctly, EXERCISE C
Answers may vary slightly; possible answers are given.
1. We saw the Louvre Museum, <u>which</u> is one of the most famous museums in the world. <u>Who</u> saw the Louvre Museum?
2. The Louvre's new entrance was designed by I. M. Pei, <u>who</u> is an American architect. By <u>whom</u> was the Louvre's new entrance designed?
3. Another famous museum is the Musée d'Orsay, <u>which</u> had been a railroad station in Paris. What had the Musée d' Orsay been?
4. We found a museum tour guide <u>whose</u> knowledge we admired. <u>Whom</u> did you admire?

Using Indefinite and Reflexive Pronouns Correctly, EXERCISE A
1. themselves
2. his or her
3. she
4. himself
5. their

Using Indefinite and Reflexive Pronouns Correctly, EXERCISE B
1. themselves
2. her
3. his or her
4. its
5. himself

Using Indefinite and Reflexive Pronouns Correctly, EXERCISE C
1. Any one of these stories will fascinate you with <u>its</u> plot.
2. Correct
3. Rolanda and Marya quizzed <u>themselves</u> on the material for the test.
4. Many of the homes had flowers or a tree near <u>their</u> front steps.
5. If everybody has memorized <u>his or her</u> script, the prompters will make <u>themselves</u> available for rehearsal of the first two scenes.

Developing Your Style: Pronouns, EXERCISE A
1. Karylle made a list of <u>her</u> friends; she sent <u>them</u> invitations.
2. Karylle then asked Mr. Lee to tell <u>her</u> the names of <u>his</u> friends.
3. Mr. Lee's friends said that <u>they</u> would be glad to come.
4. The party would be on Saturday, and <u>it</u> would start at eight o'clock.
5. When Brenda and I promised that <u>we</u> would provide the music, Karylle thanked <u>us</u>.
6. Mr. Lee made sandwiches, and were <u>they</u> ever delicious!
7. The guests played charades; each of <u>them</u> won a prize.

Developing Your Style: Pronouns, EXERCISE B
Answers may vary slightly; possible answers are given.
1. Ed sometimes tutors Vanessa and me. <u>He</u> is great at math./Ed, <u>who</u> is great at math, sometimes tutors Vanessa and me.
2. Vanessa owns two dogs. <u>Their</u> parents were both champions./Vanessa owns two dogs <u>whose</u> parents were both champions.
3. Vanessa is a special person. I can tell my secrets to her./Vanessa, to <u>whom</u> I can tell my secrets, is a special person.
4. All people need friends. <u>They</u> can trust <u>them</u>./All people need friends <u>whom</u> they can trust.

Developing Your Style: Pronouns, EXERCISE C
Answers will vary; possible answers are given.

One of the first important summer movies was *Jaws.* <u>It</u> was about a great white shark <u>who</u> attacked swimmers in a resort town called Amity. In 1982, *E.T.*, another summer box-office smash, told the story of an alien <u>who</u> is found and helped by a boy. More than ten years later, *Jurassic Park,* <u>which</u> was the biggest money-making film of all time, topped the list of spectacular summer movies.

Question Marks

Using Question Marks Correctly, EXERCISE A
1. Did Robert Louis Stevenson write for children<u>?</u>
2. I asked the librarian to recommend a book<u>.</u>
3. Correct
4. Do you like adventure stories<u>?</u>" he inquired.
5. "What do you think of when I say "treasure"?

Using Question Marks Correctly, EXERCISE B
1. The skating party last winter was great fun, wasn't it?
2. We could plan another one. Wouldn't that be great?
3. Did I just hear you say, "no way"?
4. You would rather not help. Why not?
5. Maria replied, "Why must we do all the work?"
6. I wonder why parties are always our responsibility.
7. Someone else should do the planning—but who?
8. "Who would like to assist us?" we asked the class.

Using Question Marks Correctly, EXERCISE C

Mrs. Xing asked, "Have you done much baby-sitting?"

"Certainly. Hasn't everyone done some?" I answered. I can be a bit flip at times, can't I? More politely, I continued, "Did you have time to read my references?"

"They are good, aren't they?" Mrs. Xing admitted. "What exactly did Ms. Huang mean by 'usually excellent'? Please explain that."

Quotation Marks

Using Quotation Marks Correctly, EXERCISE A
1. Mom laughed, "Come on, kids, get to work!"
2. "Must we clean the whole basement?" sighed Peter.
3. "That," said Mom, "is the basic idea."
4. "Wow!" Mom later exclaimed. "You kids did a great job!"
5. "I think," groaned Peter, "that my back is broken."

Using Quotation Marks Correctly, EXERCISE B
1. "I suppose," sighed Gus, "that we will never know the truth."
2. "I'll wait outside the store," said Carmen.
3. "These boxes are heavy!" I gasped in dismay.
4. Did I hear you say, "Give me a break"?
5. "After lunch," I promised, "I'll tell you everything."

Using Quotation Marks Correctly, EXERCISE C
Some answers may vary slightly; possible answers are given.
1. Our Scout leader said, "Be sure that the fire is out."
2. I heard her remark, "I'm glad that job is done."
3. Did he say, "There is no homework tonight"?
4. "Don't play ball here!" shouted Mr. Grasso.
5. "How," Margo wondered, "can spiders walk on the ceiling?"
6. How can you just come out and say, "I refuse to help"?
7. She moaned, "My feet are absolutely killing me!"
8. I was furious when he announced, "This is a pop quiz."
9. Who can say, "She sells seashells by the seashore"?
10. "Would you please," said Ms. King, "be kind enough to take a message?"

Other Uses of Quotation Marks, EXERCISE A
1. the author, Josephine ("Jo") McPherson
2. reads the poem "Billboards"
3. reference to the song "America, the Beautiful"
4. calls polluters "a scourge on the land"
5. oil executives' attitude, termed "laid back"

Other Uses of Quotation Marks, EXERCISE B

1. "Yankees"
2. "Yankee Jon"
3. "cool"
4. "Colonial New England"
5. "the house that [Babe] Ruth built"

Other Uses of Quotation Marks, EXERCISE C

1. The audience sang "Feelings" with great feeling.
2. "Crime on Mars," a story by Arthur C. Clarke, has a clever ending.
3. Ruth ("Rutabaga") Remarque is a funny stand-up comic.
4. We played "Swing Low, Sweet Chariot" at the ball game.
5. Did Francisco really call our party "swell"?
6. The crime was committed by Leo "The Leopard" Lamas.
7. The May issue has an article entitled "A Stitch in Time."
8. Poe's story "The Pit and the Pendulum" is unnerving.
9. I asked him to play, but he said he was just "chilling."
10. Do you prefer Rudyard Kiplings's poem "If" to Robert Frost's "Birches"?

Quotations

Distinguishing Between Direct and Indirect Quotations, EXERCISE A

1. direct
2. indirect
3. indirect
4. direct
5. indirect

Distinguishing Between Direct and Indirect Quotations, EXERCISE B

Answers may vary slightly; possible answers are given.

1. Mr. Jennings asked Keiko, "Do you know how our town got its name?" (direct)
2. Keiko replied that it was named for a famous French explorer. (indirect)
3. She added that he explored the Mississippi River at length, learning much along the way. (indirect)
4. "I'm impressed by your knowledge," Mr. Jennings admitted. (direct)

Distinguishing Between Direct and Indirect Quotations, EXERCISE C

1. "Only the Sunday paper is delivered to my house," Charisse answered./Charisse answered that only the Sunday paper was delivered to her house.
2. "Even then," she admitted, "I read just the sports section and the comics."/She admitted that, even then, she read just the sports section and the comics.
3. "I rather enjoy the Sunday comics myself," agreed Mrs. Tolbert./Mrs. Tolbert agreed that she rather enjoyed the Sunday comics herself.
4. Then she asked Charisse, "Do you know about the Metro, Arts, and Travel sections?"/Then she asked Charisse whether she knew about the Metro, Arts, and Travel sections.
5. Charisse said, "I guess there's more to a newspaper than one might think."/Charisse said that she guessed there was more to a newspaper than one might think.

Using Quotations in Essays and Research Papers, EXERCISE A

1. B
2. B
3. A
4. A
5. A
6. B
7. B
8. A
9. A
10. B

Using Quotations in Essays and Research Papers, EXERCISE B

Paragraphs will vary; a possible paragraph, on the first topic, is given.

   Oh, how I hate to get up in the morning! However, as much as I hate to get up, that's exactly how much I wanted to go to the rock concert on Saturday. To be able to go, I had to get the tickets. When the alarm clock's ugly little voice shrilled in my ear, I rolled out of bed, shivering and muttering. I remember getting dressed, because I would have frozen outside if I hadn't, but I can't remember whether I brushed my teeth—or hair. Half-asleep, I climbed into the bus; still half-asleep, I got off in front of the ticket outlet. Joy of joys, though—there were only five other kids there before me! It's just as Pop always says: "The early bird catches the worm."

Using Quotations in Essays and Research Papers, EXERCISE C

Paragraphs will vary; a possible paragraph, on the second topic, is given.

   That Mother's Day was truly memorable. It was the first time I had ever tried to put on a family party by myself. My sister, who usually heads those gatherings, was studying for final exams. "It's up to you this year, Barry," she'd said to me. Boy, was she ever right! I shopped for the food and decorations. I made my mom's favorite potato salad and a Mother's Day cake. On the big day, I set the table, put out the decorations, and grilled the hamburgers. Was Mom surprised! "I don't believe it!" she exclaimed when I escorted her to her chair. "You did this all by yourself? Without Audrey's help?" Audrey and Dad were impressed, too. "Well, what do you know!" Dad remarked, his mouth full of potato salad. "It's edible!" "Thank goodness!" Audrey said, pretending to sigh. "I thought I'd have to pretend to like it." I was pleased with the compliments, although I tried not to show it. I may have overdone it, though. Now the family wants me to cook at least one meal a week!

Writing Dialogue, EXERCISE A

Each number change indicates a new paragraph.

1. "Are you ready to go yet, Kent?" asked Ricardo.
2. "Almost. I still have to let my mother know where I will be and how long I'll be gone," Kent replied.
3. "Better hurry," urged Ricardo. "You know they won't hold up the parade for us."
4. "Do you suppose," asked Kent, "that the 1904 Oldsmobile will be in the parade again this year?"
5. "I hope so," said Ricardo. "That is my favorite. It has really been well taken care of."

Writing Dialogue, EXERCISE B

New paragraphs are denoted by /.

(1) "Terry," asked Ms. Rodriguez, "have you completed your book report?" / (2) "I have finished the book, Ms. Rodriguez, but I haven't finished the written report yet," Terry answered. / (3) "What is the book you have chosen for your report?" / (4) "I read *Big Red*. It's about an Irish setter. (5) I really liked it because Big Red reminded me of my dog." / (6) "I'm glad you liked it, Terry. Try to get that report in tomorrow."

Writing Dialogue, EXERCISE C

New paragraphs are denoted by /.

"Have you ever been inside this cave?" I asked nervously./"Sure, lots of times," Tom answered confidently./"Well, which way do we go, then?" I inquired./"If we go left, we come to a wall. The other way leads deeper into the cave," Tom explained. "Let's go deeper," he suggested./"Okay, lead on," I said./"I came this way once and found an underground stream," said Tom. "Do you want to try to find it again?" he asked./ "Sure . . . Hey, what's this?" I exclaimed, pointing my flashlight at my feet./"It looks like a treasure chest," Tom answered excitedly./"Let's take it outside where we can look at it more closely," I said./"Great idea! You grab that end," said Tom, and we tried to carry the chest out of the cave.

Developing Your Style: Quotations, EXERCISE A

Answers will vary; possible answers are given.
1. Most students admitted that they didn't care for Paulo's Pizza Palace because, as one explained, "Eating one of their pizzas is like chewing soggy cardboard!"
2. Coach Nickerson expressed regret at replacing the once-great forward, saying, "Hollinson seems to have lost his touch."
3. Principal Sherry Adamson applauded the students' willingness to help construct pavilions for the fair, explaining, "They'll appreciate it more if they help build it."
4. Claiming that seasonal lightning and thunderstorms accounted for many injuries, meteorologist Chen Li of WPXG stated, "Everyone should write to this station for our book of safety tips."
5. A few art lovers, however, disagreed vehemently, siding instead with one patron who declared, shaking her head, "His work is some of the least creative I've ever seen."

Developing Your Style: Quotations, EXERCISE B

Paragraphs will vary; a possible paragraph, based on the second item, is given.

"What a magnificent sunset!" sighed Sandy, coming to a sudden halt. The sun blazed across the evening sky, sending broad rays of crimson streaking halfway across the heavens. The clouds nearest the sun shone orange and hot pink; those farther away shaded to peach and lavender. The dome of sky untouched by the sun was a royal blue deepening to violet. "The colors are so vivid that I can almost *feel* them vibrating in the air!" She exclaimed.

Developing Your Style: Quotations, EXERCISE C
Paragraphs will vary; a possible paragraph, for the third topic, is given.

"There's no place like home." So said Dorothy as she tapped the heels of her red shoes and wished to go home. That's exactly how I feel every time I come home to the "wide open spaces" of the West. As the plane circles over the airport in Phoenix, I can see the desert stretching out for miles in every direction. No forests of trees block out the sun or throw shadows on the ground; there's just a cactus here or there, spiky arms raised in welcome. Everywhere I look I see bright blue sky and brown-red plateaus and mesas. In Phoenix, I feel free and happy. That old saying is certainly true for me: "East or west, home *is* best."

Semicolons

Using Semicolons Correctly EXERCISE A
1. Cleary had always wanted to be a writer; she finally started when her husband bought her a new pencil sharpener.
2. Cleary's first book was *Henry Huggins;* the main character was based on a boy from Cleary's childhood.
3. Characters in other stories include Ramona Quimby, a mischievous girl; Beezus, her older sister; and twins Mitch and Amy.
4. Her earlier novels were mostly humorous; however, some recent works have been concerned with realistic, serious problems.
5. Cleary's stories will remain popular because of their memorable characters; their funny, touching plots; and their subtle, inspirational encouragement.

Using Semicolons Correctly EXERCISE B
1. My mother planned a big party for me; she allowed me thirteen guests.
2. I invited Susan, my next-door neighbor; Juan, my best friend; and Lee, my cousin.
3. The food included pizza with thirteen toppings, salad with thirteen vegetables, and thirteen types of cookies.
4. Of course, my birthday is always special; it's on Halloween!
5. Among the costumed guests at my party were a green, hairy werewolf; a rock star with a guitar; and a purple and red dinosaur.

Using Semicolons Correctly EXERCISE C
Answers will vary; possible answers are given.
1. My hobbies include playing basketball, which I play with my friends; playing the guitar, which I practice alone; and learning to sing.
2. My best friend is so much fun to be with; he is always in a cheerful mood.
3. Among my heroes are Jackie Robinson, the baseball player; Martin Luther King, Jr., the civil rights leader; and my own grandmother, a social worker.
4. I always know when it's suppertime; the dog lies under the dinner table and wags her tail.
5. My three favorite movies and their stars are *Hot Shots,* with Tom Cruise; *Sister Act,* with Whoopi Goldberg; and the classic *Gunga Din* with Cary Grant.

Sentences: Structure and Types

Identifying and Using Subjects and Predicates, EXERCISE A

1. <u>Rain</u> / <u>forms</u> from moisture in the atmosphere.
2. The <u>moisture</u> in the air / <u>comes</u> from evaporation.
3. <u>Water</u> / <u>is made</u> up of molecules.
4. <u>Molecules</u> of water / <u>escape</u> into the air.
5. Warm <u>air</u> / <u>holds</u> more water than cold air.
6. <u>Droplets</u> of water / <u>may form</u> around tiny pieces of dust.
7. A <u>cloud</u> / <u>is</u> a collection of these droplets.
8. A lower air <u>temperature</u> / <u>causes</u> more droplets to form.
9. Air <u>currents</u> / <u>can hold</u> them up no longer.
10. <u>They</u> / <u>fall</u> to the earth as rain.

Identifying and Using Subjects and Predicates, EXERCISE B
Sentences will vary; possible sentences are given.
1. complete subject; <u>The post office on the corner</u> sells stamp-collecting kits.
2. complete predicate; The plumber <u>is working in the basement</u>.
3. complete subject; <u>Excellent cities for vacations</u> are San Francisco and New Orleans.
4. complete subject; <u>Plenty of photographs</u> filled the albums.
5. complete subject; <u>That piece of material</u> would make a pretty tablecloth.
6. complete predicate; The two painters <u>were arguing about the color</u>.
7. complete subject; <u>Broccoli and cauliflower</u> are on sale at the store today.
8. complete predicate; Trees, grass, and other plants <u>become scarce at high altitudes</u>.
9. complete subject; <u>Quiet strains of music</u> filled the room.
10. complete predicate; The girl standing in the rain <u>pulled her hat lower</u>.

Identifying and Using Subjects and Predicates, EXERCISE C
Sentences will vary; possible sentences are given.
1. An overstuffed couch <u>sat against the back wall</u>.
2. A delicate, old-fashioned birdcage <u>was stuffed with old rags</u>.
3. <u>The vase on the desk</u> would look wonderful decorated with flowers.
4. <u>The furniture</u> could be fixed, cleaned, and repainted.

Identifying and Using Complements, EXERCISE A
1. object complement
2. direct object, object complement
3. indirect object
4. indirect object, direct object
5. object complement
6. indirect object, direct object
7. indirect object
8. direct object
9. direct object
10. indirect object, direct object

Identifying and Using Complements, EXERCISE B
Complements appear in the order given. Sentence breaks are denoted by /.

Grand Canyon (direct object) / Grand Canyon (direct object), national park (object complement) Grand Canyon (direct object) / beautiful (object complement) / walls (direct object), colorful (object complement) ourselves (indirect object), canteens (direct object), boots (direct object) / water (direct object) / bottom (direct object), home (object complement) / me (indirect object), passion (direct object)

Identifying and Using Complements, EXERCISE C
Answers will vary; possible answers are given.

   Leon told <u>us</u> a story about a tornado. His story made me <u>weak</u>. One day he had left <u>home</u> for school. It was 8:00 A.M. Leon said that the sky turned emerald green suddenly and that dogs began barking loudly. A high-pitched whine made him <u>dizzy</u>. He lost consciousness. The next he knew, he was sitting on his porch, and it was two hours later!

Identifying and Using Sentence Patterns, EXERCISE A
Answers may vary; possible answers are given.
  1. was
  2. my friend
  3. thanked
  4. we
  5. wonderful

Identifying and Using Sentence Patterns, EXERCISE B
Answers will vary; possible answers are given.
  1. does not match; She eagerly awaited my opinion.
  2. matches
  3. does not match; "You should give other people portraits.
  4. does not match; Yolanda grinned and looked quite proud.
  5. matches

Identifying and Using Sentence Patterns, EXERCISE C
Sentences will vary; possible sentences are given.
  1. The skating rink is my favorite after-school place.
  2. I practice my routines two or tree times a week.
  3. How graceful I look!
  4. Would Olympic judges award me a medal?
  5. I would accept the prize, wave, and enjoy myself.

Identifying and Using Types of Sentences, EXERCISE A
  1. declarative.
  2. exclamatory!
  3. declarative.
  4. imperative.
  5. interrogative?

Identifying and Using Types of Sentences, EXERCISE B
Answers may vary; possible answers are given.
  1. How fragile its wings appear!
  2. Those wings are strong enough to reach a speed of sixty miles per hour.
  3. Aren't the wings shimmering like little rainbows?
  4. Notice how the insect's entire body shines.
  5. What remarkable eyes the dragonfly has!

Identifying and Using Types of Sentences, EXERCISE C
Answers will vary; possible answers are given.
  1. DAVID: I haven't decided. What kind of music will the band be playing?
  2. MARCY: Most of the program is rock, but there's some rap music, too. Don't miss this chance to hear some great music.
  3. DAVID: Are the tickets expensive? I don't have much money to spare.
  4. MARCY: The tickets are free. Go to the office and pick one up.
  5. DAVID: What a bargain that is! I guess I'll see you there.

Identifying and Using Simple and Compound Sentences, EXERCISE A
1. simple; human
2. simple; skeleton
3. compound; skeleton, bones
4. simple; hands, arms
5. simple; bones
6. simple; allow
7. compound; swing, rotate, do
8. compound; have, may last
9. simple; get
10. compound; eat, take

Identifying and Using Simple and Compound Sentences, EXERCISE B
1. compound; She sells real estate on weekends, <u>but</u> during the week she works at the hospital.
2. simple
3. compound; Mindy lost her purse, <u>and</u> her whole family was upset.
4. compound; Chip doesn't want to go to the party, <u>nor</u> does he want to meet us for lunch.
5. simple

Identifying and Using Simple and Compund Sentences, EXERCISE C
Answers will vary; possible answers are given.

Apples are one of the oldest-known fruits eaten by humans. Remains of apples have been found in Stone Age villages! The Greeks were growing apples 2,200 years ago, and the Romans carried them to Europe. Pilgrims and Puritans brought apple seeds and seedlings to America. The colonists dried apples, or they used them to make cider and apple butter.

Pioneer Johnny Appleseed is credited with planting apple trees along the early American frontier. Many short stories and poems tell of Johnny's deeds, but none of these folktales has ever been proven true.

Identifying and Using Complex and Compound-Complex Sentences, EXERCISE A
1. one main clause + one subordinate clause = complex
2. two main clauses + one subordinate clause = compound-complex
3. two main clauses + one subordinate clause = compound-complex
4. one main clause + one subordinate clause = complex
5. two main clauses + one subordinate clause = compound-complex

Identifying and Using Complex and Compound-Complex Sentences, EXERCISE B
New sentences will vary; possible sentences are given.
1. compound-complex; Juan, <u>who is my cousin</u>, keeps buying stamps, although he has hundreds already.
2. complex; Juan isn't the only person <u>who is a stamp collector</u>.
3. complex; Briana, <u>who likes to show off her marble collection</u>, has special display cases.
4. complex; Roxana, <u>who keeps a collection of shells at home,</u> bought special insurance to protect the items.
5. complex; Art collectors <u>who have sculptures and paintings</u> may install burglar alarms.

Identifying and Using Complex and Compound-Complex Sentences, EXERCISE C

Answers will vary; possible answers are given.

1. I went to the movies with Ivan, <u>whom I like very much</u>. (complex)
2. Bret interrupted Martha before she finished speaking; <u>consequently, we never knew the end of her story</u>. (compound-complex)
3. When lunch is over, Seth has gym, <u>but I go to math</u>. (compound-complex)
4. Although Marty looked everywhere, <u>he couldn't find his favorite shirt</u>. (complex)
5. Jack, who is his best friend, is not here, <u>but Mike may have a good time, anyway</u>. (compound-complex)
6. <u>The garden that Mom planted bloomed beautifully</u>, but Aunt Rita's didn't. (compound-complex)
7. <u>Even though I paid close attention</u>, I didn't understand the explanation. (complex)
8. <u>When the school elections are held</u>, Bob and Alison will probably win. (complex)
9. Have a haircut and then mail these letters, <u>since you pass the post office anyway</u>? (compound-complex)
10. <u>When she leaves, we will follow her</u>, for we want her to get home safely. (compound-complex)

Spelling

Adding Prefixes and Suffixes, EXERCISE A
1. incorrect; illegally
2. incorrect; coordinate
3. incorrect; copiloted
4. incorrect; unbelievable
5. correct
6. incorrect; legislative
7. correct
8. incorrect; infamous
9. correct
10. incorrect; rearranging

Adding Prefixes and Suffixes, EXERCISE B
1. useless
2. irresponsible
3. untying
4. hopeful
5. stubbornness
6. arrival
7. horribly
8. peacefully
9. confusing
10. immobile

Adding Prefixes and Suffixes, EXERCISE C
1. amazing
2. gracefully
3. reorganized
4. beautiful
5. happiest

Choosing Correct Homophones, EXERCISE A
1. brake
2. all ready
3. capital
4. passed
5. principal

Choosing Correct Homophones, EXERCISE B
1. My favorite <u>course</u> this year is language arts.
2. Barbara did <u>accept</u> my invitation to the dance.
3. Do you think this dress is too <u>plain</u> for the prom?
4. Trucks have to use that <u>weigh</u> station before they continue.
5. You should never <u>desert</u> your teammates during a game.
6. Everyone is going to the event <u>except</u> Vince.
7. Has Julie <u>shown</u> you her new dress?
8. The students left <u>their</u> books in homeroom.
9. What <u>effect</u> does nicotine have on your body?
10. This old ring has lost <u>its</u> shine.

Choosing Correct Homophones, EXERCISE C
My family decided that <u>it's</u> time for a vacation. <u>Two</u> years had <u>passed</u> since our last trip. We drove to Richmond, the <u>capital</u> of Virginia. We hoped that the <u>weather</u> would be warm enough for swimming—but it was <u>altogether</u> <u>too</u> cold for water sports! Since we had not packed warm clothes, we had to <u>alter</u> our plans. We traveled eastward <u>through</u> the state toward Virginia Beach. We spent one <u>week</u> basking in the sunlight of this coastal town. Before leaving for home, we made reservations for next year!

Applying Other Spelling Rules and Tips, EXERCISE A
1. con<u>cede</u>
2. accept<u>ance</u>
3. proc<u>eed</u>
4. rec<u>ei</u>pt
5. <u>ei</u>ghteen
6. experi<u>ence</u>
7. caff<u>ei</u>ne
8. viol<u>ence</u>
9. suc<u>ceed</u>ed
10. disbel<u>ief</u>

Applying Other Spelling Rules and Tips, EXERCISE B
1. proceed
2. conceit
3. unnatural
4. truthfully
5. baroness
6. weird
7. seize
8. knowledge
9. necessary
10. supersede

Applying Other Spelling Rules and Tips, EXERCISE C

<u>Usually</u>, the boys <u>agreed</u> on how to <u>schedule</u> <u>their</u> day. One afternoon, however, they were <u>arguing</u> over how to spend some <u>leisure</u> time. Tim <u>believed</u> that they <u>should</u> <u>bicycle</u> to the lake and go fishing. Dan's <u>choice</u> of activity was <u>hiking</u> <u>through</u> the woods with a <u>picnic</u> lunch. How should they <u>proceed</u>? <u>Finally</u>, after much <u>discussion</u>, they <u>compromised</u>. They hiked to the lake and had a <u>picnic</u> lunch after fishing! As it turned out, it was a <u>wonderful</u> <u>experience</u>!

Spelling Commonly Misspelled Words Correctly, EXERCISE A

1. disease
2. cemetery
3. business
4. laboratory
5. February
6. eighth
7. occasion
8. performance
9. recommend
10. truly
11. embarrass
12. license
13. infinite
14. variety
15. all right
16. library
17. jewelry
18. harass
19. definite
20. misspell

Spelling Commonly Misspelled Words Correctly, EXERCISE B

1. They had a display on the <u>environment</u>.
2. The display is part of the <u>permanent</u> collection.
3. One book was all about the <u>rhythms</u> of nature.
4. Another book presented facts about my <u>neighborhood</u>.
5. I picked up a <u>pamphlet</u> about building a bird feeder.

Spelling Commonly Misspelled Words Correctly, EXERCISE C

Answers will vary; possible sentences are given.

1. Our <u>neighbor</u> has a <u>mischievous</u> cat.
2. I <u>recommend</u> this book on computer <u>technology</u>.
3. For the <u>benefit</u> of those who were unable to be there, won't you please <u>describe</u> the scene?
4. It doesn't take a <u>genius</u> to prove the <u>existence</u> of snow.
5. The <u>government</u> of a <u>foreign</u> country may differ from our own.
6. I <u>sincerely</u> hope that you'll take your prescription to the new <u>pharmacy</u>.
7. It has been a real <u>privilege</u> to view this display of antique <u>jewelry</u>.
8. It's <u>all right</u>; you won't <u>embarrass</u> yourself.
9. The <u>library</u> system in that large city has <u>forty</u> branches.
10. If you don't behave, I'll have to <u>separate</u> you—and that's <u>definite</u>!

Underlining/Italics

Using Underlining/Italics Correctly, EXERCISE A

1. *Treasure Island*
2. *Newsweek*
3. *Wall Street Journal*
4. *z*
5. *The Thinker*
6. *semper fidelis*
7. *serendipity*
8. *7*'s
9. *Merrimac*
10. *Gone with the Wind*

Using Underlining/Italics Correctly, EXERCISE B

1. Larry read both *The Yearling* and *The Incredible Journey*.
2. He wrote his book report, however, on the *Odyssey*.
3. Larry's hometown paper *The Boston Globe*, reviews only current books, however.
4. This classic by Homer gave James Joyce the idea to title his novel, *Ulysses*.
5. In Greek mythology, some characters have a flaw called *hubris*.
6. This Greek word is nearly a synonym for the word *pride*.
7. I wonder if some athletes featured in *Sports Illustrated* have too much pride.
8. Another Homer created the painting called *Snap the Whip*.
9. In another myth, Jason and the Argonauts sailed on the ship *Argo*.
10. Larry remembered to dot his *i*'s and cross his *t*'s in his report.

Using Underlining/Italics Correctly, EXERCISE C

Answers and numbers of sentences will vary; sample answers are given.

1. My brother subscribes to *Popular Mechanics*, but I prefer to read *National Geographic*.
2. In many places, you can read *The New York Times*.
3. The science-fiction movie *Blade Runner* was based on the novel *Do Androids Dream of Electric Sheep?*
4. The musical *Sunday in the Park with George* brings to life Georges Seurat's famous painting *Sunday Afternoon on the Island of La Grande Jatte*.
5. Does *accommodate* contain one *m* or two?

Verbals

Identifying and Using Participles and Participial Phrases, EXERCISE A

1. thrilling
2. referred to as "mushers"
3. pumping with one foot
4. completing the race in slightly more than eleven days
5. Sharing the winner's podium with her dogs

Identifying and Using Participles and Participial Phrases, EXERCISE B

1. <u>known</u> to only a few people (facts)
2. <u>swallowing</u> hard (Miguel)
3. <u>cut</u> from yeaterday's newspaper, (articles)
4. <u>Trying</u> to be helpful (children)

Identifying and Using Participles and Participial Phrases, EXERCISE C

Answers will vary; possible answers are given.

1. The elephants were eating peanuts <u>scattered</u> on the ground. (peanuts)
2. The monkeys, <u>chewing</u> on bananas, peered at their curious visitors. (monkeys)
3. The crocodiles, <u>hidden</u> from view beneath the surface of the pond, waited for their supper. (crocodiles)
4. <u>Disguised</u> in their spots, leopards lounged among some fallen leaves. (leopards)
5. A child pointed to the snakes <u>slithering</u> across a rock. (snakes)
6. Two exotic birds, <u>perched</u> on a limb, cautiously watched the snakes. (birds)
7. <u>Stretching</u> his neck, the giraffe looked for some fresh foliage. (giraffe)
8. Peacocks <u>screeching</u> in the distance captured my attention. (Peacocks)
9. The male, <u>spreading</u> his tail feathers, attracted the attention of a nearby bird. (male)
10. The rhinoceros, <u>caked</u> with mud, watched the peacocks. (rhinoceros)

Identifying and Using Gerunds and Gerund Phrases, EXERCISE A
1. Quilting
2. "Piecing" the quilt
3. sewing a large single piece of fabric onto the back of the patchwork top
4. naming their quilts with titles drawn from everyday life
5. Joining long strips of fabric into squares

Identifying and Using Gerunds and Gerund Phrases, EXERCISE B
1. <u>picking</u> fruits and vegetables for half the year (direct object)
2. <u>attending</u> school regularly (direct object)
3. <u>Getting</u> an education (subject)
4. <u>growing</u> up as a worker in the field (object of the preposition)
5. <u>Writing</u> the book *y no se lo trago la tierra* (*Earth Did Not Swallow*) (subject)

Identifying and Using Gerunds and Gerund Phrases, EXERCISE C
Answers will vary; possible answers are given.
1. <u>Smelling the food</u> makes my mouth water. (subject)
2. <u>Devouring a pizza</u> satisfies my hunger. (subject)
3. I can have fun at the mall without <u>spending much money</u>. (object of the preposition)
4. I enjoy <u>looking at new styles</u>. (direct object)
5. At the audio store, my favorite activity is <u>listening to new music</u>. (predicate nominative)
6. How <u>watching other shoppers</u> amuses me! (subject)
7. The mall is the perfect place for <u>meeting friends</u>. (object of the preposition)
8. At the mall's arcade, most of my friends like <u>playing video games</u>. (direct object)
9. To me, a great activity is <u>studying the window displays</u>. (predicate nominative)
10. Most shoppers appreciate <u>browsing in the bookstore</u>. (direct object)

Identifying and Using Infinitives and Infinitive Phrases, EXERCISE A
1. to find a husband for his daughter
2. to wed her
3. to see her in his mirror
4. to fly to her in a magic hammock
5. to marry

Identifying and Using Infinitives and Infinitive Phrases, EXERCISE B
1. <u>to achieve</u> (adverb)
2. <u>to become</u> an engineer (adjective)
3. <u>to understand</u> everything about computers (noun)
4. <u>to sail</u> around the world in his own boat (noun)
5. <u>to choose</u> a teaching career (adjective)

Identifying and Using Infinitives and Infinitive Phrases, EXERCISE C
Answers will vary; possible answers are given.
1. The kicker positioned himself <u>to kick</u> the ball to the receiver. (adverb)
2. <u>To catch</u> the ball proved difficult for the receiver. (noun)
3. The opposing team tried <u>to tackle</u> him. (noun)
4. He ran out of bounds <u>to avoid</u> them. (adverb)
5. Our coach signaled that it was time <u>to huddle</u>. (adjective)
6. Our team attempted all evening <u>to make</u> a touchdown. (noun)
7. <u>To cheer</u> the team, the band played a pep song. (adverb)
8. During the second half, the other team managed <u>to fumble</u>. (noun)
9. We were finally able <u>to score</u> twice. (adverb)
10. It was our night <u>to win</u>, after all! (adjective)

Using Verbals Correctly, EXERCISE A
1. misplaced modifier, breathing a sigh of relief
2. dangling participle, Painting the ceiling
3. split infinitive, to quickly shield
4. dangling participle, Dropping his brush
5. split infinitive, to slowly and carefully climb

Using Verbals Correctly, EXERCISE B
Answers may vary; possible answers are given.
1. Mrs. Canton planned <u>to work slowly</u> today.
2. <u>Holding the machine in her hands</u>, the inventor inspected it carefully.
3. Placing it back on the table, <u>she noticed that the machine was out of batteries.</u>
4. Correct
5. The machine, <u>whirring loudly</u>, started to break apart.

Using Verbals Correctly, EXERCISE C
Answers may vary; possible answers are given.

   The salesclerk <u>slyly tried to hide</u> the sale sign. <u>Realizing what had happened, Darnell</u> asked to see the manager. <u>Apologizing for the mistake, the manager</u> tore up the sign. <u>Paying half price for the shoes, Darnell</u> noticed that the manager smiled weakly. <u>Hanging his head in shame, the clerk</u> handed Darnell the package.

Developing Your Style: Verbals, EXERCISE A
Answers will vary; possible answers are given.
1. <u>Guiding the team, the coach wasn't scheming</u> to win an award as the best coach of the year.
2. The honor of <u>winning</u> isn't half as satisfying to Coach Eliot as <u>knowing</u> that his players tried their best.
3. <u>Arriving first at the victory party, Coach Eliot</u> remembers congratulationg each member of the team.
4. <u>Starting as the players' drill instructor, Coach Eliot</u> became their lifelong friend.

Developing Your Style: Verbals, EXERCISE B
Answers may vary; possible answers are given.
1. <u>Addressing her fellow graduates, Elaine</u> quoted a line from a poem to inspire them.
2. She remembers <u>using</u> gestures <u>to emphasize</u> her main points.
3. Elaine praised her audience for <u>accomplishing</u> many things in junior high school.
4. She urged them <u>to continue</u> their good work in high school.
5. <u>Applauding loudly</u>, the audience gave her a standing ovation.

Developing Your Style: Verbals, EXERCISE C
Answers may vary; possible answers are given.

   <u>Spending a grueling week to promote his economic policies, the President talked</u> to lawmakers on Capitol Hill. He labored <u>to gain</u> the support of members of Congress. Of course, the President didn't expect <u>to win</u> their approval automatically. That's why he decided <u>to appear</u> on television. <u>Recognizing the importance of the public's support, the President took</u> to the airwaves "<u>to sell</u>" his message.

Verbs

Identifying and Using Action Verbs and Linking Verbs, EXERCISE A
1. action
2. linking
3. linking
4. linking
5. action

Identifying and Using Action Verbs and Linking Verbs, EXERCISE B
1. action; physical
2. action; physical
3. linking; ride/long, boring
4. linking; classmates/noisy
5. action; physical
6. linking; Jonah/sorry
7. action; mental
8. action; mental
9. linking; Ricardo/handsome
10. action; physical

Identifying and Using Action Verbs and Linking Verbs, EXERCISE C
Answers will vary; possible answers are given.

Walnut Street school <u>sponsored</u> (action) a canned-food drive. Everyone <u>seemed</u> (linking) excited about the activity. Their school spirit <u>must have been</u> (linking) contagious! Even the faculty <u>participated</u> (action) in the drive. The principal alone <u>collected</u> (action) 127 cans. The drive <u>lasted</u> (action) three weeks and <u>produced</u> (action) 842 cans. Local charities <u>took</u> (action) the boxes and <u>delivered</u> (action) them to needy families. Everyone <u>seemed</u> (linking) pleased with the success of the drive.

Identifying and Using Transitive Verbs and Intransitive Verbs, EXERCISE A
Verbs appear in the order given. Sentence breaks are denoted by /.

holds (transitive) / enjoy (transitive) / like (transitive), stretches (intransitive) / play (transitive) / are donated (intransitive) / received (transitive) / is (intransitive) / prepare (transitive) / tastes (intransitive)

Identifying and Using Transitive Verbs and Intransitive Verbs, EXERCISE B
1. are—intransitive
2. have joined—transitive, team
3. run—transitive, races
4. enjoy—transitive, hurdles
5. loves—transitive, jump
6. seems—intransitive
7. had—transitive, race
8. was—intransitive
9. have worked—intransitive
10. looks—intransitive

Identifying and Using Transitive Verbs and Intransitive Verbs, EXERCISE C
Answers will vary; possible answers are given.
1. Dorothy <u>believes</u> everything she reads./I <u>believe</u> in the importance of freedom.
2. We <u>cooked</u> chili for the picnic./I often <u>cook</u> on Saturdays.
3. Garrett <u>has sung</u> his solo perfectly./Joyce and I <u>have been singing</u> together all summer.
4. Mrs. Sato <u>answered</u> our questions patiently./<u>Can</u> you <u>answer</u> before the buzzer sounds?
5. Bethany <u>looked</u> the stubborn child squarely in the eye./How happy you <u>look</u> today!

Identifying and Using Main Verbs and Helping Verbs, EXERCISE A
1. were <u>waiting</u>
2. had <u>been</u>
3. were <u>expecting</u>
4. were <u>watching</u>
5. had been <u>repainting</u>
6. should have been <u>watching</u>
7. was <u>speeding</u>
8. could have <u>been</u>
9. might have <u>been</u>
10. did <u>break</u>

Identifying and Using Main Verbs and Helping Verbs, EXERCISE B
Answers will vary; possible answers are given.
1. Someone <u>should have</u> closed the window.
2. Your friend <u>is</u> feeling better this morning.
3. Amanda <u>has been</u> looking for you all day.
4. A report about the accident <u>must be</u> written.
5. Your guinea pigs <u>have</u> escaped from their cage again.

Identifying and Using Main Verbs and Helping Verbs, EXERCISE C
Answers will vary; possible answers are given.
1. Penny <u>will write</u> a report about Japan.
2. Her uncle, Jared, <u>has toured</u> the island nation.
3. Did Stella <u>choose</u> Thailand for her report?
4. She <u>had eaten</u> Thai food in a restaurant.
5. The students <u>will be presenting</u> their reports all next week.

Identifying and Using Verb Forms, Number, and Person, EXERCISE A
1. did know, second person singular; have joined, first person singular
2. knows, third person singular; finds, third person singular
3. walk, first person plural; eat, first person plural
4. began, first person singular; hurt, third person singular
5. says, third person singular; is, third person singular

Identifying and Using Verb Forms, Number, and Person, EXERCISE B
1. Correct; second person plural
2. He <u>has improved</u> his serve and his forehand; third person singular
3. Richard's level of skill <u>surpasses</u> mine; third person singular
4. Anh's love of tennis <u>inspires</u> and <u>challenges</u> me; third person singular, third person singular
5. Both tennis and golf <u>require</u> much hand-eye coordination; third person plural
6. Correct; first person singular
7. Correct; are registering, second person plural
8. We will <u>sign up</u> and <u>play</u> doubles; first person plural, first person plural

Identifying and Using Verb Forms, Number, and Person, EXERCISE C
Dialogues will vary; a possible dialogue is given.
OLIVIA: I don't think so.
GRACE: Why won't you go?
OLIVIA: I want to go, but my parents are going out of town.
GRACE: They should go out of town some other time.

Identifying and Using Simple Tenses, EXERCISE A
1. miss/misses, missed, will miss
2. watch/watches, watched, will watch
3. scamper/scampers, scampered, will scamper
4. select/ selects, selected, will select
5. play/plays, played, will play
6. plan/plans, planned, will plan
7. prepare/prepares, prepared, will prepare
8. copy/copies, copied, will copy
9. think/thinks, thought, will think
10. go/goes, went, will go

Identifying and Using Simple Tenses, EXERCISE B
1. Virgina Hamilton <u>was</u> the youngest of five children.
2. Hamilton's childhood experiences <u>influenced</u> her writing.
3. Her grandfather <u>escaped</u> from slavery to Ohio.
4. Historians <u>will remember</u> Hamilton's hometown in Ohio as an important stop on the Underground Railroad.
5. Her novel *Arilla Sun Down* <u>focuses</u> on stories about her grandmother.
6. <u>M.C. Higgins, the Great</u> <u>won</u> the National Book Award and the Newbery Award in the same year.
7. Many of Hamilton's books <u>concern</u> themselves with the past.
8. She also <u>writes</u> stories about today's problems.
9. Today she and her husband <u>live</u> in Yellow Springs, Ohio.
10. Virginia Hamilton <u>will continue</u> to write novels for young adults on contemporary issues and historical events.

Identifying and Using Simple Tenses, EXERCISE C
Answers will vary; possible answers are given.
1. We <u>jump</u> for joy when we go to the pool. / Damien <u>jumped</u> from the high board. / When the signal goes off, I <u>will jump</u> into the pool.
2. Bobby <u>carries</u> all his books home every day. / Mr. Hutton <u>carried</u> the crates into the garage. / <u>Will</u> we <u>carry</u> these flags in the parade?
3. The museum <u>displays</u> a variety of folk art./Irv proudly <u>displayed</u> his coin collection. / The art teachers <u>will display</u> our projects in the front hall.
4. The ball <u>drops</u> through the hoop, and we win! / Ricky <u>dropped</u> the hot platter. / That juggler <u>will</u> not <u>drop</u> his clubs.
5. We <u>write</u> poetry about once a week in Ms. Cooper's class. / Stan <u>wrote</u> a story called "Eagles in Flight." / <u>Will</u> you <u>write</u> more stories soon?

Identifying and Using Perfect Tenses, EXERCISE A
1. present perfect
2. future perfect
3. present perfect
4. past perfect
5. future perfect

Identifying and Using Perfect Tenses, EXERCISE B
1. We <u>have moved</u> the furniture in the den.
2. After dinner Ron <u>had grumbled</u> about doing the dishes.
3. Each contestant <u>will have spelled</u> difficult words.
4. Vi <u>had built</u> the new computer by herself.
5. Who <u>has used</u> all the adhesive tape?

Identifying and Using Perfect Tenses, EXERCISE C

Answers will vary; possible answers are given.

1. I <u>have cleaned</u> the table and <u>have washed</u> the dishes.
2. <u>Had</u> Mrs. Roberts <u>heard</u> the good news?
3. Mickey <u>has read</u> the book, but last week he <u>had</u> not even <u>begun</u> it.
4. When <u>will</u> the committee <u>have reached</u> a decision?
5. What a long time it <u>has taken</u> to reach a verdict!

Identifying and Using Progressive Forms of Verb Tenses, EXERCISE A

1. is climbing
2. will be reading
3. has been visiting
4. was explaining
5. will have been studying
6. will be practicing
7. had been acting
8. was traveling
9. has been lying
10. had been seeing

Identifying and Using Progressive Forms of Verb Tenses, EXERCISE B

1. are taking (present progressive)
2. will have been working (future perfect progressive)
3. will be competing (future progressive)
4. had been thinking (past perfect progressive), have been thinking (present perfect progressive)

Identifying and Using Progressive Forms of Verb Tenses, EXERCISE C

Sentences will vary; possible sentences are given.

1. Last week, we <u>were discussing</u> ancient Greece.
   I wonder what they <u>were doing</u> before they went to art class?
2. This week, we <u>have been seeing</u> similarities between the two cultures.
   My art teacher <u>has been talking</u> about the use of light and shadow.
3. Right now, we <u>are viewing</u> a video about some of the services that the Roman government <u>was providing</u> for its people on a daily basis.
   She <u>is telling</u> us to go through our portfolios to see how we <u>were using</u> light in our earlier work.
4. Our teacher says that she <u>will be quizzing</u> us on this material soon!
   Now <u>I will be thinking</u> about light in a whole new way.

Identifying and Using Irregular Verbs, EXERCISE A

1. sing, <u>sang</u>, <u>sung</u>
2. <u>draw</u>, drew, <u>drawn</u>
3. <u>go</u>, <u>went</u>, gone
4. see, <u>saw</u>, <u>seen</u>
5. <u>drink</u>, drank, <u>drunk</u>
6. <u>speak</u>, <u>spoke</u>, spoken
7. <u>think</u>, thought, <u>thought</u>
8. write, <u>wrote</u>, <u>written</u>
9. <u>ring</u>, <u>rang</u>, rung
10. <u>grow</u>, grew, <u>grown</u>

Identifying and Using Irregular Verbs, EXERCISE B
1. spoken, past participle
2. thought, past
3. left, past participle
4. begun, past participle
5. swam, past

Identifying and Using Irregular Verbs, EXERCISE C
Some answers may vary slightly; possible answers are given.
1. RHONDA: In which department did she find it?
2. DONNA: She <u>found</u> it in the Broadway Limited Collection. (past)
3. RHONDA: How did she get the money for it?
4. DONNA: She <u>had gotten</u> the money from her baby-sitting. (past participle)
5. RHONDA: Did she wear it to school yet?
6. DONNA: She <u>wore</u> it to school on Monday. (past)
7. RHONDA: Did Aimee really buy the same sweater?
8. DONNA: Aimee <u>had bought</u> the same sweater! (past participle)
9. RHONDA: Do you think that she'll take it back?
10. DONNA: She <u>has</u> already <u>taken</u> it back. (past participle)

Identifying and Using Active and Passive Voice, EXERCISE A
Verbs appear in the order given. Sentence breaks are denoted by /.
is eaten, passive / knows, active / was brought, passive / made, active / added, active; was created, passive / were carried, passive / was made, passive / was established, passive / is produced, passive

Identifying and Using Active and Passive Voice, EXERCISE B
1. passive; My family <u>has visited</u> a restaurant.
2. passive; All of us <u>ate</u> favorite desserts.
3. active; Custard pie <u>was favored</u> by my sister.
4. active; The bill <u>was paid</u> by Dad.
5. passive; Now my family <u>will need</u> some exercise!

Identifying and Using Active and Passive Voice, EXERCISE C
Answers will vary; possible answers are given.
1. The balloons for the party <u>have been bought</u>.
2. Jay <u>bought</u> a new baseball card for his collection.
3. <u>Did</u> you <u>read</u> that magazine yet?
4. This novel <u>will be read</u> by everyone in class.
5. When <u>will</u> the rest of the book <u>have been read</u>?

Using Easily Confused Verbs Correctly, EXERCISE A
1. sitting
2. lay
3. let
4. laid
5. set

Using Easily Confused Verbs Correctly, EXERCISE B
Some answers may vary; possible answers are given.
1. sat
2. laid
3. set
4. lie
5. Leave

Using Easily Confused Verbs Correctly, EXERCISE C
1. The workers have just <u>laid</u> new tiles around the fountain.
2. Correct
3. They'll <u>let</u> anybody play in the fountain.
4. Yesterday, I <u>sat</u> in the rose garden.
5. Some rose petals <u>lay</u> on the flower bed.

Using Principal Parts of Verbs Correctly, EXERCISE A
1. taken
2. rode
3. wore
4. known
5. blew

Using Principal Parts of Verbs Correctly, EXERCISE B
1. Native Americans <u>taught</u> the Pilgrims to plant corn.
2. Correct
3. Every day the corn <u>rose</u> higher and higher.
4. They <u>left</u> it to dry in the sun.
5. Some of the Pilgrims' first crop <u>was taken</u> back to Europe.

Using Principal Parts of Verbs Correctly, EXERCISE C
1. I <u>bit</u> into one without thinking.
2. I probably should have <u>chosen</u> a sweet pepper.
3. How that spicy pepper <u>stung</u> my tongue!
4. I could have <u>drunk</u> a gallon of water.
5. I never <u>knew</u> that anything could be so hot!

Using Tense Sequence Correctly, EXERCISE A
1. had mistreated
2. had been
3. had changed
4. misjudged

Using Tense Sequence Correctly, EXERCISE B
1. Janice felt sorry that she <u>had disturbed</u> our sleep.
2. We were nervous until we <u>had flown</u> a few times.
3. Correct
4. Don't you wish that you <u>had answered</u> him first?
5. Correct
6. I feel better now that I <u>have filled</u> out my application.
7. Correct
8. Gerald polished the silver although he <u>had done</u> it earlier.
9. When Sis has written, I <u>have</u> always <u>answered</u>.
10. Correct

Using Tense Sequence Correctly, EXERCISE C
1. have responded
2. had spoken
3. had caught
4. had written
5. have flown

Developing Your Style: Using Vivid, Precise Verbs, EXERCISE A
Answers will vary; possible answers are given.
 1. The visitors <u>stroll</u> through the gallery and <u>study</u> the paintings.
 2. Some artists <u>sign</u> their names on their artwork in clear, bold letters while others <u>scribble</u> theirs carelessly.
 3. "You see, the glass frames <u>preserve</u> the paintings," the guide <u>explains</u>.
 4. Although many people <u>appreciate</u> the paintings, they <u>prefer</u> the sculpture garden more.

Developing Your Style: Using Vivid, Precise Verbs, EXERCISE B
Answers will vary; possible answers are given.
 1. One guest <u>discussed</u> politics with the host; another guest <u>gossiped</u> about Hollywood stars.
 2. The singer <u>strode</u> into the spotlight and <u>bowed</u>.
 3. The people <u>whistled</u> and <u>cheered</u> for their favorite rock star.
 4. When the comedienne <u>slipped</u> on the polished floor, she <u>laughed</u>.
 5. Because she <u>had bruised</u> her knee, she <u>limped</u> off the stage.

Developing Your Style: Using Vivid, Precise Verbs, EXERCISE C
Answers will vary; possible answers are given.

 The ill-mannered passenger <u>stumbled</u> aboard the train and <u>tramped</u> down the aisle. First, the passenger <u>lounged</u> in his chair and then <u>leafed</u> quickly through the newspaper. Later, he <u>guzzled</u> some water and <u>snored</u> loudly when he fell asleep. As the train <u>crawled</u> into the station, the conductor <u>shouted</u>, "Last stop!" Suddenly, the startled passenger <u>bounded</u> from his seat and <u>sprang</u> from the train onto the platform.

Developing Your Style: Choosing the Active Voice, EXERCISE A
 1. a
 2. b
 3. a
 4. b

Developing Your Style: Choosing the Active Voice, EXERCISE B
 1. The cleaning crew washed all the windows in the house.
 2. The birth of the kittens fascinated the whole family.
 3. The treasurer is maintaining the financial records.
 4. Will the school board recommend all our changes?
 5. You have defended your position well.
 6. The poor farmers had fought and won the battle.
 7. How wonderfully Lenore is playing the piano!
 8. This year Mr. Hirsch will coach the team.
 9. Had a girl in the back row asked one question?
10. Our girls' basketball team has won the championship!

Developing Your Style: Choosing the Active Voice, EXERCISE C
Sentences will vary; possible sentences are given.
 1. Dr. Hicks <u>brought</u> me into the world.
 2. When I was three, I <u>broke</u> my arm in a fall.
 3. How that arm <u>hurt</u>!
 4. In second grade, Dad <u>moved</u> us to Denver.
 5. We <u>were</u> all sorry to leave Detroit.
 6. In Denver, however, I <u>met</u> my best friend.
 7. Dennis <u>lives</u> across the street from us.
 8. He and I <u>do</u> almost everything together.
 9. At school, I <u>like</u> science the best.
10. A career in medical research <u>sounds</u> pretty good to me.

Overview

Throughout their scholastic careers, most students are expected to take a variety of standardized tests. Developing skill in taking standardized tests will be of great value to students as they proceed through the grades and encounter such tests.

Most standardized tests, including the Scholastic Aptitude Test (SAT), include a verbal component that tests students' knowledge of vocabulary. In order to perform up to their potential and achieve competitive scores on these tests of verbal skills, students need substantive preparation.

To achieve success on standardized tests, students must be able to apply their knowledge of vocabulary to the types of items encountered on these tests. Therefore, in addition to developing their vocabularies, students should learn the format of standardized tests and practice answering the various types of items included on the tests.

Description of the Vocabulary Practice Tests

The following pages are designed to familiarize students with standardized test formats and to give students practice in taking the verbal portions of these tests. Each of the practice tests includes one or more of the following types of questions: synonyms, antonyms, verbal analogies, and sentence completions.

Organization

The vocabulary practice tests are structured so that the tests become increasingly challenging as students progress from grade to grade. This progression will enable students to continue developing their vocabulary and test-taking skills throughout their scholastic careers and will prepare them for the pivotal standardized tests they are likely to encounter in their last few years of high school.

The structure of the vocabulary practice tests for Grade 7 enables students to develop confidence and skill with each type of vocabulary item before they encounter a full test with all types of items. Tests 1–5 focus on a single vocabulary skill. Tests 6–9 encompass different types of vocabulary skills.

The Vocabulary Practice Tests for Grade 7 are as follows:

Test 1   Synonyms

Test 2   Antonyms

Test 3   Verbal Analogies

Test 4   Sentence Completions

Test 5   Antonyms

Test 6   Synonyms
Verbal Analogies
Sentence Completions

Test 7   Sentence Completions

How to Use the Vocabulary Practice Tests

Before you begin administering the tests to your students, give each of them a copy of Test-Taking Strategies for Students, beginning on page 267. This section provides students with proven test-taking strategies that should help to improve their performance on standardized tests.

We urge you to use these vocabulary tests for practice, not for grades, in order to allow students to develop comfort and facility with test items and situations. Although you may choose to provide students with a limited amount of time in which to complete each test, try to allow at least one minute for each item on the test. Tests 6, 7, and 8 have more test items than your students could probably complete in one class period. You may wish to subdivide those tests.

Answer Sheet

The answer sheet included here (page 321) is a blackline master. You may duplicate copies for your classes. Please be aware that these blackline copies cannot be read in a scanner.

Test-Taking Strategies for Students

General Strategies

Over the course of your school career, you will probably encounter many standardized tests. To perform well on these tests, you must be well-prepared and have a solid background in the subjects being tested. In addition, you will benefit from using the following proven test-taking strategies.

1. Before taking any standardized test, you should learn about the types of items included on the test. Familiarize yourself with the instructions and examples for each type of item on the test. Then, when you take the test you will be comfortable with the instructions and examples.

2. Difficult questions often take much more time to answer answer than easier questions. If you cannot answer a question quickly, skip over it and focus on answering easier ones. Once you have reached the end of the section, return to the questions you passed over and try to answer them.

3. Avoid making wild guesses. If you are unsure of the correct answer to a question, examine the choices to see if any can be eliminated. Once you have eliminated two or more choices, you can make an educated guess.

4. Trust your first instincts. Avoid going back and changing your answers, unless you are reasonably certain that your original answer was incorrect.

5. Make sure that you enter each of your answers beside the appropriate number on your answer sheet. If you pass over a question, make sure that you do not forget to skip over the corresponding number on your answer sheet.

Taking Standardized Vocabulary Exams

Prentice Hall's Vocabulary Practice Tests include four types of items: synonyms, antonyms, verbal analogies, and sentence completions. In each of the synonym items, you are given one word and asked to select the word most similar in meaning. In each of the antonym items, you are given one word and asked to select the word most opposite in meaning. In each of the verbal analogies, you are given a pair of words and asked to determine the relationship between the two words and then select the word pair with the most similar relationship. Finally, the sentence completions provide a sentence with one blank space for which you must select the most appropriate word.

Synonyms

Synonym items require you to choose the word most similar in meaning to the given word. Before you begin a group of synonym items, you will encounter the following instructions. Read them thoroughly now and study the example.

Directions: Each question below consists of a word in CAPITAL LETTERS, followed by five lettered words or phrases. Choose the word or phrase that is most *similar* in meaning to the word in CAPITAL LETTERS. Blacken the letter of your answer on the answer sheet. Because some choices may be close in meaning, consider all the choices before deciding which is best.

Example:

VANISH:
(A) return
(B) disappear
(C) go
(D) magic
(E) dim

Disappear is the correct answer. You would have filled in the circle marked B on your answer sheet.

Explanation: Because VANISH is a verb, you can immediately eliminate the noun *magic*. The verb *go* is unsuitable because it means "to move." The verb *return* has the opposite meaning of VANISH, and the meaning of the verb *dim* is lesser in degree than the meaning of VANISH. Finally, the verb *disappear* is the best choice because it is the word most similar in meaning.

Tips for Answering Synonym Questions

1. Remember, many words have more than one meaning. First, determine the meaning of the given word. Then, carefully read the word choices and select the word that is the most similar.

2. If you are not completely sure of the given word's meaning, try using it in a sentence.

3. Choose the word or phrase that is similar to the given word. Take care that you do not mistakenly choose a word that is opposite to the original word.

4. Most synonyms do not have exactly the same meaning. Always choose the word most nearly similar in meaning to the given word.

5. If the correct answer is not immediately apparent, try to eliminate as many choices as possible.

Antonyms

Antonym items require you to choose the best opposite of a given word. Before you begin a group of antonym items, you will encounter the following instructions. Read them thoroughly now and study the example.

Directions: Each question below consists of a word in CAPITAL LETTERS, followed by five lettered words or phrases. Choose the word or phrase that is most nearly *opposite* in meaning to the word in CAPITAL LETTERS. Blacken the letter of your answer on the answer sheet. Because some of the choices are close in meaning, consider all the choices before deciding which is best.

Example:

CORRECTLY:
(A) falsely
(B) unjust
(C) wrong
(D) simply
(E) sadly

Falsely is the correct answer. You would have filled in the circle marked A on your answer sheet.

Explanation: Because CORRECTLY is an adverb, you can immediately eliminate the adjectives *unjust* and *wrong*. Although *simply* and *sadly* are also adverbs, they are not opposite in meaning to CORRECTLY. This leaves the word *falsely*, which is the best opposite of CORRECTLY.

Tips for Answering Antonym Questions

1. Remember, many words have more than one meaning. First, read the word and determine its meaning. Then, carefully read the word choices and choose the word that is most nearly opposite in meaning.

2. If you are not completely sure of the given word's meaning, try using it in a sentence.

3. Make sure that you choose the word or phrase that is opposite to the given word. Do not mistakenly choose a word that is similar to the original word.

4. Many words do not have exact opposites or antonyms. Therefore, consider the choices carefully. Always choose the word most nearly opposite in meaning to the given word.

5. If the correct answer is not immediately apparent, try to eliminate as many choices as possible by thinking of their opposites.

Verbal Analogies

An analogy is a relationship between two things. Verbal analogies require you to determine how two words in a pair are related to each other. Then, from the five other word pairs, you must select the pair of words with the relationship most similar to the original pair. Before you begin a group of verbal analogies, you will encounter directions similar to the following. Read these directions thoroughly and study the example.

Directions: Each question below consists of a related pair of words in CAPITAL LETTERS, followed by five lettered pairs of words. Choose the pair that best expresses a relationship similar to that expressed in the pair in CAPITAL LETTERS. Blacken the letter of your answer on the answer sheet.

Example:

FOOLISH is to SILLY as

(A) **confuse** is to **explain**
(B) **wheel** is to **motorcycle**
(C) **tree** is to **oak**
(D) **fall** is to **rise**
(E) **brilliant** is to **bright**

Brilliant is to *bright* is the correct answer. You would have filled in the circle marked E on your answer sheet.

Explanation: To answer verbal analogies, you must first determine the relationship between the two words in the original pair. In the preceding example you would look at the relationship between the words *foolish* and *silly*. You should note that they are synonyms. Choice E is correct because the words in that pair are the only synonyms. In choice A the words are antonyms. In choice B the relationship is that of part (wheel) to whole (motorcycle). In choice C the relationship is one of group (tree) to example (oak). In choice D the words are antonyms.

You may find it helpful to formulate a sentence expressing the relationship between the original pair. Use the words first and second in your sentence, showing the order in which the words appear in the item. For example, if the two words were *walk* and *stroll*, you might create the following sentence: The first word is a verb and the second word is a synonym of the verb.

Typical Relationships

The following are some of the most common types of relationships used in verbal analogies:

Synonyms	**Clue** is to **Hint** **Angry** is to **Mad**
Antonyms	**Shy** is to **Outgoing** **Advance** is to **Retreat**
Lesser to Greater	**Walk** is to **Run**
Greater to Lesser	**Pound** is to **Tap**
Group and Example	**Color** is to **Red**
Example and Group	**Baseball Player** is to **Athlete**
Sequence	**Before** is to **After**
Person or Thing and Function or Action	**Minister** is to **Preaches**

Tips for Answering Analogy Questions

1. First, determine the relationship in the given pair of words. Then, look at all of the word pairs and select the pair that has the same relationship as the given pair.

2. Parts of speech may be a clue. Generally, the correct answer will consist of a pair of words that are the same parts of speech as the original pair.

3. Make sure that your choice has the same similarity of the given word pair. If the relationship of the given pair is greater to lesser, the relationship of the words in the pair you choose must also be greater to lesser, not lesser to greater.

4. Because a number of the pairs of words may express relationships somewhat similar to that of the original pair, make sure that the relationship of the pair you choose is the most similar to that of the original pair.

Sentence Completions

Sentence completion items require you to choose a word that correctly completes the meaning of a sentence. Before you begin a group of sentence completions, you will encounter directions similar to the following. Read these directions thoroughly now and study the example.

Directions: Each of the following sentences has a blank space, indicating that a word has been omitted. Beneath the sentence are five lettered words. Choose the word that best completes the meaning of the sentence as a whole. Blacken the letter of your answer on the answer sheet.

Example:

It was early in the morning and Phil walked along _____, trying not to disturb anyone on our way to the docks to go fishing.

(A) happily
(B) loudly
(C) quietly
(D) silence
(E) moody

Quietly is the correct answer. You would have filled the circle marked C on your answer sheet.

Explanation: If you try all of the answer choices, you will notice that none makes sense except for C. Because the answer requires an adverb, *silence* and *moody* can be eliminated. You would eliminate *loudly* because Phil would not walk that way if he was trying not to disturb anyone. Because he was trying not to disturb anyone, *quietly* fits the meaning of the sentence better than *happily* does.

The best way to approach answering a sentence completion question is by first reading only the sentence and supplying your own word to fill the gap. Then, look at the answer choices and cross out those that do not make sense. If that leaves you with more than one answer choice, pick the one that seems most logical and convincing.

Tips for Answering Sentence Completions

1. Use context clues to help you unlock the meaning of the sentence.

2. Look for signal words, such as *because, therefore, but, however,* or *although,* that indicate a relationship in the incomplete sentence.

3. If you are unfamiliar with one of the word choices, try fitting each of the remaining choices into the sentence. If one of them fits perfectly into the sentence, select it as your answer. On the other hand, if the remaining four choices all seem unsuitable, the unknown word is probably the right one.

Test 1

Synonyms

Directions: Each question below consists of a word in CAPITAL LETTERS, followed by five lettered words or phrases. Choose the word or phrase that is most *similar* in meaning to the word in CAPITAL LETTERS. Blacken the letter of your answer on the answer sheet. Because some choices may be close in meaning, consider all the choices before deciding which is best.

Example:

DESPAIR:

(A) repair
(B) sad
(C) hopelessness
(D) optimism
(E) regret

Hopelessness is the correct answer. You would have filled in the circle marked C on your answer sheet.

---

1. WONDERMENT:
   (A) wonderful
   (B) amazement
   (C) basement
   (D) ordinary
   (E) unknowing

2. PROVISIONS:
   (A) revisions
   (B) exceptions
   (C) groups
   (D) beliefs
   (E) supplies

3. PUMMELED:
   (A) kick
   (B) tumbled
   (C) ridiculed
   (D) pounded
   (E) yelled

4. FLINCHED:
   (A) glimpsed
   (B) flicked
   (C) robbed
   (D) recoiled
   (E) grabbed

5. UNDELETERIOUS:
   (A) relieved
   (B) undefined
   (C) healthful
   (D) sane
   (E) unhealthy

6. RECONNOITER:
   (A) sleep
   (B) scout
   (C) refill
   (D) reconnect
   (E) warn

7. SOMNOLENT:

(A) sleepy
(B) lazy
(C) slow
(D) energetic
(E) confident

8. ELEVATION:

(A) height
(B) recline
(C) simple
(D) revelation
(E) portion

9. CONSOLATION:

(A) runner up
(B) comfort
(C) relieved
(D) control panel
(E) isolation

10. HENCEFORTH:

(A) why not
(B) before
(C) forthwith
(D) advance
(E) hereafter

11. CREVASSE:

(A) survey
(B) impasse
(C) glacier
(D) crack
(E) climb down

12. FRAUDULENT:

(A) below standards
(B) reluctant
(C) snobby
(D) cold
(E) deceitful

13. SHEEN:

(A) transparent
(B) yell
(C) savage
(D) shininess
(E) female

14. PRONE:

(A) unlikely
(B) standing up
(C) lying down
(D) uncomfortable
(E) dark

15. SYLVAN:

(A) golden
(B) forestlike
(C) slender
(D) drowsy
(E) expensive

16. CUNNINGLY:

(A) sneakily
(B) smart
(C) cleverly
(D) sloppily
(E) snake-like

17. AWE:

(A) amazement
(B) drill
(C) expectancy
(D) relief
(E) disappointment

18. STEALTHY:

(A) ill
(B) jealous
(C) quiet
(D) illegally
(E) sneaky

19. TAUT:
   (A) nervous
   (B) tight
   (C) bought
   (D) learned
   (E) bottom

20. COLLABORATED:
   (A) agreed
   (B) congratulated
   (C) spent
   (D) cooperated
   (E) labored

21. MOURNING:
   (A) grieving
   (B) evening
   (C) tomorrow
   (D) realizing
   (E) greeting

22. LACKADAISICAL:
   (A) uninterested
   (B) shortage
   (C) musical
   (D) confused
   (E) sloppy

Test 2

Antonyms

Directions: Each question below consists of a word in CAPITAL LETTERS, followed by five lettered words or phrases. Choose the word or phrase that is most nearly *opposite* in meaning to the word in CAPITAL LETTERS. Blacken the letter of your answer on the answer sheet. Because some of the choices are close in meaning, consider all the choices before deciding which is best.

Example:

NIMBLE:

(A) light-footed
(B) stupid
(C) old
(D) forgetful
(E) clumsy

Clumsy is the correct answer. You would have filled in the circle marked E on your answer sheet.

1. ABETTING:

   (A) betting
   (B) waking
   (C) regretting
   (D) discouraging
   (E) denying

2. REPROACH:

   (A) blame
   (B) approach
   (C) distance
   (D) praise
   (E) avoid

3. GNAWING:

   (A) soothing
   (B) drinking
   (C) annoying
   (D) build
   (E) agreeing

4. CRAFTY:

   (A) artsy
   (B) blunder
   (C) stationary
   (D) shifted
   (E) straightforward

5. SOLEMN:

   (A) splendid
   (B) monotonous
   (C) joyous
   (D) relief
   (E) insecure

6. OMINOUSLY:

   (A) honestly
   (B) encouragingly
   (C) threateningly
   (D) grumbling
   (E) encourage

7. FIASCO:

   (A) tango
   (B) prize
   (C) triumph
   (D) secretive
   (E) somber

8. SAUCINESS:

   (A) lively
   (B) smoothness
   (C) humorous
   (D) dryness
   (E) sulkiness

9. CONFOUND:

   (A) retrieve
   (B) convex
   (C) amaze
   (D) rebound
   (E) clarify

10. RIGOROUSLY:

   (A) squarely
   (B) undisciplined
   (C) unfortunately
   (D) sloppily
   (E) vigorously

11. DISPELLED:

   (A) removed
   (B) misspelled
   (C) spelled
   (D) reinforced
   (E) built

12. INCREDULOUSLY:

   (A) trustingly
   (B) believe
   (C) incredibly
   (D) credited
   (E) vaguely

13. INTERWOVEN:

   (A) underground
   (B) separated
   (C) unwound
   (D) woven
   (E) interstate

14. PASSIVE:

   (A) active
   (B) enduring
   (C) awake
   (D) furtive
   (E) uncontrollable

15. INFLAMMATORY:

   (A) extinguished
   (B) soothing
   (C) painful
   (D) cool
   (E) stiffness

16. DAWDLED:

   (A) trundled
   (B) run
   (C) hastened
   (D) waddled
   (E) hurrying

17. SANCTION:

   (A) suction
   (B) fear
   (C) disapproval
   (D) advance
   (E) inactivity

18. PERPETUAL:

   (A) alternating
   (B) exceptional
   (C) disposal
   (D) conceptual
   (E) momentary

19. RESIGNEDLY:

(A) rebelliously
(B) hired
(C) hastily
(D) half-heartedly
(E) memorably

20. REVERIE:

(A) sleep
(B) unimportant
(C) hidden
(D) concentration
(E) imagination

21. FEINTED:

(A) attacked
(B) revived
(C) awakened
(D) faked
(E) climbed

22. WILY:

(A) sly
(B) unintelligent
(C) straightforward
(D) pleasing
(E) unthreatening

23. TRIUMPHANT:

(A) surrender
(B) unfortunate
(C) silent
(D) redundant
(E) despairing

24. DEBUT:

(A) rebuttal
(B) final appearance
(C) flimsy excuse
(D) redo
(E) foreign debt

25. SANCTUARY:

(A) unholy statement
(B) itinerary
(C) vulnerable place
(D) forgotten knowledge
(E) fortress

Test 3

Verbal Analogies

Directions: Each question below consists of a related pair of words in CAPITAL LETTERS, followed by five lettered pairs of words. Choose the pair that best expresses a relationship similar to that expressed in the pair in CAPITAL LETTERS. Blacken the letter of your answer on the answer sheet.

Example:

SHROUDED is to **UNCOVERED** as

(A) **foggy** is to **misty**
(B) **sail** is to **wind**
(C) **covered** is to **blanketed**
(D) **lacked** is to **wanted**
(E) **pushed** is to **pulled**

Pushed is to pulled is the correct answer. You would have filled in the circle marked E on your answer sheet.

1. **MAJESTIC** is to **ORDINARY** as

   (A) **alone** is to **apart**
   (B) **barbaric** is to **civilized**
   (C) **justice** is to **judge**
   (D) **look** is to **see**
   (E) **salt** is to **pepper**

2. **REFUGE** is to **SHELTER** as

   (A) **ship** is to **vessel**
   (B) **rain** is to **April**
   (C) **difficult** is to **hard**
   (D) **chair** is to **table**
   (E) **grand** is to **nice**

3. **RESILIENT** is to **RIGID** as

   (A) **bounce** is to **hop**
   (B) **excellent** is to **excited**
   (C) **air** is to **water**
   (D) **attack** is to **retreating**
   (E) **superior** is to **inferior**

4. **BRAVADO** is to **NERVOUSNESS** as

   (A) **bravery** is to **courage**
   (B) **shaking** is to **steadying**
   (C) **last** is to **final**
   (D) **weakness** is to **strength**
   (E) **reset** is to begin **again**

5. **TEMPEST** is to **HURRICANE** as

   (A) **thunder** is to **lightning**
   (B) **during** is to **ongoing**
   (C) **tornado** is to **cyclone**
   (D) **twine** is to **rope**
   (E) **annoying** is to **helpful**

6. **CHIVALROUS** is to **DISCOURTEOUS** as

   (A) **courteous** is to **devious**
   (B) **opening** is to **closed**
   (C) **generous** is to **selfish**
   (D) **closet** is to **pantry**
   (E) **racket** is to **bat**

7. **CONCUSSION** is to **JOLT** as

    (A) **crack** is to **crunch**
    (B) **jolly** is to **happy**
    (C) **vibration** is to **trembling**
    (D) **scooter** is to **motorcycle**
    (E) **elephant** is to **mouse**

8. **LETHAL** is to **POISON** as

    (A) **bullet** is to **arrow**
    (B) **worry** is to **concern**
    (C) **sniff** is to **smell**
    (D) **nourishing** is to **food**
    (E) **solid** is to **heavy**

9. **RESOLUTELY** is to **UNCERTAINLY** as

    (A) **dolphin** is to **porpoise**
    (B) **super** is to **great**
    (C) **repeated** is to **restated**
    (D) **forcefully** is to **aggressively**
    (E) **forcefully** is to **gently**

10. **EVIDENTLY** is to **APPARENTLY** as

    (A) **falsely** is to **genuinely**
    (B) **not** is to **nor**
    (C) **blackened** is to **lightened**
    (D) **stiffly** is to **sloppily**
    (E) **completely** is to **utterly**

11. **CURRENCY** is to **MONEY** as

    (A) **timepiece** is to **clock**
    (B) **tortoise** is to **hare**
    (C) **prepare** is to **repair**
    (D) **simple** is to **difficult**
    (E) **song** is to **musical**

12. **IMMENSE** is to **TINY** as

    (A) **fly** is to **spider**
    (B) **huge** is to **average**
    (C) **silly** is to **funny**
    (D) **disgusting** is to **appealing**
    (E) **brown** is to **yellow**

13. **KEENER** is to **DULLER** as

    (A) **longer** is to **shorten**
    (B) **laughter** is to **tears**
    (C) **faster** is to **slower**
    (D) **problem** is to **difficulty**
    (E) **call** is to **summon**

14. **DEMEANOR** is to **MANNER** as

    (A) **sloppy** is to **clean**
    (B) **activity** is to **project**
    (C) **sick** is to **healthy**
    (D) **offensive** is to **defensive**
    (E) **calender** is to **clock**

15. **HAUGHTILY** is to **SCORNFULLY** as

    (A) **hastily** is to **quickly**
    (B) **confidently** is to **doubtfully**
    (C) **respect** is to **honor**
    (D) **foolish** is to **unwise**
    (E) **garbage** is to **smelly**

16. **DISTRACTED** is to **FOCUSED** as

    (A) **installed** is to **removed**
    (B) **reported** is to **heard**
    (C) **daily** is to **weekly**
    (D) **concentrate** is to **study**
    (E) **collapsed** is to **fell**

17. **MARTIAL** is to **PEACEFUL** as

    (A) **wedding** is to **marriage**
    (B) **valiant** is to **cowardly**
    (C) **bat** is to **cave**
    (D) **older** is to **elder**
    (E) **lonely** is to **alone**

18. **TUMULTUOUSLY** is to **STORMILY** as

    (A) **relaxed** is to **mellowed**
    (B) **joyfully** is to **happily**
    (C) **nervous** is to **stagefright**
    (D) **riverboat** is to **tugboat**
    (E) **mistakenly** is to **purposfully**

19. **MELANCHOLY** is to **CHEERFUL** as

   (A) **floating** is to **sinking**
   (B) **busy** is to **hurried**
   (C) **down** is to **elevator**
   (D) **hopeful** is to **optimistic**
   (E) **embarrassed** is to **proud**

20. **DECIPHER** is to **DECODE** as

   (A) **deflate** is to **inflate**
   (B) **forest** is to **meadow**
   (C) **blow up** is to **explode**
   (D) **belonging** is to **joining**
   (E) **hello** is to **goodbye**

21. **SUPERCILIOUSLY** is to **MEEKLY** as

   (A) **mechanically** is to **automatically**
   (B) **crab** is to **lobster**
   (C) **meek** is to **gentle**
   (D) **supernatural** is to **natural**
   (E) **loudly** is to **quietly**

22. **DOMESTIC** is to **HOUSEHOLD** as

   (A) **slave** is to **worker**
   (B) **private** is to **personal**
   (C) **chicken** is to **egg**
   (D) **itchy** is to **painful**
   (E) **sour** is to **lemon**

23. **ARCHED** is to **STRAIGHT** as

   (A) **flat** is to **level**
   (B) **door** is to **window**
   (C) **beside** is to **above**
   (D) **obvious** is to **unclear**
   (E) **flower** is to **rose**

24. **INDIFFERENTLY** is to **ATTENTIVELY** as

   (A) **oddly** is to **strangely**
   (B) **moon** is to **sun**
   (C) **yell** is to **whisper**
   (D) **happily** is to **angrily**
   (E) **seal** is to **walrus**

25. **OBLIGING** is to **GOOD-NATURED** as

   (A) **going** is to **coming**
   (B) **playing** is to **performed**
   (C) **leaf** is to **tree**
   (D) **nagging** is to **bothersome**
   (E) **gully** is to **ditch**

26. **SLACKENING** is to **SLOWING DOWN** as

   (A) **slithering** is to **snake**
   (B) **towing** is to **pushing**
   (C) **throwing** is to **tossing**
   (D) **slowly** is to **quickly**
   (E) **familiar** is to **recognizable**

27. **IRREVOCABLY** is to **CHANGEABLY** as

   (A) **dirty** is to **muddy**
   (B) **irregular** is to **strange**
   (C) **common** is to **extraordinary**
   (D) **week** is to **year**
   (E) **trumpet** is to **instrument**

28. **INCREDULOUS** is to **TRUSTFUL** as

   (A) **boring** is to **exciting**
   (B) **sleepy** is to **drowsy**
   (C) **alive** is to **lively**
   (D) **pretend** is to **make believe**
   (E) **shopping** is to **stores**

29. **INCOMPREHENSIBLE** is to **UNDERSTANDABLE** as

   (A) **crowded** is to **empty**
   (B) **valid** is to **acceptable**
   (C) **crunchy** is to **crispy**
   (D) **enjoy** is to **like**
   (E) **father** is to **daughter**

30. **SAVORED** is to **ENJOYED** as

   (A) **sunshine** is to **darkness**
   (B) **planet** is to **Saturn**
   (C) **willing** is to **resistant**
   (D) **grabbed** is to **placed**
   (E) **faded** is to **evaporated**

Test 4

Sentence Completions

Directions: Each of the following sentences has a blank space, indicating that a word has been omitted. Beneath the sentence are five lettered words. Choose the word that best completes the meaning of the sentence as a whole. Blacken the letter of your answer on the answer sheet.

Example:

Because of Arnold's _____ refusal to have anything to do with girls, he was left alone when his friends began playing softball with girls from another neighborhood.

(A) fitting
(B) obstinate
(C) coarse
(D) unbiased
(E) opaque

Obstinate is the correct answer. You would have filled in the circle marked B on your answer sheet.

---

1. After the jurors had seated themselves in the jury box, the judge sternly asked the foreman, "Jury, have you reached a _____?"

   (A) fitting
   (B) impartiality
   (C) verdict
   (D) wheedle
   (E) crevasses

2. The young bear _____ sniffed the porcupine, puzzled by its strange appearance.

   (A) triumphantly
   (B) diligently
   (C) tentatively
   (D) insolent
   (E) somberly

3. The director and the entire cast were filled with _____ when the lead singer arrived for the opening performance with a sore throat.

   (A) consternation
   (B) staccato
   (C) turmoil
   (D) verdict
   (E) intricacy

4. The _____ of a caterpillar into a butterfly is one of the many wonders of nature.

   (A) inert
   (B) emerged
   (C) consternation
   (D) technology
   (E) transformation

5. My mother stores all of our _____ china in a glass cabinet in the dining room.

   (A) pathetic
   (B) hexagonal
   (C) lacy
   (D) succulent
   (E) fragile

6. The sheets on the clothes-line _____ out like white sails when a breeze blows across our backyard.

   (A) tether
   (B) reproach
   (C) endow
   (D) billow
   (E) concave

7. Honey bees are extremely _____ insects who will fly up to six miles from the hive in their endless search for honey.

   (A) industrious
   (B) relevant
   (C) impetuous
   (D) fragile
   (E) obstinate

8. The champion strode _____ into the sta-dium as her adoring fans showered her with deafening applause.

   (A) emphatic
   (B) triumphantly
   (C) tentatively
   (D) staccato
   (E) resolutely

9. As the _____ improves, computers will be made smaller, will work faster, and will be easier to use.

   (A) clan
   (B) industrious
   (C) technology
   (D) transformation
   (E) hexagonal

10. During the autumn months, apple trees are filled with ripe, _____ apples.

    (A) billowed
    (B) concave
    (C) inert
    (D) coarse
    (E) succulent

11. The meeting of the Men's Club erupted into a _____ of shouts and scuffling when it was discovered that there was a mouse in the room.

    (A) derive
    (B) consternation
    (C) turmoil
    (D) intricacy
    (E) verdict

12. The marchers at the funeral procession walked _____ toward the cemetery.

    (A) somberly
    (B) tentatively
    (C) resolutely
    (D) pathetic
    (E) diligently

13. Liza and Willie _____ white-faced and shaken from the "House of Horrors" at the state fair.

    (A) derived
    (B) reproached
    (C) endowed
    (D) emerged
    (E) billowed

14. The judge continually had to interrupt the talkative witness and ask him to re-late only _____ information.

    (A) insolent
    (B) relevant
    (C) impetuous
    (D) obstinate
    (E) succulent

15. Although the children enjoyed the movie tremendously, Miss Snodgrass thought it was _____ and simple-minded.

(A) wheedle
(B) opaque
(C) fitting
(D) coarse
(E) unbiased

16. The _____ little boy yanked off the beard of the department-store Santa Claus and yelled, "You're nothing but a fake!"

(A) fragile
(B) insolent
(C) lacy
(D) relevant
(E) tethered

17. Determined to overcome her shyness, Maria walked _____ toward the group of girls in the school yard.

(A) triumphantly
(B) resolutely
(C) somberly
(D) impartiality
(E) turmoil

18. The baseball team ended its terrible season in a(n) _____ manner, losing a doubleheader 12-0 and 8-2.

(A) industrious
(B) verdict
(C) insolent
(D) inert
(E) fitting

19. The _____ of the plot and the multitude of characters made the novel too difficult to read.

(A) transformation
(B) turmoil
(C) technology
(D) impartiality
(E) intricacy

20. Unable to ignore the _____ whining and uncontrollable shaking of the scruffy, skinny puppy, Roberto decided to take it home with him.

(A) emphatic
(B) opaque
(C) pathetic
(D) fragile
(E) impetuous

21. Aware of the dangers involved in scuba diving, Li was _____ about learning all there was to know about the sport.

(A) pathetic
(B) staccato
(C) unbiased
(D) reproached
(E) emphatic

22. Glenda _____ herself for not studying harder for the vocabulary test.

(A) reproached
(B) endowed
(C) billowed
(D) derived
(E) emerged

23. Although he was _____ to a tree, the bulldog's growling and barking was enough to scare people to the other side of the street.

(A) emerged
(B) wheedled
(C) clan
(D) tethered
(E) somberly

24. Rhonda, who was _____ with the ability to persuade, found it easy to convince people that she was the woman for the job.

(A) endowed
(B) industrious
(C) tethered
(D) hexagonal
(E) coarse

25. After working _____ for several hours, Philip decided to take a break and get something to eat.

(A) triumphantly
(B) diligently
(C) technology
(D) tentatively
(E) intricacy

Test 5

Antonyms

Directions: Each question below consists of a word in CAPITAL LETTERS, followed by five lettered words or phrases. Choose the word or phrase that is most nearly *opposite* in meaning to the word in CAPITAL LETTERS. Blacken the letter of your answer on the answer sheet. Because some of the choices are close in meaning, consider all the choices before deciding which is best.

Example:

SEVERE:

(A) sincere
(B) join
(C) quiet
(D) mild
(E) good

Mild is the correct answer. You would have filled in the circle marked D on your answer sheet.

1. DEFIANT:

   (A) nice
   (B) tiny
   (C) despairing
   (D) moving
   (E) obedient

2. MASTERFUL:

   (A) meaningful
   (B) weakling
   (C) beginner
   (D) feeble
   (E) lazy

3. VOID:

   (A) large
   (B) avoid
   (C) fullness
   (D) genius
   (E) gap

4. PEEVED:

   (A) concerned
   (B) weaved
   (C) peered
   (D) delighted
   (E) relaxed

5. GLEEFULLY:

   (A) gloomily
   (B) cheerfully
   (C) carefully
   (D) sickening
   (E) anger

6. MOROSE:

   (A) jolly
   (B) gross
   (C) talkative
   (D) simple
   (E) quick

7. AUDIBLE:

   (A) unseen
   (B) inaudible
   (C) heard
   (D) sound
   (E) dishonorable

8. ASSENT:

   (A) assert
   (B) descent
   (C) disagreement
   (D) helpless
   (E) buffer

9. COMPULSION:

   (A) complexion
   (B) repulse
   (C) force
   (D) relation
   (E) persuasion

10. ASTONISH:

   (A) startle
   (B) surprise
   (C) yawn
   (D) bore
   (E) frighten

11. DESTITUTE:

   (A) prosperous
   (B) institute
   (C) compute
   (D) fortunate
   (E) hateful

12. CORROBORATE:

   (A) collaborate
   (B) support
   (C) anticipate
   (D) contradict
   (E) forget

13. SCAPEGOAT:

   (A) billy goat
   (B) hero
   (C) entrance
   (D) sitting duck
   (E) epic

14. MEAGER:

   (A) stronger
   (B) plentiful
   (C) stillness
   (D) loud
   (E) miniature

15. IMPLORE:

   (A) explore
   (B) folklore
   (C) imply
   (D) demand
   (E) ask

16. REMONSTRANCE:

   (A) solidity
   (B) display
   (C) agreement
   (D) demonstrate
   (E) inability

17. SLUGGISHLY:

   (A) sullenly
   (B) briskly
   (C) peacefully
   (D) awakening
   (E) superbly

18. MISANTHROPE:

   (A) humanitarian
   (B) ogre
   (C) scrooge
   (D) sissy
   (E) antelope

19. SUBSCRIBED:

   (A) inscribed
   (B) presented
   (C) disapproved
   (D) removed
   (E) allowed

20. THREADBARE:

   (A) new
   (B) repair
   (C) dispair
   (D) covered
   (E) sewn

21. FLUSTERED:

   (A) custard
   (B) quieted
   (C) whirled
   (D) flipped
   (E) calmed

22. DISPELLED:

   (A) continued
   (B) misspelled
   (C) proven
   (D) gathered
   (E) signed

23. PONDEROUS:

   (A) bulky
   (B) medium
   (C) rare
   (D) silly
   (E) light

24. PERSISTENTLY:

   (A) insistently
   (B) undetermined
   (C) resistingly
   (D) awfully
   (E) waveringly

Test 6

Synonyms

Directions: Each question below consists of a word in CAPITAL LETTERS, followed by five lettered words or phrases. Choose the word or phrase that is most *similar* in meaning to the word in CAPITAL LETTERS. Blacken the letter of your answer on the answer sheet. Because some choices may be close in meaning, consider all the choices before deciding which is best.

Example:

GRIEVING:

(A) sad
(B) mourning
(C) retrieving
(D) weeping
(E) happy

Mourning is the correct answer. You would have filled in the circle marked B on your answer sheet.

---

1. LIABILITY:

   (A) honesty
   (B) vulnerability
   (C) disability
   (D) bonus
   (E) expense

2. INTERROGATION:

   (A) interruption
   (B) delegation
   (C) communicate
   (D) locking
   (E) questioning

3. COMMOTION:

   (A) release
   (B) quiet
   (C) locomotion
   (D) emotion
   (E) uproar

4. ASSORTMENT:

   (A) kind
   (B) variety
   (C) recollection
   (D) compartment
   (E) sort

5. AESTHETICALLY:

   (A) officially
   (B) foolishly
   (C) artistically
   (D) athletically
   (E) randomly

6. MENACE:

   (A) threat
   (B) angry
   (C) attacking
   (D) dangerously
   (E) evil

7. MOBILIZED:

   (A) activated
   (B) civilized
   (C) motored
   (D) returned
   (E) simplified

8. APTITUDE:

   (A) likely
   (B) attitude
   (C) talent
   (D) height
   (E) intelligence

9. MANEUVER:

   (A) invention
   (B) stunted
   (C) rover
   (D) thought
   (E) procedure

10. PREVALENT:

   (A) relevant
   (B) truth
   (C) ordinary
   (D) common
   (E) unknown

11. COMPARABLE:

   (A) friendly
   (B) alike
   (C) reliable
   (D) consistent
   (E) story

12. APPRAISAL:

   (A) rehearsal
   (B) conference
   (C) assortment
   (D) evaluation
   (E) promotion

13. RADIANT:

   (A) radical
   (B) unhappy
   (C) vast
   (D) beaming
   (E) angled

14. CONSULTATION:

   (A) argument
   (B) discussion
   (C) assistance
   (D) visit
   (E) operation

15. CATASTROPHE:

   (A) disaster
   (B) feline
   (C) apostrophe
   (D) symphony
   (E) event

16. CRUCIAL:

   (A) rusty
   (B) certain
   (C) simple
   (D) special
   (E) vital

17. PERSISTENTLY:

   (A) fluently
   (B) questioningly
   (C) constantly
   (D) flawlessly
   (E) assisting

18. OOZED:

   (A) liquored
   (B) slept
   (C) seeped
   (D) complimented
   (E) ridiculed

19. IMMEASURABLY:
   (A) tall
   (B) incalculably
   (C) huge
   (D) mistakenly
   (E) repeatedly

20. MAXIM:
   (A) completely
   (B) proverb
   (C) coffee
   (D) sin
   (E) failure

21. ELUSIVE:
   (A) evasive
   (B) exclusive
   (C) slimey
   (D) wandering
   (E) floppy

22. FORMIDABLE:
   (A) fortress
   (B) impressive
   (C) frightened
   (D) past
   (E) impressive

23. UTILIZING:
   (A) working
   (B) praising
   (C) singing
   (D) using
   (E) aging

24. PAUPER:
   (A) poor person
   (B) carpenter
   (C) correct
   (D) poet
   (E) editor

25. ACCESSIBLE:
   (A) entrance
   (B) possible
   (C) approachable
   (D) openly
   (E) reliable

Sentence Completions

Directions: Each of the following sentences has a blank space, indicating that a word has been omitted. Beneath the sentence are five lettered words. Choose the word that best completes the meaning of the sentence as a whole. Blacken the letter of your answer on the answer sheet.

Example:
   Mortimer decided it was _____ to coat himself with greasy insect repellent than to risk being feasted upon by mosquitoes.

   (A) ominous
   (B) conventional
   (C) consolation
   (D) pungent
   (E) preferable

Preferable is the correct answer. You would have filled in the circle marked E on your answer sheet.

26. In _____, Julia decided that she would have performed better at her dance recital if she had not eaten two banana splits an hour before her performance.

(A) retrospect
(B) prose
(C) data
(D) fortitude
(E) intrigue

27. As the ladder fell away from him, Tony grabbed the window ledge and realized he was in a _____ predicament.

(A) inevitable
(B) vital
(C) perilous
(D) deteriorated
(E) compelling

28. The scruffy coat and _____ body of the young dog convinced us that he was badly in need of a home.

(A) provisional
(B) definitive
(C) desolate
(D) distraught
(E) emaciated

29. In addition to her fine works of _____, Gwendolyn Brooks has won the Pulitzer Prize for her poetry.

(A) retrospect
(B) prose
(C) emblems
(D) sieve
(E) bias

30. Because of overgrazing by cattle and an extreme drought, much of the area had become a(n) _____ wasteland.

(A) emaciated
(B) camouflaged
(C) arid
(D) despondent
(E) grotesquely

31. The dancers wore masks with _____ carved features that startled and puzzled the audience.

(A) surreptitiously
(B) inevitability
(C) grotesquely
(D) mortality
(E) conspiring

32. We discovered that my little sister had been the _____ who had played a series of practical jokes on all of us.

(A) allay
(B) preferable
(C) translucent
(D) culprit
(E) deluge

33. The young child became _____ when the ice cream cone she was eating slipped from her hand and splattered all over the floor.

(A) sauntered
(B) perilous
(C) extricate
(D) arid
(E) distraught

34. Due to the recent shortage of blood, Claudia felt it was _____ that she donate during the blood drive.

(A) vital
(B) inevitable
(C) conventional
(D) compelling
(E) interact

35. The abandoned house _____ to the point where it was dangerous to enter.

(A) encountered
(B) desolate
(C) sauntered
(D) intrigued
(E) deteriorated

36. The professor was _____ by the possibility that there was life on other planets.

(A) definitive
(B) intrigued
(C) camouflaged
(D) deluged
(E) despondent

37. As usual, Elaine avoided _____ costumes and arrived at the party dressed as a lima bean.

(A) ominous
(B) conventional
(C) provisional
(D) preferable
(E) culprit

38. Following the dismantling of the Berlin Wall, it was _____ that West and East Germany would reunite.

(A) mortality
(B) inevitable
(C) bias
(D) inevitability
(E) consolation

39. The _____ aroma wafting up from the kitchen made Jessica's mouth water and her stomach growl.

(A) conspiring
(B) arid
(C) translucent
(D) pungent
(E) culprit

40. The _____ action taken by the government was to ration gasoline and encourage conservation of other fuels until another source of crude oil could be found.

(A) allay
(B) provisional
(C) conventional
(D) retrospect
(E) vital

41. In Sheila's first _____ with her new neighbors, she was quiet and shy, but they soon became fast friends.

(A) emblem
(B) interact
(C) encounter
(D) provisional
(E) prose

42. To keep our treehouse a secret, we _____ it with branches and leaves.

(A) camouflaged
(B) extricated
(C) deteriorated
(D) encountered
(E) fortitude

43. Despite a(n) _____ of protest, the governor raised income taxes for everyone in the state.

(A) deluge
(B) sieve
(C) pungent
(D) inevitability
(E) data

44. As soon as Mary Beth's back was turned, Kelvin _____ placed the valentine on her desk and quickly walked to the other side of the room.

(A) mortality
(B) ominously
(C) surreptitiously
(D) grotesquely
(E) conspiring

45. The thick, black clouds and the _____ rumble of distant thunder convinced us to return to the house.

(A) distraught
(B) perilous
(C) pungent
(D) ominous
(E) surreptitiously

46. Mr. and Mrs. Johnson were _____ to throw their son a surprise party, unaware that he was in the next room listening to every word.

(A) sauntering
(B) compelling
(C) emblems
(D) intrigued
(E) conspiring

47. During our cruise in the Caribbean, we passed through waters so _____ that you could see fish swimming fifty feet beneath the surface.

(A) translucent
(B) grotesquely
(C) perilous
(D) desolate
(E) deteriorated

48. In an effort to _____ her fears of the dark, I always leave the door to my sister's room slightly open when she goes to sleep.

(A) sieve
(B) allay
(C) camouflage
(D) fortitude
(E) encounter

49. Being in no hurry, I _____ slowly through town, windowshopping and watching the crowds of people.

(A) retrospect
(B) emaciated
(C) extricated
(D) sauntered
(E) allayed

50. Herman hemmed and hawed, stammered and stewed, as he tried to think of a way to _____ himself from his most recent social blunder.

(A) arid
(B) consolation
(C) deluge
(D) extricate
(E) bias

Verbal Analogies

Directions: Each question below consists of a related pair of words in CAPITAL LETTERS, followed by five lettered pairs of words. Choose the pair that best expresses a relationship similar to that expressed in the pair in CAPITAL LETTERS. Blacken the letter of your answer on the answer sheet.

Example:

LATENT is to DEVELOPED as

(A) **labored** is to **worked**
(B) **foreign** is to **alien**
(C) **mast** is to **rudder**
(D) **aggressive** is to **passive**
(E) **single** is to **double**

Aggressive is to passive is the correct answer. You would have filled in the circle marked D on your answer sheet.

51. **CLAMORING** is to **YELLING** as

   (A) **rope** is to **cable**
   (B) **here** is to **now**
   (C) **grapefruit** is to **yellow**
   (D) **paddling** is to **canoeing**
   (E) **holding** is to **grasping**

52. **APT** is to **UNLIKELY** as

   (A) **fortunate** is to **lucky**
   (B) **salad** is to **lettuce**
   (C) **bowl** is to **spoon**
   (D) **large** is to **huge**
   (E) **generous** is to **selfish**

53. **UNIQUE** is to **ORDINARY** as

   (A) **radio** is to **television**
   (B) **background** is to **foreground**
   (C) **softly** is to **painfully**
   (D) **obvious** is to **unclear**
   (E) **sorted** is to **mixed**

54. **BRUTALITY** is to **SAVAGERY** as

   (A) **focused** is to **blurry**
   (B) **gentleness** is to **tenderness**
   (C) **thief** is to **police**
   (D) **point** is to **direct**
   (E) **human** is to **mammal**

55. **JUDICIOUS** is to **UNREASONABLE** as

   (A) **relief** is to **calm**
   (B) **long** is to **short**
   (C) **ocean** is to **salt water**
   (D) **open-minded** is to **unsure**
   (E) **layered** is to **piled**

56. **CONVEY** is to **COMMUNICATE** as

   (A) **speak** is to **listen**
   (B) **spark** is to **fire**
   (C) **retrieve** is to **regain**
   (D) **lesson** is to **assignment**
   (E) **creep** is to **sprint**

57. **CANTANKEROUS** is to **PLEASANT** as

   (A) **rough** is to **smooth**
   (B) **pony** is to **horse**
   (C) **right** is to **correct**
   (D) **speak** is to **whisper**
   (E) **pull** is to **push**

58. **TEPID** is to **LUKEWARM** as

   (A) **tap** is to **bounce**
   (B) **awful** is to **dreadful**
   (C) **wash** is to **dry**
   (D) **finer** is to **finest**
   (E) **control** is to **command**

59. **EXPECTANTLY** is to **INDIFFERENTLY** as

   (A) **sadly** is to **farewell**
   (B) **vaguely** is to **barely**
   (C) **soup** is to **broth**
   (D) **properly** is to **incorrectly**
   (E) **piano** is to **flute**

60. **SERENITY** is to **ANXIETY** as

   (A) **calming** is to **excited**
   (B) **awareness** is to **ignorance**
   (C) **super** is to **great**
   (D) **after** is to **before**
   (E) **lick** is to **bite**

61. **ENTICING** is to **TEMPTING** as

   (A) **entering** is to **departing**
   (B) **shining** is to **dulling**
   (C) **roofing** is to **shingles**
   (D) **foaming** is to **subsiding**
   (E) **grabbing** is to **snatching**

62. **INVARIABLE** is to **CHANGING** as

   (A) **marble** is to **slate**
   (B) **imaginary** is to **real**
   (C) **confusing** is to **bewildering**
   (D) **sound** is to **silence**
   (E) **grumble** is to **complain**

63. **DISTINCTION** is to **SIMILARITY** as

    (A) **extinct** is to **dinosaur**
    (B) **reflection** is to **mirror**
    (C) **emptiness** is to **fullness**
    (D) **song** is to **tune**
    (E) **cow** is to **calf**

64. **USURPED** is to **RELINQUISHED** as

    (A) **crude** is to **primitive**
    (B) **about** is to **exactly**
    (C) **took** is to **gave**
    (D) **sadly** is to **sorrowfully**
    (E) **anger** is to **contentment**

65. **SUBTLE** is to **OBVIOUS** as

    (A) **success** is to **achievement**
    (B) **knowing** is to **informed**
    (C) **original** is to **common**
    (D) **bicycle** is to **skateboard**
    (E) **absurd** is to **ridiculous**

66. **CONCEIVABLE** is to **IMAGINABLE** as

    (A) **crept** is to **crawled**
    (B) **boring** is to **interesting**
    (C) **unthinkable** is to **impossible**
    (D) **stop** is to **intersection**
    (E) **harvest** is to **crops**

67. **VANQUISHED** is to **DEFEATED** as

    (A) **cried** is to **laughed**
    (B) **label** is to **mark**
    (C) **father** is to **son**
    (D) **jumped** is to **vaulted**
    (E) **am** is to **was**

68. **SUSCEPTIBLE** is to **INSENSITIVE** as

    (A) **reckless** is to **careful**
    (B) **comma** is to **question mark**
    (C) **healthy** is to **health food**
    (D) **cool** is to **cold**
    (E) **careful** is to **cautious**

69. **SUCCESSION** is to **SEQUENCE** as

    (A) **recess** is to **excess**
    (B) **color** is to **blue**
    (C) **whale** is to **dolphin**
    (D) **satisfaction** is to **pleasure**
    (E) **enjoyment** is to **displeasure**

70. **SUBSERVIENT** is to **SUPERIOR** as

    (A) **subset** is to **set**
    (B) **quality** is to **quantity**
    (C) **airborne** is to **jet**
    (D) **mature** is to **undeveloped**
    (E) **active** is to **energetic**

Test 7

Sentence Completions

Directions: Each of the following sentences has a blank space, indicating that a word has been omitted. Beneath the sentence are five lettered words. Choose the word that best completes the meaning of the sentence as a whole. Blacken the letter of your answer on the answer sheet.

Example:

My baby sister does a lot of silly things because she is young; the other day she tried to eat an entire orange, _____ and all!

(A) rind
(B) rouge
(C) candy
(D) moor
(E) cremated

Rind is the correct answer. You would have filled in the circle marked A on your answer sheet.

---

1. Our dog Sally hates taking baths so much that she _____ and shakes when we wash her.

   (A) withers
   (B) scowls
   (C) hisses
   (D) whimpers
   (E) strives

2. The slugger crushed the ball deep into the right-field _____ for a home run.

   (A) bleachers
   (B) sepulcher
   (C) cascade
   (D) beams
   (E) breeches

3. We discovered that the refrigerator contained some rotten vegetables and _____ meat that had been left over from the summer before.

   (A) tawny
   (B) rancid
   (C) ghastly
   (D) curdled
   (E) tiered

4. Unable to contain herself, Pauline gushed forth with a _____ of words describing every detail of her first date.

   (A) torrent
   (B) scour
   (C) whimper
   (D) covet
   (E) bleacher

5. The hot sun _____ down on the soldiers, making each step more and more difficult.

   (A) brandished
   (B) cascaded
   (C) cremated
   (D) torrent
   (E) beamed

6. The witchdoctor cast her spells, danced about, and begged the gods to help her rid the house of the _____ that inhabited it.

   (A) rind
   (B) sepulcher
   (C) rancid
   (D) demons
   (E) bleachers

7. Although he was known more for his brains than his _____, Leo made the football team because of his intelligence and quickness.

   (A) grisly
   (B) stern
   (C) brawn
   (D) rinds
   (E) demons

8. The river rapids lead to a glittering _____ that drops twenty feet into a quiet pool.

   (A) beam
   (B) torrent
   (C) rouge
   (D) brawn
   (E) cascade

9. When she heard that she had not been chosen, Daisy _____ and stamped her feet in anger.

   (A) scowled
   (B) loathed
   (C) related
   (D) curdled
   (E) tiered

10. I immediately knew we had a puncture because I heard the tire _____ as I stepped out of the car.

    (A) whimper
    (B) relating
    (C) hissing
    (D) whithering
    (E) striving

11. A deer's _____ coat and ability to move quickly and silently are its best weapons against predators.

    (A) rancid
    (B) grisly
    (C) stern
    (D) tawny
    (E) ghastly

12. While we were away on vacation, several house plants _____ and died due to a lack of light and water.

    (A) coveted
    (B) withered
    (C) brandished
    (D) loathed
    (E) scoured

13. After playing with my mother's makeup, my youngest sister looked hilarious with her entire face reddened with _____ and her lips shining with bright pink lipstick.

    (A) bleachers
    (B) rouge
    (C) demons
    (D) candy
    (E) breeches

14. Mort was disappointed that *Night of the Killer Ladybugs, Part II* did not have as many _____ scenes as in *Night of the Killer Ladybugs, Part I*.

    (A) tawny
    (B) rancid
    (C) grisly
    (D) hissing
    (E) curdled

15. As the fortune teller began to _____ the strange and mysterious tale of her life, she leaned back and put her feet up on the table.

    (A) relate
    (B) whimper
    (C) hiss
    (D) beam
    (E) scowl

16. Although she failed in her first attempt, Vanessa continued to _____ to reach her goal of running a mile in less than four minutes, thirty seconds.

    (A) cascade
    (B) covet
    (C) relate
    (D) scour
    (E) strive

17. Archie _____ mathematics but continued to work hard at the subject because he wanted to earn a scholarship to college.

    (A) moor
    (B) cremated
    (C) brandished
    (D) brawn
    (E) loathed

18. Virgil did not enjoy the book about the Civil War because it contained _____ descriptions of death on the battlefield.

    (A) tawny
    (B) tiered
    (C) sepulcher
    (D) ghastly
    (E) stern

19. In her hurry to go outside and play, Janet did not _____ the pans thoroughly, leaving them greasy and dirty.

    (A) candy
    (B) rouge
    (C) scour
    (D) torrent
    (E) strive

20. Elvin's large collection of baseball cards was _____ by many boys and girls in the neighborhood who had smaller collections of their own.

    (A) withered
    (B) coveted
    (C) scowled
    (D) ghastly
    (E) loathed

Verbal Analogies

Directions: Each question below consists of a related pair of words in CAPITAL LETTERS, followed by five lettered pairs of words. Choose the pair that best expresses a relationship similar to that expressed in the pair in CAPITAL LETTERS. Blacken the letter of your answer on the answer sheet.

Example:

POMP is to **CEREMONY** as

(A) **party** is to **celebration**
(B) **dog** is to **puppy**
(C) **sing** is to **yell**
(D) **on** is to **off**
(E) **room** is to **house**

Party is to celebration is the correct answer. You would have filled in the circle marked A on your answer sheet.

21. **QUARRIED** is to **MINED** as

   (A) **hunted** is to **hunter**
   (B) **picked** is to **harvested**
   (C) **labor** is to **rest**
   (D) **relief** is to **respite**
   (E) **gone** is to **arrived**

22. **TESTIMONY** is to **STATEMENT** as

   (A) **conversation** is to **discussion**
   (B) **stiff** is to **flexible**
   (C) **harden** is to **soften**
   (D) **above** is to **below**
   (E) **simpleton** is to **genius**

23. **TOTTER** is to **STEADY** as

   (A) **excite** is to **uplift**
   (B) **run** is to **ran**
   (C) **sandy** is to **rocky**
   (D) **willow** is to **tree**
   (E) **bend** is to **straighten**

24. **FEED** is to **FOOD** as

   (A) **mountain** is to **anthill**
   (B) **respect** is to **disregard**
   (C) **gasoline** is to **fuel**
   (D) **simple** is to **easy**
   (E) **corner** is to **bend**

25. **HYMN** is to **SONG** as

   (A) **poem** is to **drama**
   (B) **rowboat** is to **oar**
   (C) **fairy** tale is to **story**
   (D) **large** is to **compact**
   (E) **music** is to **heavy metal**

26. **SOMBER** is to **CHEERFUL** as

   (A) **cheer** is to **applaud**
   (B) **red** is to **color**
   (C) **suitable** is to **appropriate**
   (D) **ugly** is to **attractive**
   (E) **modern** is to **futuristic**

27. **SAUNTER** is to **STROLL** as

   (A) **choose** is to **decide**
   (B) **still** is to **motion**
   (C) **movie** is to **cartoon**
   (D) **apple** is to **apple tree**
   (E) **walk** is to **run**

28. **AMISS** is to **MISTAKENLY** as

   (A) **oddly** is to **normally**
   (B) **easily** is to **simply**
   (C) **fallen** is to **dropping**
   (D) **star** is to **constellation**
   (E) **ladder** is to **steps**

29. **SQUAT** is to **STUMPY** as

   (A) **alive** is to **dead**
   (B) **crept** is to **crawled**
   (C) **balloon** is to **swell**
   (D) **small** is to **huge**
   (E) **active** is to **energetic**

30. **MEEK** is to **BOLD** as

   (A) **shy** is to **quiet**
   (B) **long** is to **stretched**
   (C) **sensitive** is to **unfeeling**
   (D) **break** is to **mend**
   (E) **disguise** is to **camouflage**

31. **BROOCH** is to **JEWELRY** as

   (A) **diamond** is to **ruby**
   (B) **avoid** is to **meet**
   (C) **salad** is to **dessert**
   (D) **beef** is to **meat**
   (E) **foreign** is to **familiar**

32. **GLINT** is to **FLASH** as

   (A) **liquid** is to **solid**
   (B) **slide** is to **bounce**
   (C) **lost** is to **found**
   (D) **slash** is to **cut**
   (E) **cheer** is to **happy**

33. **MUSLIN** is to **CLOTH** as

    (A) **maple** is to **tree**
    (B) **sewing** is to **mending**
    (C) **monkey** is to **banana**
    (D) **globe** is to **circle**
    (E) **crack** is to **open**

34. **SCORN** is to **ADMIRATION** as

    (A) **ant** is to **grasshopper**
    (B) **probable** is to **likely**
    (C) **fill** is to **empty**
    (D) **pain** is to **comfort**
    (E) **rabbit** is to **fox**

Antonyms

Directions: Each question below consists of a word in CAPITAL LETTERS, followed by five lettered words or phrases. Choose the word or phrase that is most nearly *opposite* in meaning to the word in CAPITAL LETTERS. Blacken the letter of your answer on the answer sheet. Because some of the choices are close in meaning, consider all the choices before deciding which is best.

Example:

DOWNY:

    (A) hardly
    (B) relief
    (C) outside
    (D) above
    (E) hard

Hard is the correct answer. You would have filled in the circle marked E on your answer sheet.

35. SAGE:

    (A) release
    (B) fool
    (C) king
    (D) jest
    (E) gentleman

36. BANISH:

    (A) begin
    (B) invite
    (C) vanish
    (D) appeal
    (E) arrive

37. ODIOUS:

    (A) perfumed
    (B) evil
    (C) attractive
    (D) sweet
    (E) mean

38. DOTE:

    (A) like
    (B) note
    (C) large
    (D) drop
    (E) dislike

39. SUPPLE:

    (A) stiff
    (B) difficult
    (C) awkward
    (D) breakfast
    (E) replace

40. BOG:

    (A) fog
    (B) dry ground
    (C) large insect
    (D) assist
    (E) clear sky

41. WEE:

   (A) no
   (B) late
   (C) extreme
   (D) gigantic
   (E) extremely small

42. QUAIL:

   (A) confront
   (B) quiver
   (C) yell
   (D) forget
   (E) run

43. ESTEEMED:

   (A) opposition
   (B) exactly
   (C) repeated
   (D) scorned
   (E) guessed

44. ADHESIVE:

   (A) forgotten
   (B) original
   (C) tape
   (D) slippery
   (E) active

45. PROFOUND:

   (A) serious
   (B) alike
   (C) shallow
   (D) lost again
   (E) wonder

46. INCESSANTLY:

   (A) infrequently
   (B) repeatedly
   (C) often
   (D) sometimes
   (E) obviously

Test 8

Synonyms

Directions: Each question below consists of a word in CAPITAL LETTERS, followed by five lettered words or phrases. Choose the word or phrase that is most *similar* in meaning to the word in CAPITAL LETTERS. Blacken the letter of your answer on the answer sheet. Because some choices may be close in meaning, consider all the choices before deciding which is best.

Example:

GLOSSY:

(A) glamorous
(B) obedient
(C) new
(D) shiny
(E) feathered

Shiny is the correct answer. You would have filled in the circle marked D on your answer sheet.

1. FLOCK:

(A) solitary
(B) opening
(C) fail
(D) apron
(E) herd

2. APPEASED:

(A) satisfied
(B) annoyed
(C) emerged
(D) relaxed
(E) forgot

3. FARE:

(A) ticket
(B) honest
(C) food
(D) elf
(E) average

4. FORLORNLY:

(A) oddly
(B) lovely
(C) despairingly
(D) moisten
(E) half-heartedly

5. HEED:

(A) attention
(B) his
(C) heard
(D) allowance
(E) advice

6. SURPASS:

(A) surprise
(B) extending
(C) hop
(D) exceed
(E) leave behind

7. ARROGANTLY:
  (A) dangerously
  (B) awfully
  (C) straight
  (D) ridiculously
  (E) proudly

8. CUNNING:
  (A) sly
  (B) carrying
  (C) separating
  (D) treacherous
  (E) evil

9. DESPISED:
  (A) ignored
  (B) replied
  (C) unbound
  (D) hated
  (E) uncovered

10. HEARTILY:
  (A) bravely
  (B) sincerely
  (C) strangely
  (D) loving
  (E) violently

Sentence Completions

Directions: Each of the following sentences has a blank space, indicating that a word has been omitted. Beneath the sentence are five lettered words. Choose the word that best completes the meaning of the sentence as a whole. Blacken the letter of your answer on the answer sheet.

Example:

The great lollipop theft succeeded due to a _____ plan involving a woman and an infant who turned out to be a midget in disguise.

  (A) deluded
  (B) pious
  (C) clever
  (D) haggard
  (E) shrewdest

Clever is the correct answer. You would have filled in the circle marked C on your answer sheet.

11. Rodney's _____ decision to go sailing without checking the weather report nearly cost him his life when his boat almost capsized in a violent rain storm.

  (A) ominous
  (B) rash
  (C) snug
  (D) immeasurable
  (E) lament

12. "The _____ who rules these lands is Queen Hortense de Blume," announced the border guard. "What are your names and what is your business?"

  (A) monarch
  (B) amber
  (C) mortal
  (D) fledgling
  (E) councilor

13. The orchestra's performance was _____ by a baby in the audience who cried and screamed throughout the show.

   (A) marred
   (B) courted
   (C) implored
   (D) veered
   (E) anointed

14. "It's all in the wrist and the follow-through," claimed Noreen as she _____ shot another basketball through the hoop.

   (A) gravely
   (B) sustained
   (C) rash
   (D) deftly
   (E) insolently

15. The young knight was _____ with fear as he approached the castle of the dreaded Count Foulbreath.

   (A) kindling
   (B) marred
   (C) precipitous
   (D) quavering
   (E) asunder

16. "Welcome to my humble _____," he chuckled as he ushered us into an immense and luxurious living room.

   (A) dominion
   (B) monarch
   (C) abode
   (D) vacancy
   (E) realm

17. During the three days that she was lost in the wilderness, Gladys _____ herself on nuts and berries.

   (A) bustled
   (B) despised
   (C) defied
   (D) dissuaded
   (E) sustained

18. Rebecca was able to _____ Herman from renting a surfboard by pointing out that the waves were ten-feet tall and that he did not know how to swim.

   (A) intervene
   (B) dissuade
   (C) disdain
   (D) delude
   (E) deftly

19. Being a kind, honest, and considerate fellow, the _____ youth was a model citizen.

   (A) unrequited
   (B) deference
   (C) quavering
   (D) cunning
   (E) pious

20. Although her most trusted _____ advised against it, the queen decided to marry the tall stranger whom she had only met a week before.

   (A) mortal
   (B) councilor
   (C) monarch
   (D) hearth
   (E) abode

21. Because I _____ myself into believing that I did not need to rehearse, I made a fool of myself during the recital by forgetting the words to the song.

   (A) implored
   (B) dissuaded
   (C) deluded
   (D) bustled
   (E) veered

22. As Sebastian shook and whimpered in fear, the evil sorcerer shrieked, "Why has such a feeble _____ dared to enter my chamber of death?"

   (A) mortal
   (B) hearth
   (C) councilor
   (D) fledgling
   (E) dominion

23. After being struck by two enemy torpedoes, the warship burst _____ and sank without a trace.

(A) gravely
(B) unrequited
(C) insolently
(D) asunder
(E) deftly

24. After she was ill for several days, her face was pale and _____.

(A) snug
(B) amber
(C) pious
(D) ominous
(E) haggard

25. Because she was not paying attention to where she was going, Hazel suddenly found herself hiking on a(n) _____ trail that climbed to a dizzying height.

(A) immeasurable
(B) rash
(C) kindling
(D) quavering
(E) precipitous

26. "The citizens of my _____ are being terrorized by this dragon and we must get rid of it!" cried the king. "Who will volunteer to slay the hideous beast?"

(A) realm
(B) hearth
(C) rash
(D) monarch
(E) abode

27. Although she was _____ by several attractive young men, Miss Jeffers chose to marry the short and balding librarian, Mr. Owlsly.

(A) anointed
(B) sustained
(C) courted
(D) despised
(E) disdained

28. Although my father is clever, my Uncle Louie is definitely the _____ member of our family.

(A) asunder
(B) shrewdest
(C) precipitous
(D) marred
(E) haggard

29. As my brothers and sisters put up decorations and tidied up the living room, my mother _____ around the kitchen preparing food for my father's birthday party.

(A) disdained
(B) defied
(C) intervened
(D) courted
(E) bustled

30. The judge _____ asked the youth, "Do you realize the consequences of your actions?"

(A) insolently
(B) gravely
(C) kindling
(D) lament
(E) deftly

31. When our car hit the patch of ice, we _____ left, spun completely around, and slid into a snowbank on the side of the road.

(A) implored
(B) shrewdest
(C) bustled
(D) veered
(E) marred

32. Being a solitary man by nature, Hal _____ the company of others and went off to live alone in the woods.

(A) deluded
(B) anointed
(C) dissuaded
(D) sustained
(E) disdained

33. "Why don't you join us for the week-end?" Shirley exclaimed, "My grand-mother has a(n) _____ little cottage on the seashore that I know you would just love!"

(A) cunning
(B) ominous
(C) snug
(D) haggard
(E) amber

34. When my sister and I have a loud dis-agreement, my mother usually _____ and settles the dispute.

(A) despises
(B) laments
(C) veers
(D) intervenes
(E) defies

35. "Have you no respect?" sneered the sniveling jester, "Kneel, you worm, and kiss the floor in _____ to his majesty the king!"

(A) deference
(B) dominion
(C) councilor
(D) vacancy
(E) pious

Antonyms

Directions: Each question below consists of a word in CAPITAL LETTERS, followed by five lettered words or phrases. Choose the word or phrase that is most nearly *opposite* in meaning to the word in CAPITAL LETTERS. Blacken the letter of your answer on the answer sheet. Because some of the choices are close in meaning, consider all the choices before deciding which is best.

Example:

AVARICE:

(A) exceptional
(B) generosity
(C) courage
(D) skill
(E) helpful

Generosity is the correct answer. You would have filled in the circle marked B on your answer sheet.

36. GAUNT:

(A) show
(B) polite
(C) modest
(D) return
(E) chubby

37. DECREED:

(A) declared
(B) relieved
(C) faithful
(D) requested
(E) implant

38. EXTRACTED:

(A) detract
(B) pulled
(C) inserted
(D) on track
(E) found

39. ACKNOWLEDGE:

(A) learning
(B) information
(C) deny
(D) remember
(E) admit

40. FLAUNTED:

(A) concealed
(B) launched
(C) stripped
(D) flopped
(E) caressed

41. PAUPER:

(A) stern
(B) jester
(C) richer
(D) piper
(E) millionaire

42. BESIEGED:

(A) left alone
(B) unleashed
(C) filled up
(D) uncorked
(E) relieved

43. PROFFERED:

(A) offered
(B) withdrew
(C) forgot
(D) unseen
(E) helped

44. EMITTING:

(A) denying
(B) receiving
(C) disagreeing
(D) encouraging
(E) knitting

45. VANQUISH:

(A) surrender
(B) appear
(C) starve
(D) greenish
(E) topple

46. REFUTE:

(A) acceptable
(B) prove
(C) worry
(D) intense
(E) allow

47. DREADED:

(A) woven
(B) repaired
(C) unafraid
(D) fancy
(E) terrible

48. YEARNED:

(A) avoided
(B) driven away
(C) learned
(D) mine
(E) confirmed

49. TEDIOUS:

(A) anxious
(B) energy
(C) interesting
(D) hideous
(E) alive

50. HARASSED:

(A) enjoyment
(B) super
(C) bothered
(D) comforted
(E) annoyed

51. RELISHED:

(A) unbound
(B) embellished
(C) hot dog
(D) disliked
(E) wrapped

Test 9

Synonyms

Directions: Each question below consists of a word in CAPITAL LETTERS, followed by five lettered words or phrases. Choose the word or phrase that is most *similar* in meaning to the word in CAPITAL LETTERS. Blacken the letter of your answer on the answer sheet. Because some choices may be close in meaning, consider all the choices before deciding which is best.

Example:

CAUTIOUS:

(A) determined
(B) anxious
(C) careful
(D) precious
(E) clumsy

Careful is the correct answer. You would have filled in the circle marked C on your answer sheet.

---

1. QUAVERING:

   (A) trembling
   (B) lying
   (C) jamming
   (D) stumbling
   (E) protecting

2. WINCED:

   (A) announced
   (B) annoyed
   (C) flinched
   (D) grinned
   (E) screamed

3. RUNT:

   (A) giant
   (B) loser
   (C) giant
   (D) parent
   (E) midget

4. BAYING:

   (A) barking
   (B) whispering
   (C) talking
   (D) bowing
   (E) whistling

5. MOMENTUM:

   (A) moment
   (B) steadiness
   (C) instance
   (D) force
   (E) readiness

6. NONCHALANTLY:

   (A) instinctively
   (B) playfully
   (C) importantly
   (D) casually
   (E) similarly

7. BELLIGERENT:

(A) friendly
(B) hostile
(C) peaceful
(D) believable
(E) stubborn

8. SLOUGH:

(A) field
(B) inlet
(C) swamp
(D) arch
(E) lake

Verbal Analogies

Directions: Each question below consists of a related pair of words in CAPITAL LETTERS, followed by five lettered pairs of words. Choose the pair that best expresses a relationship similar to that expressed in the pair in CAPITAL LETTERS. Blacken the letter of your answer on the answer sheet.

Example:

FULL is to EMPTY as

(A) pack is to unpack
(B) stocked is to stored
(C) crammed is to jammed
(D) crowded is to vacant
(E) whole is to complete

Crowded is to vacant is the correct answer. You would have filled in the circle marked D on your answer sheet.

9. LEERING is to SNEERING as

(A) mumbling is to muttering
(B) screaming is to whispering
(C) thinking is to reading
(D) leaning is to standing
(E) listening is to watching

12. HAGGARD is to ENERGETIC as

(A) tired is to weary
(B) sleepy is to wakeful
(C) active is to busy
(D) spirited is to rested
(E) worn is to used

10. JUBILANT is to DISAPPOINTED as

(A) sorrowful is to cheerful
(B) triumphant is to joyful
(C) happily is to sadly
(D) victorious is to defeated
(E) bright is to glowing

13. PREDATORY is to VICIOUS as

(A) harmful is to playful
(B) natural is to artificial
(C) destructive is to violent
(D) vegetable is to carrot
(E) citrus is to lemon

11. GLOATED is to GRINNED as

(A) scolded is to rewarded
(B) discovered is to concealed
(C) scowled is to frowned
(D) played is to scored
(E) applaud is to clap

14. SINEW is to TENDON as

(A) navel is to bellybutton
(B) teeth are to mouth
(C) elbow is to arm
(D) vein is to artery
(E) ring is to finger

15. **BERSERK** is to **VIOLENT** as
    (A) **pleased** is to **dissatisfied**
    (B) **outraged** is to **content**
    (C) **joined** is to **separated**
    (D) **peaceful** is to **calm**
    (E) **new** is to **used**

16. **LITHE** is to **INFLEXIBLE** as
    (A) **curious** is to **scary**
    (B) **determined** is to **positive**
    (C) **tall** is to **high**
    (D) **important** is to **essential**
    (E) **fragile** is to **sturdy**

17. **SCOURGE** is to **TROUBLE** as
    (A) **rain** is to **flood**
    (B) **vitamin** is to **medicine**
    (C) **sneaker** is to **shoe**
    (D) **picture** is to **frame**
    (E) **health** is to **illness**

18. **ENTRAILS** is to **SKIN** as
    (A) **bracelet** is to **wrist**
    (B) **book** is to **pages**
    (C) **letter** is to **envelope**
    (D) **inside** is to **outside**
    (E) **record** is to **chart**

Name _____ Date _____

Test Number _____

ANSWER SHEET

Using pencil, completely blacken the answer space of your choice. Mark only one answer for each questions. Erase stray marks.

1. Ⓐ Ⓑ Ⓒ Ⓓ Ⓔ   26. Ⓐ Ⓑ Ⓒ Ⓓ Ⓔ   51. Ⓐ Ⓑ Ⓒ Ⓓ Ⓔ

2. Ⓐ Ⓑ Ⓒ Ⓓ Ⓔ   27. Ⓐ Ⓑ Ⓒ Ⓓ Ⓔ   52. Ⓐ Ⓑ Ⓒ Ⓓ Ⓔ

3. Ⓐ Ⓑ Ⓒ Ⓓ Ⓔ   28. Ⓐ Ⓑ Ⓒ Ⓓ Ⓔ   53. Ⓐ Ⓑ Ⓒ Ⓓ Ⓔ

4. Ⓐ Ⓑ Ⓒ Ⓓ Ⓔ   29. Ⓐ Ⓑ Ⓒ Ⓓ Ⓔ   54. Ⓐ Ⓑ Ⓒ Ⓓ Ⓔ

5. Ⓐ Ⓑ Ⓒ Ⓓ Ⓔ   30. Ⓐ Ⓑ Ⓒ Ⓓ Ⓔ   55. Ⓐ Ⓑ Ⓒ Ⓓ Ⓔ

6. Ⓐ Ⓑ Ⓒ Ⓓ Ⓔ   31. Ⓐ Ⓑ Ⓒ Ⓓ Ⓔ   56. Ⓐ Ⓑ Ⓒ Ⓓ Ⓔ

7. Ⓐ Ⓑ Ⓒ Ⓓ Ⓔ   32. Ⓐ Ⓑ Ⓒ Ⓓ Ⓔ   57. Ⓐ Ⓑ Ⓒ Ⓓ Ⓔ

8. Ⓐ Ⓑ Ⓒ Ⓓ Ⓔ   33. Ⓐ Ⓑ Ⓒ Ⓓ Ⓔ   58. Ⓐ Ⓑ Ⓒ Ⓓ Ⓔ

9. Ⓐ Ⓑ Ⓒ Ⓓ Ⓔ   34. Ⓐ Ⓑ Ⓒ Ⓓ Ⓔ   59. Ⓐ Ⓑ Ⓒ Ⓓ Ⓔ

10. Ⓐ Ⓑ Ⓒ Ⓓ Ⓔ   35. Ⓐ Ⓑ Ⓒ Ⓓ Ⓔ   60. Ⓐ Ⓑ Ⓒ Ⓓ Ⓔ

11. Ⓐ Ⓑ Ⓒ Ⓓ Ⓔ   36. Ⓐ Ⓑ Ⓒ Ⓓ Ⓔ   61. Ⓐ Ⓑ Ⓒ Ⓓ Ⓔ

12. Ⓐ Ⓑ Ⓒ Ⓓ Ⓔ   37. Ⓐ Ⓑ Ⓒ Ⓓ Ⓔ   62. Ⓐ Ⓑ Ⓒ Ⓓ Ⓔ

13. Ⓐ Ⓑ Ⓒ Ⓓ Ⓔ   38. Ⓐ Ⓑ Ⓒ Ⓓ Ⓔ   63. Ⓐ Ⓑ Ⓒ Ⓓ Ⓔ

14. Ⓐ Ⓑ Ⓒ Ⓓ Ⓔ   39. Ⓐ Ⓑ Ⓒ Ⓓ Ⓔ   64. Ⓐ Ⓑ Ⓒ Ⓓ Ⓔ

15. Ⓐ Ⓑ Ⓒ Ⓓ Ⓔ   40. Ⓐ Ⓑ Ⓒ Ⓓ Ⓔ   65. Ⓐ Ⓑ Ⓒ Ⓓ Ⓔ

16. Ⓐ Ⓑ Ⓒ Ⓓ Ⓔ   41. Ⓐ Ⓑ Ⓒ Ⓓ Ⓔ   66. Ⓐ Ⓑ Ⓒ Ⓓ Ⓔ

17. Ⓐ Ⓑ Ⓒ Ⓓ Ⓔ   42. Ⓐ Ⓑ Ⓒ Ⓓ Ⓔ   67. Ⓐ Ⓑ Ⓒ Ⓓ Ⓔ

18. Ⓐ Ⓑ Ⓒ Ⓓ Ⓔ   43. Ⓐ Ⓑ Ⓒ Ⓓ Ⓔ   68. Ⓐ Ⓑ Ⓒ Ⓓ Ⓔ

19. Ⓐ Ⓑ Ⓒ Ⓓ Ⓔ   44. Ⓐ Ⓑ Ⓒ Ⓓ Ⓔ   69. Ⓐ Ⓑ Ⓒ Ⓓ Ⓔ

20. Ⓐ Ⓑ Ⓒ Ⓓ Ⓔ   45. Ⓐ Ⓑ Ⓒ Ⓓ Ⓔ   70. Ⓐ Ⓑ Ⓒ Ⓓ Ⓔ

21. Ⓐ Ⓑ Ⓒ Ⓓ Ⓔ   46. Ⓐ Ⓑ Ⓒ Ⓓ Ⓔ   71. Ⓐ Ⓑ Ⓒ Ⓓ Ⓔ

22. Ⓐ Ⓑ Ⓒ Ⓓ Ⓔ   47. Ⓐ Ⓑ Ⓒ Ⓓ Ⓔ   72. Ⓐ Ⓑ Ⓒ Ⓓ Ⓔ

23. Ⓐ Ⓑ Ⓒ Ⓓ Ⓔ   48. Ⓐ Ⓑ Ⓒ Ⓓ Ⓔ   73. Ⓐ Ⓑ Ⓒ Ⓓ Ⓔ

24. Ⓐ Ⓑ Ⓒ Ⓓ Ⓔ   49. Ⓐ Ⓑ Ⓒ Ⓓ Ⓔ   74. Ⓐ Ⓑ Ⓒ Ⓓ Ⓔ

25. Ⓐ Ⓑ Ⓒ Ⓓ Ⓔ   50. Ⓐ Ⓑ Ⓒ Ⓓ Ⓔ   75. Ⓐ Ⓑ Ⓒ Ⓓ Ⓔ

Answer Key

© Prentice-Hall, Inc.

Test 1

1. B	9. B	17. A
2. E	10. E	18. E
3. D	11. D	19. B
4. D	12. E	20. D
5. C	13. D	21. A
6. B	14. C	22. A
7. A	15. B	
8. A	16. C	

Test 2

1. D	10. D	19. A
2. D	11. D	20. D
3. A	12. A	21. A
4. E	13. B	22. C
5. C	14. A	23. E
6. B	15. B	24. B
7. C	16. C	25. C
8. E	17. C	
9. E	18. E	

Test 3

1. B	11. A	21. E
2. A	12. D	22. B
3. E	13. C	23. D
4. D	14. B	24. D
5. C	15. A	25. D
6. C	16. A	26. C
7. C	17. B	27. C
8. D	18. B	28. A
9. E	19. E	29. A
10. E	20. C	30. E

Test 4

1. C	10. E	19. E
2. C	11. C	20. C
3. A	12. A	21. E
4. E	13. D	22. A
5. E	14. B	23. D
6. D	15. D	24. A
7. A	16. B	25. B
8. B	17. B	
9. C	18. E	

Test 5

1. E	9. E	17. B
2. D	10. D	18. A
3. C	11. A	19. C
4. D	12. D	20. A
5. A	13. B	21. E
6. A	14. B	22. D
7. B	15. D	23. E
8. C	16. C	24. E

Test 6

1. B	25. C	49. D
2. E	26. A	50. D
3. E	27. C	51. E
4. B	28. E	52. E
5. C	29. B	53. D
6. A	30. C	54. B
7. A	31. C	55. B
8. C	32. D	56. C
9. E	33. E	57. A
10. D	34. A	58. B
11. B	35. E	59. D
12. D	36. B	60. B
13. D	37. B	61. E
14. B	38. B	62. B
15. A	39. D	63. C
16. E	40. B	64. C
17. C	41. C	65. C
18. C	42. A	66. C
19. B	43. A	67. D
20. B	44. C	68. A
21. A	45. D	69. D
22. E	46. E	70. D
23. D	47. A	
24. A	48. B	

Test 7

1.	D	17.	E	33.	A
2.	A	18.	D	34.	D
3.	B	19.	C	35.	B
4.	A	20.	B	36.	B
5.	E	21.	B	37.	C
6.	D	22.	A	38.	E
7.	C	23.	E	39.	A
8.	E	24.	C	40.	B
9.	A	25.	C	41.	D
10.	C	26.	D	42.	A
11.	D	27.	A	43.	D
12.	B	28.	B	44.	D
13.	B	29.	E	45.	C
14.	C	30.	C	46.	A
15.	A	31.	D		
16.	E	32.	D		

Test 9

1.	A	7.	B	13.	C
2.	C	8.	C	14.	A
3.	E	9.	A	15.	D
4.	A	10.	D	16.	E
5.	D	11.	C	17.	A
6.	D	12.	B	18.	C

Test 8

1.	E	19.	E	37.	D
2.	A	20.	B	38.	C
3.	C	21.	C	39.	C
4.	C	22.	A	40.	A
5.	A	23.	D	41.	E
6.	D	24.	E	42.	A
7.	E	25.	E	43.	B
8.	A	26.	A	44.	B
9.	D	27.	C	45.	A
10.	B	28.	B	46.	B
11.	B	29.	E	47.	C
12.	A	30.	B	48.	A
13.	A	31.	D	49.	C
14.	D	32.	E	50.	D
15.	D	33.	C	51.	D
16.	C	34.	D		
17.	E	35.	A		
18.	B	36.	E		